Financial Services in the Twenty-First Century

John JA Burke

Financial Services in the Twenty-First Century

The Present System and Future Developments in Fintech and Financial Innovation

palgrave
macmillan

John JA Burke
RISEBA University
Rīga, Latvia

ISBN 978-3-030-63966-2   ISBN 978-3-030-63967-9 (eBook)
https://doi.org/10.1007/978-3-030-63967-9

Illustrator: All illustrations created by Svetlana Vladimirovna Panina-Burke.

This Palgrave Macmillan imprint is published by the registered company Springer Nature Switzerland AG.
The registered company address is: Gewerbestrasse 11, 6330 Cham, Switzerland

Contents

List of Figures

Part I

Financial Services: Public Framework and Relationship to Capital and Income

Introduction

1

Un visionnaire imagine des choses autres.[1]

Introduction

This textbook builds upon standard texts in the domain of international banking and markets and merges them with the post-2008 developments in technology applying to financial services. It also is a textbook about the possibility of imagination. Reconstruction of the extant financial services system is required to meet customer demand and respond to the new *status quo*. Since the 2008 financial crisis, *The Economist* observes: we live in a "strange new world" of global economics. "Rich-world economics consist of a billion consumers and millions of firms taking their own decisions. But they also feature mighty public institutions that try to steer the economy, including central banks, which set monetary policy, and governments, which decide to spend and borrow" (*The Economist*). The arrangement is collapsing. Low unemployment is no longer correlated to increased inflation rates. Quantitative easing, supposedly an emergency measure to counteract the negative effects of the 2008 financial crisis, is the new normal for central banks. Lenders now pay borrowers to hold negative-yielding investment-grade bonds to maturity, turning the concept of credit on its head. Disregard of consumer demands for mobile-enabled financial services by legacy institutions opened the door to FinTech neo-banks and facile and cheap payment systems. Distributed ledger technology (DLT) is not constrained by Bitcoin, and DLT is establishing a new infrastructure to conduct financial transactions. Equally important is the rise of artificial intelligence and its application to banking, investment, and financial markets. "The institutions that steer the economy must be remade [or eliminated and replaced] for today's strange new world" (*The Economist*).

This textbook reviews historical events, as a necessary precondition, for understanding the present, tracks the post-2008 changing landscape of finance, and

J. JA Burke, *Financial Services in the Twenty-First Century*,
https://doi.org/10.1007/978-3-030-63967-9_1

examines the consequences of rebuilding the financial services edifice upon "first principles thinking". If governments and/or large institutions do not co-opt or warp innovation, FinTech, blockchain, artificial intelligence, and BRICS will likely produce a revolution, or major evolution, in the field of finance: (1) elimination, or reduced role, of intermediaries, (2) reinventing the understanding of money, (3) introduction of innovative banking and payment systems, and (4) reform, if not demise, of the financial system established under the Bretton Woods agreement.[2] The confluence of emerging technologies and emerging markets have the capacity to challenge the dominance of the dollar and the financial system created by the Western bloc subsequent to World War Two. Asian platforms, such as the Ant Group, already provide financial services to almost a billion customers and reveal the new architecture of banking services. In Africa, M-Pesa has constructed a different but novel platform to provide banking to the unbanked and underbanked.

The title of this textbook, *Financial Services in the Twenty-First Century*, is ambitious, if not pretentious, as no one can predict the future. However, the constellation of developments in various fields and bold rethinking of conventional financial institutions and services since the 2008 financial crisis justify an attempt to record these developments and make projections about the future. The forward-looking purposes of this book are important, but that does not mean one can eschew the centuries of wisdom found in classic textbooks on these similar topics. Numerous textbooks cover the topics of economics, banking, financial intermediation and institutions, investment instruments and strategies, diverse markets, and central bank policy. This textbook does not restate these principles but tries to build upon, expand, and where necessary, question the fundamental principles contained in these books.

Take "Starling Bank" to illustrate this point. Starling Bank is a digital challenger bank founded in 2014 by Anne Boden. The bank is headquartered in London and is licensed by the United Kingdom's Prudential Regulation Authority and the Financial Conduct Authority. Hence Starling Bank is authorised to provide services to residents of the United Kingdom. This restriction means that, if a customer does not have a physical address in the United Kingdom, the customer cannot open an account with the bank. Prior to Brexit, Starling Bank had the legal right to "passport" its services to residents of Member States of the European Union, upon notice to the individual financial regulators of each Member State. Post-Brexit, unless Starling Bank is licensed in a Member State of the European Union, the bank is limited to offering services within its licensed jurisdiction. Hence, Nation State licensing and regulatory requirements block the possibility of a global bank.

Notes

1. "A visionary sees what others cannot see." A billboard advertisement placed by HSBC in Paris Charles de Gaulle Airport. I doubt if the bank means it. But the sentence is a perfect opening for this text.
2. Blockchain technology is not equivalent to "e-finance", a term referring to traditional financial services that are delivered or executed on the Internet. Blockchain is a network based on novel protocols. The most famous incarnation is Bitcoin. However, blockchain is a technology having many business applications encompassing financial services and going beyond that domain.

Bibliography

Jonathan Ashworth, *Quantitative Easing: The Great Central Bank Experiment* (Agenda Publishing 2020).
Zvi Bodie, Alex Kane, and Alan Marcus, *Essentials of Investments* (McGraw-Hill 2020).
Stephen Cecchetti and Kermit Schoenholtz, *Money, Banking and Financial Markets* (McGraw-Hill 2020)
Sidney Homer and Richard Sylla, A History of Interest Rates (John Wiley & Sons 4th ed. 2005).
Frederic S. Mishkin, *The Economics of Money, Banking, and Financial Markets* (Pearson 12th Global Ed. 2019).
Stephen Valdez and Philip Molyneux, *An Introduction to Global Financial Markets* (Macmillan Education UK 8th ed. 2015).

Essential History and Fundamental Purposes

2

Introduction

Nation States play a critical role in the financial system by making it impossible to achieve a seamless "global" financial system. The United Nations Charter is the fundamental document intended to harmonise the actions of Nation States to achieve the principles embodied in Article 1.[1] The United Nations was founded in 1945 and is currently made up of 193 Member States. The United Nations recognises the absolute sovereignty of each Member State, meaning that absent agreement, each Member State is free to adopt its own policy, including financial matters. Paraphrasing Pauwelyn in a different context, international finance "is a universe of interconnected islands".[2] Pronouncements that there is a global financial system are fiction. Sovereign Nation States make impossible the establishment of a seamless single financial system extending across the globe. Rather, financial systems, if deemed a universe, comprise distinct and interconnected island jurisdictions, infrastructures, and services. This chapter provides a cursory overview of the major public institutions effecting financial systems.

The United Nations

Chapter 1 of the United Nations Charter sets its purposes, principally to maintain international peace, following two major world wars; prevent aggression and the use of force by Member States; and provide a mechanism to resolve international conflicts without the use of violence.[3] The UN Charter is based on the principle "of the sovereign equality of all its Members".[4] Contrary to reality, where Nation States are unequal in economic, political, and military power, each Member State of the United Nations is equal within its purview. A principal, if not foundational, provision of the UN Charter governs the use of force. Article 2(4) states: "Members shall refrain from the threat or use of force against the territorial integrity or political

J. JA Burke, *Financial Services in the Twenty-First Century*,
https://doi.org/10.1007/978-3-030-63967-9_2

independence of any state, or in any other manner inconsistent with the Purposes of the United Nations." Legal scholars have written books and articles to interpret this single sentence and no unified interpretation exists (Shaw 2010). Municipal law of Nation States co-exists with international law. Therefore, at least conceivably, a Nation State may use force against another Nation State, pursuant to political judgment or municipal legislation, when the Nation State deems there is no violation of Article 2(4) or other obligation flowing from the membership rules outlined in the UN Charter. This conclusion explains the widespread existence of international military conflict in the absence of Security Council approval.

Chapter 3 of the UN Charter sets forth the organs of the UN: a General Assembly, a Security Council, an Economic and Social Council, a Trusteeship Council, an International Court of Justice, and a Secretariat. The Security Council consists of ten elected members, serving terms of two years, and five permanent Member States: The United States, China, France, the United Kingdom, and the Russian Federation. The Security Council has exclusive jurisdiction to determine a "breach of peace" or "act of aggression" and to take "measures" to maintain or restore international peace or security. Measures taken range from economic sanctions to the use of military force. However, a resolution from the Security Council authorising measures available under Chap. 7 requires the unanimous consent of the five permanent members. A "no" vote from any permanent member of the Security Council defeats the passage of a proposed Security Council resolution.

Logically, Nation States may not undertake unilateral action when a dispute falls within the exclusive jurisdiction of the Security Council. However, relying upon the ambiguity of Article 2(4) and/or the right of self-defence embodied in Article 51, Nation States historically and presently use economic sanctions against Nation States or use military force deemed necessary and proportionate in response to "international incidents".[5] Economic sanctions are wide ranging, beginning with legal proscription against dealing with designated individuals or entities, and ending with full economic embargo. Economic sanctions use financial systems to destabilise or punish a Nation State, with the aim of stimulating domestic unrest and regime change. Economic sanctions are the major instrument of contemporary foreign policy to achieve political ends. Former President Donald Trump, following in the footsteps of Barack Obama, realised their potential to the fullest degree (*The Economist* 2019). Trump "tweeted" that he would wipe off the face of the earth Afghanistan, Iran, and North Korea. He also would wipe out the economies of: Turkey, Venezuela, and presumably 150% of China's economy (how can you wipe out more than 100% of an economy; a rhetorical question). *The Economist* article is perverse in its enthusiasm for this questionable foreign policy tool. The sub-title is "Financial carpet-bombing". The article also contains the following text: "What has driven this surge in sanctions? According to Marshall Billingslea, an assistant secretary in the Treasury department, the growth reflects Donald Trump's innovative "financial statecraft". In a word, financial carpet-bombing or misuse of the financial system now is transformed into "innovative financial statecraft".

Take for example the Russian Federation's 2014 incorporation of the Republic of Crimea and the City of Sevastopol. In response, the United States and the European Union imposed numerous economic sanctions "against both Russian national and Russian businesses, including Russian government entities".[6] President Barack Obama, invoking the 1977 International Emergency Economic Powers Act, declared a "state of national emergency"[7] and issued an Executive Order authorizing the use of economic sanctions against anyone involved in the Ukraine crisis.[8] Several additional Executive Orders followed including an order forbidding any trade with the Republic of Crimea, effectively an economic embargo. In the United States, economic sanctions are interpreted and enforced by the Office of Foreign Assets Control (OFAC). The regulations issued by OFAC, pursuant to an Executive Order pertaining to economic sanctions, results in an impenetrable quagmire of rules imposing immense costs upon businesses striving for legal compliance.[9] As the next chapter demonstrates, financial systems also may be used (misused) to gain international trade advantage.

The International Court of Justice

The International Court of Justice (ICJ) was established in 1945 at the time of adoption of the UN Charter. The Statute of the ICJ is appended to the UN Charter.[10] The ICJ is a continuation of the Permanent Court of International Justice established under Article 14 of the Covenant of the League of Nations. Because of the brevity of this description, and aside from noting that there are 15 members of the ICJ, this synopsis focuses upon the competence of the ICJ. The latter is competent to adjudicate cases between and among Nation States. Individuals or juridical entities lack standing to bring a case to the ICJ. Article 36 provides: "The jurisdiction of the Court comprises all cases which the parties refer to it and all matters specially provided for in the Charter of the United Nations or in treaties and conventions in force". The jurisdiction of the ICJ theoretically is quite wide. In addition, the ICJ has issued numerous and significant judgments, and, as of 2020, has entered 179 cases on its docket. No matter how constructively written, however, enforcement of an ICJ decision is the "Achilles heel" of the ICJ. Absent Nation State acquiescence, or Security Council backing, the decisions of the ICJ cannot be enforced. "The role of "great Power unanimity" was seen in the case that Nicaragua brought against the US in 1984. Several attempts to use the UN system to enforce the ICJ ruling ordering the US to pay reparations failed. The ruling was never complied with, and a frustrated Nicaragua abandoned the ICJ process in 1991" (Amandala 2009). "United Nations (UN) member countries have the option of submitting cases for final and binding determination to the International Court of Justice (ICJ); but nothing in the UN Charter or the Statute of the ICJ guarantees any country full enforcement of any ICJ ruling" (Ibid). In sum, the ICJ is pragmatically without authority to enforce its decision, though it clarifies international law.

The Bank of International Settlements

The Bank of International Settlements (BIS) was established in Basel, Switzerland in 1930 by Belgium, France, Germany, Italy, Japan, the UK, and Switzerland. At inception, its primary mission was to settle payments imposed upon Germany under the Treaty of Versailles; a secondary mission was to coordinate central bank activity. In 1932, when, under the Lausanne Agreement, Germany's debts were cancelled, the BIS mission primarily, though not exclusively, served to provide a forum for central banks to coordinate policy. The BIS also supported the European Monetary Cooperation from 1950 through 1993. However, when the Bretton Woods system collapsed, followed by the failure of two banks: Bankhaus Herstatt in Germany and the Franklin National Bank in the USA, the "Group of Ten industrialized countries" convened "The Committee on Banking Regulations and Supervisory Practices" in 1975 (Deane and Pringle 1994). Renamed the Basel Committee on Banking Supervision (BCBS), the Committee, headquartered at the Bank for International Settlements in Basel, "was established to enhance financial stability by improving the quality of banking supervision worldwide, and to serve as a forum for regular cooperation between its member countries on banking supervisory matters. The Committee's first meeting took place in February 1975, and meetings have been held regularly three or four times a year since" (BIS). The Committee provides a forum for central banks to coordinate their activities in response to multi-national banks and increased cross-border financial activity.

Due to its mission to stabilise monetary policy, the Committee has two primary goals: (1) assurance of capital adequacy; and (2) transparency of reserve requirements. The Committee therefore sets capital adequacy requirements and encourages the transparency of reserve requirements. The coordinated bank regulations and standards are known as Basel Capital Accords. There are three existing accords: Basel I: the Basel Capital Accord; Basel II: the new capital framework; and Basel III: responding to the 2008 financial crisis. The BIS lacks any authority to make law or to enforce its Accords. Rather, central bank members go to their respective governments and request that the Accords be given the force of law and implemented. The international character of the BIS is important given the problems of coordinating financial regulation among diverse and fractionalised domestic systems.

The Bretton Woods System and Institutions

"The international monetary system is broadly defined as the set of conventions, rules, procedures, and instruments that govern the conduct of financial relations between nations".[11] Subsequent to World War Two, the United States and the United Kingdom, in conjunction with 42 countries, undertook a reconstruction of the international monetary system "to avoid the breakdown in international monetary relations" that took place during the 1920s and 1930s: (1) hyperinflation in Germany, (2) the 1929 US stock market collapse, (3) the Great Depression, (4) trade imbalances leading to protectionism, (5) deflation and currency devaluation designed to gain competitive advantage in international trade, and (6) abandonment of the gold exchange standard. The Bretton Woods system emerged to impose order upon exchange rates and created two key institutions: The International Monetary Fund and the International Bank for Reconstruction and Development.[12]

The International Monetary Fund

Bretton Woods established a regime of fixed but adjustable exchange rates under the supervision of the International Monetary Fund (IMF). The Articles of Agreement of the IMF assigned each currency a central parity against the US dollar, and this parity was permitted to fluctuate by plus or minus 1% on either side. The US dollar was pegged to gold at the price of $35 per ounce. Convertibility of the US dollar into gold was deemed necessary to inspire confidence of central banks to hold dollars in their reserves. In 1945, the United States held 70% of gold reserves in the world; hence, the dollar was "good as gold". The conversion price of $35 per ounce of gold committed the US to preserve the purchasing power of the dollar and therefore provide a further backing of its reliability and staying power.

Under the new monetary regime, countries were expected to preserve the par value of their currencies vis-à-vis the dollar, but the Bretton Woods system provided flexibility in cases of a "fundamental disequilibrium" in a country's balance of payments (BOP). In such case, a country could devalue or revalue its currency by a margin of 10% from its parity without the approval of the IMF. Larger realignments required IMF authorisation. Allowing countries to alter the par rate of their currencies provided an alternative to measures deemed more destructive to the "new order": deflation or import controls to correct "persistent balance of payments imbalances".[13] In addition, countries were permitted immediately to make their currencies available to buy goods and services from other countries, as these imports effected only the "current account" of the BOP. Hence, governments could still employ capital controls effecting the capital account of the BOP; the omission was considered necessary to curtail the destabilising effects of free capital movement.

The IMF was funded by Member State contributions called "quotas": the amount determined by the Member State's economic importance as reflected in its size of subscription to the IMF. A Member State placed one-quarter of its quota in reserve assets (mainly gold) and the remaining three-quarters in its currency. The IMF began operations in March 1947 with a total quota of $8.8 billion. The IMF credit facility thereby had the capital necessary to lend to countries encountering balance of payments difficulties. In the event a country required funding to correct an imbalance in its BOP, the country was entitled automatically to the first 25% of its quota, and a further four tranches each of 25% known as credit tranches. However, any tranche above the first 25% was subject to IMF conditions imposing increasing austerity measures on the Member State with each drawn tranche. In total, a country could draw 125% of its quota. "The conditions attached to the latter tranches are known as 'IMF conditionality' and constitute a set of measures designed to improve a country's balance of payments".[14] Drawing from the IMF credit facility required the country to borrow US dollars in exchange for further deposits of its currency. "The Fund decides what assets and currencies the drawing country receives".[15] In general, the maturity period of the loan ranges from three to five years. The debtor repays the IMF by purchasing its domestic currency with foreign reserves, that is, gold or US dollars.

The new international monetary system encountered strains from its inception: primarily the demand for US dollars, the amount of which was restricted on the foreign exchange market. The United States ran current account surpluses by selling its goods and services abroad while European countries ran current account deficits since they needed to purchase goods and capital equipment to rebuild their economies. The demand for US dollars exceeded the supply on the foreign exchange market. In response, the United States Secretary of State George Marshall announced a package of aid to European economies. Between 1948 and 1952, the "Marshall aid" package provided grants in the approximate amount of $11.6 billion and $1.8 billion in loans to enable European reconstruction and development of their post-war economies. Marshall aid was contingent upon increased cooperation among European states and led to setting up the Organisation for European Economic Co-operation that later became the Organisation for Economic Co-operation and Development (OECD). The "Marshall aid" programme also benefited the United States by supplying US dollars to European countries enabling them to purchase US manufactured goods and equipment.

The Bretton Woods international monetary system experienced additional fractures as early as 1950. In 1949, European deficits led to a series of devaluations in the UK, France, and Scandinavian countries. The IMF then realised that the parities of European currencies to the US dollar were overvalued and unsustainable thereby leading to approval of European currency devaluations. In contrast to its initial post-war current account surpluses, the United States, beginning in the early 1950s, began to run current account deficits of approximately $1.5 billion per year. By contrast, Germany and Japan began to run current account surpluses as both relied upon export-driven growth. The shifting current account balances among the US, Germany, and Japan initially posed no risk as Germany and Japan did not object to augmenting their dollar reserves. In addition, "Marshall aid" combined with a recovery of European economies allowed Europe to acquire sufficient reserves to make their currencies freely convertible.

Subsequently, the United States current account deficits continued to deteriorate during the period between 1958 and 1961, sparking a demand by foreign central banks to convert dollar reserves into gold, and requiring the formation of a bailout committee called the General Arrangements to Borrow (GAB), to forestall speculation against the dollar. In 1954, the London gold bullion market reopened for private trading in gold. Combined with a belief in an overvalued US dollar, the private gold market pushed the price of gold, on the open and private market, higher than the US peg price of $35 per ounce. In 1965, President de Gaulle of France extolled the virtues of gold as compared to the dollar and the French began to convert their dollar reserves into gold. By 1967, US dollar liabilities exceeded its gold reserves. Any attempt by foreign central banks to convert dollars into gold would break the Bretton Woods system. Consequently, the United States managed to obtain agreement among foreign central banks not to convert dollars into gold.

Nevertheless, in spite of interim indications of recovery, the US balance of payments deteriorated during the 1960s, due partially to the Vietnam War. Concurrently, current account deficits in Europe led the UK to devalue the pound by 14.6%; France to devalue the French franc by 11%; and Germany to devalue the deutsche mark by 9.3%. These adjustments convinced speculators that trading currencies was potentially profitable and that the US dollar was overvalued. The persistent increases in the US balance of payments, involving all accounts, led to massive speculation against the US dollar; speculators bought yen and deutsche marks in anticipation of a revaluation of the US dollar. No degree of central bank intervention to support the dollar had the capacity to stem speculation against the dollar. Sensing the inevitable, President Richard M. Nixon in 1971, announced that the dollar was no longer convertible into gold, and imposed a 10% tax on all US imports until trading partners revalued their currencies against the US dollar. While efforts were made to reset the Bretton Woods system, no political measure worked, and by 1973, the world adopted a floating exchange rate system, marking an end to Bretton Woods. The IMF lost its mission as caretaker of the Bretton Woods system. Its role shrank to surveillance of international monetary transactions and use of its credit facility.

The World Bank

The World Bank was created at Bretton Woods in 1944. Its goal is to provide "financial and technical assistance to developing countries around the world" in an effort to "reduce poverty and support development." It consists of five underlying institutions, the first two of which are collectively referred to as "The World Bank": (1) International Bank for Reconstruction and Development, (2) International Development Association, (3) International Finance Corporation, (4) Multilateral Investment Guarantee Agency, and (5) International Centre for Settlement of Investment Disputes. The World Bank *per se* provides financial assistance to creditworthy middle- and low-level-income nations (Nation States). The International Development Association provides loans and grants to poor nations. The International Finance Corporation supplements these activities by lending to the private sector in eligible countries.

Important for this textbook are contracts, usually under a bilateral investment treaty, between a private entity of one Nation State and a public entity of another Nation State. Conflicts arising from these contracts generally are resolved under the International Centre for Settlement of Investment Disputes (Washington Convention).

The World Trade Organization

The General Agreement on Trade and Tariffs (GATT) came into existence in 1947 (Matsushita et al. 2005). At that time, Nation State members failed to agree upon an umbrella organisation. The purpose of the GATT was to harmonise trade rules for goods and services among its Member States, limit impediments to trade to tariffs, and to incentivise free trade and ultimately the abolishment of any obstacle to free trade including tariffs. Nation States having grievances against other Nation States brought their claims to the GATT. The GATT provided arbitration panels and an Appellate Court to resolve disputes. In 1995, Member States finally agreed upon a unitary organisation called the World Trade Organization to administer international trade regulations. The 1948 GATT, as well as its jurisprudence, and the 1993 General Agreement on Trade in Services, were incorporated into the 1995 WTO. In addition, numerous other agreements (called Annexes) were appended: for example, (1) the General Agreement on Trade in Services (GATS), (2) Agreement on Trade-Related Aspects of Intellectual Property Rights (TRIPS), and (3) the Dispute Settlement Understanding (DSU). The WTO jurisdiction extends to goods, services, and intellectual property. In addition, the DSU set forth the dispute settlement system in which conflicts among Nation State would be argued and settled.

Conclusion

The public institutional infrastructure established after World War Two was ambitious, well-intended, and prudent, given the atrocities committed during World War One and World War Two, not to mention the events that took place during the interregnum. The Bretton Woods system, bearing directly upon financial systems, crashed and burned within 26 years. Functions of surviving entities are warped: notably, the IMF and WTO. The IMF watches and provides reports on international monetary policy and provides loans to Nation States subject to conditions, generally severe austerity measures, as experienced by Greece. IMF conditionality for using its credit facility is the subject of criticism by noted economists Joseph Stiglitz and James K. Galbraith.[16] While the US dollar retains its status as the international reserve currency, emerging economies repeatedly express discontent with US hegemony over the international monetary system. The move to floating exchange rates has not given rise to a stable international monetary system.

Questions for Students

1. How do Nation States prevent the construction and existence of a global financial network?
2. How do Nation States use economic sanctions without violating the UN Charter Article 2(4)? What does Article 2(4) state? What does Article 51 state? In 1974, the General Assembly approved the Charter of Economic Rights and Duties of

States. Taken together, do these legal instruments prohibit the use of finance to push for regime change in another Nation State?
3. What is the Bretton Woods Agreement on International Monetary Policy and why did it fail?
4. What are the respective roles of the IMF and World Bank?
5. The World Trade Organization allows states to lower tariffs and to bind themselves to tariffs. In 2018, the US breached its WTO obligations toward China. China started a WTO dispute and the panel ruled in favor of China. What can China do to enforce the decision of the WTO?

Notes

1. Charter of the United Nations, Chapter 1, Article 1 frames the purposes and principles as: (1) international peace and security, (2) friendly relations respecting equal rights and self-determination of peoples, (3) international cooperation to solve economic, social, and cultural problems, and (4) harmonising the actions of nations to achieve the foregoing ends. The UN Charter is available at http://www.un.org/en/sections/un-charter/chapter-i/index.html
2. Joost Pauwelyn, Bridging Fragmentation and Unity: International Law as a Universe of Inter-Connected Islands, 25 Mich. J. Int'l L. 903 (2004).
3. UN Charter Ch.1, Arts 1, 2, 3, and 4.
4. United Nations Charter, Ch. 1, Art. 2(1).
5. Comment, Nicholas Marin, *All is Fair in Law and Warfare in the Ukrainian Crisis: A Look at the Growing Increase of Economic Sanctions as a Weapon of War and the Effects on the International Community*, 40 Southern Illinois U. L. J. 323 (2016).
6. Council Decision 2014/145/ CFSP [CD 145], the first legal response of the EU is worth reviewing for its succinct language, limited range of sanctions, and references to Articles of the Consolidated Treaties to support the EU sanction regime. The title of Council Decision concerns "restrictive measures in respect of actions undermining or threatening the territorial integrity, sovereignty, and independence of Ukraine". The Council Decision invokes Article 29 of the TEU as the legal ground empowering the Council to take the Decision. Article 29 provides: "The Council shall adopt decisions which shall define the approach of the Union to a particular matter of a geographical or thematic nature. Member States shall ensure that their national policies conform to the Union positions."
7. The legal justification for imposing economic sanctions against Russia and Crimea (whether denominated Specially Designated Persons, or Organisations) derives primarily from the US law entitled "The National Emergency Act" found in Title 50 (itself entitled "War and National Defence") of the United States Code, specifically Subchapter III, sections 1601–50, and secondarily from the International Emergency Economic Powers Act, also found in Title 50 of the USC, specifically sections 1701–07. Remarkably, neither law defines the terms "national emergency" or "international economic emergency". Excepting required reports to Congress, the laws give the President of the United States *carte blanche* to declare "national emergencies" in response to any event or threat, whether real or imaginary to whatever is conceived as national security.
8. Executive Order (E.O.) 13660.
9. President Trump signed into law a bill (H.R. 3364 entitled "Countering America's Adversaries Through Sanctions Act") that contains sanctions against Iran, North Korea, and the Russian Federation. Matters related to the Russian Federation are the sole focus of this chapter. The legislation deprives the Executive branch of government from revoking, modifying, or altering existing sanctions against the Russian Federation, without the approval of Congress. In other words, the law transforms former President Obama's Executive Orders into legislation.

10. Statute of the International Court of Justice comprising 70 articles contained within five chapters.
11. Keith Pilbeam, *International Finance* 257 (Palgrave Macmillan 4th ed. 2013).
12. The International Finance Corporation is affiliated with the World Bank "and provides risk capital directly to least developed countries". *Id.* at 259.
13. *Id.* at 260.
14. *Id.* at 261.
15. *Id.*
16. James K. Galbraith, Welcome to the Poisoned Chalice: The Destruction of Greece and the Future of Europe (Yale 2016).

Bibliography

Amandala, ICJ Stats – Enforcement of ICJ Rulings, January 30th, 2009 at http://amandala.com.bz/news/icj-stats-enforcement-of-icj-rulings/

Bank of International Settlements (BIS) at https://www.bis.org/bcbs/history.htm

Marjorie Deane & Robert Pringle, The Central Banks (Viking 1994).

The Economist, Financial carpet bombing, Donald Trump uses sanctions more keenly than any of his predecessors, 25 Nov. 2019 at https://www.economist.com/united-states/2019/11/24/donald-trump-uses-sanctions-more-keenly-than-any-of-his-predecessors

James K. Galbraith, Welcome to the Poisoned Chalice: The Destruction of Greece and the Future of Europe, (Yale 2016).

Mitsuo Matsushita, Thomas J. Schoenbaum & Petros C. Mavroidis, The World Trade Organization: Law, Practice, and Policy (Oxford 2nd ed. 2005).

Keith Pilbeam, *International Finance* (Palgrave Macmillan 4th ed. 2013).

Malcolm N. Shaw, *International Law* (Cambridge 6th ed. 2010).

The Financial System 3

Introduction

This chapter uses the UK financial system as a microcosm of financial systems generally. The UK serves as a lens to view and understand financial institutions, financial services and transactions, and the role of government and its central bank. The UK has diverse financial institutions: for example, commercial banks, investment banks, insurance companies, pension funds, exchange-traded funds, unit trusts, private equity, and hedge funds. The UK financial system delivers a wide range of financial products such as public and commercial debt, equity for enterprises, provision of services to households, and functions as a hub for international money movements. Therefore, understanding this single instance of a Nation State financial system is an effective methodology for understanding like financial systems in different Nation States. The individual systems are linked inelegantly to give the impression of a single global financial system.

Mapping the UK Financial System

In 2015, Oliver Burrows and Katie Low of the Bank of England published a bulletin entitled "Mapping the UK Financial System" (Oliver Burrows and Katie Low 2015). The bulletin "paints a picture of the financial system" by reviewing the balance sheets of financial firms. They start with a summary map and then use a sequence of sub-mapping to show the interconnections among financial firms, non-financial firms, and economic agents acting in the market. More sophisticated mapping demonstrates the link between the financial system and the real economy. The work provides a platform to identify financial institutions, economic agents, financial assets and instruments, and services provided by the financial system. The bulletin answers the question why the provision of financial services matter. The authors state financial institutions: "facilitate the wage payments companies make

J. JA Burke, *Financial Services in the Twenty-First Century*,
https://doi.org/10.1007/978-3-030-63967-9_3

to staff and the transactions households make when they use credit and debit cards to buy goods and services; provide loans to households and companies to allow some to consume and invest today, while managing savings for tomorrow on behalf of others; and provide insurance against all sorts of adverse outcomes, from ships sinking to pets needing medical care". In sum, the financial system provides four essential functions: (1) payments, (2) moving money from today to tomorrow (saving and investment), (3) moving money from tomorrow to today (credit), and (4) manging risks.

The bulletin states that, in 2014, UK GDP amounted to £1.8 trillion ($3 trillion) and that the balance sheets of UK financial firms were around £20 trillion. The authors note: "The UK financial system is bigger, relative to the size of the economy, than that of most other countries". In addition, of the £1.8 trillion, £1 trillion was paid in wages and salaries. This raises two questions: (1) why is the UK Banking sector large? and (2) what is its relationship to the real economy? Question one is explored first. Oliver Bush published a separate bulletin entitled "Why is the UK banking system so big and is that a problem?" (Oliver Bush 2014). The author first notes that the UK banking sector assets are 450% of nominal GDP, to give an impression of size. Bush posits four hypotheses for this astonishing disequilibrium in size between the real economy and the financial sector: (1) the international nature of the system, (2) comparative advantage, that is, the UK may be able to deliver financial services more efficiently than other countries, (3) first-mover advantage, meaning its historical role as an important financial centre, and (4) the implicit government subsidy, that is, the government will bail out the system in event of failure at a cost to the taxpayer. No hypothesis is proved or validated by empirical data.

To say that the UK banking sector is large requires a method of measurement. Bush uses two metrics: ownership basis and residence basis. Ownership basis measures size by combining the assets of all UK-owned monetary institutions, including the assets of non-resident branches and subsidiaries, and excluding the assets of foreign-owned banks having branches or subsidiaries in the UK. Residency basis measures size by the "assets of monetary financial institutions located in the United Kingdom regardless of the nationality of the ultimate owner" (Bush) Since foreign banks are a prominent feature of the UK financial landscape, residency measurement is substantial as it includes assets of foreign banks' UK subsidiaries and branches. The result: the UK banking system is big relative to the size of the banking sectors compared to other advanced economies. Bush notes: the UK banking sector "is the largest banking sector on a residency basis compared to Japan, the United States, and the ten largest EU economies" (Bush).

Aside from size, the UK banking system has about "150 deposit-taking foreign branches and 98 deposit-taking foreign subsidiaries from 56 countries" (Bush). Foreign banks also constitute about half of UK banking assets and "nearly a fifth of global banking is booked in the United Kingdom" (Bush). Contrary to common understanding of banks, UK banks do not have large loan portfolios. "Only around half of UK-owned banks' assets are loans to non-bank borrowers". For the largest foreign subsidiaries, the figure is lower, less than 10% of their assets are held in loans to non-bank borrowers. For these banks, most assets are held in derivatives and reverse repos. The "flip side" of this composition of assets is that the major liabilities of UK banks are not customer deposits, but "derivatives and inter-bank deposits. This raises the question of what has this gargantuan financial structure got to do with the real economy, when the classic texts tell us the function of banks is to lend to productive users to accelerate economic growth.

Data from the UK Office of National Statistics indicates the "real economy" consists of four sectors: manufacturing, production (e.g. oil and gas), construction, and services, with the latter accounting for the largest part (Office of National Statistics).[1] Bush suggests that UK Banks, based on residency, are not focused upon lending to non-bank borrowers. In addition, the assets held in the UK banking system dwarf the annual national income of the UK, in 2014 about £1 trillion. Even if the entire national income were saved, it would not make a statistical dent in the asset composition of the UK resident banking system. Therefore, it follows that the UK financial system serves interests other than lending to the real economy. While the bulletins do not identify which foreign interests are served, it is reasonable to infer that international and wholesale finance, and private banking and wealth management comprise an important activity of the UK banking system. "Wholesale banking consists in large transactions between financial institutions, or the provision of banking services to large customers (pension funds, large corporates, asset managers and other institutional customers) with specific needs in terms of cash management, access to capital markets, large trade transactions and foreign exchange exposures. They play an essential role in helping big issuers (large corporates, governments, financial institutions) reach out to investors (asset managers, hedge funds, insurers, pension funds) and therefore benefit from the network effects of London as a global financial centre" (European Parliament Briefing, Brexit: the United Kingdom and EU Financial Services 2016). The UK banking system further is an important money manager having large positions in asset management for the EU and the rest of the world.

The summary map of the UK financial system is reproduced, as it introduces common financial firms and their sizes relative to one another (Fig. 3.1).

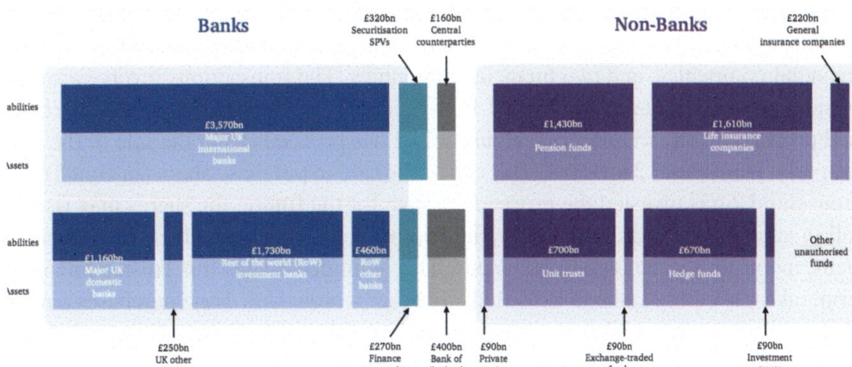

Fig. 3.1 A map of the UK financial system. (Source: UK Bank of England, Quarterly Bulletin 2015 Q2)

The map comprises two horizontal rectangles and two vertical rectangles separating the larger counterparts. The rectangle labelled "Banks" shows the architecture of the banking system in the UK and its size populated by major UK international banks (£3,570 billion); major UK domestic banks (£1,160 billion); rest of the world (ROW) investment banks (£1,730 billion); and ROW other banks (£460 billion). The rectangle labelled "Non-Banks" shows the architecture of the non-banking system in the UK and its size, populated by pension funds (£1,430 billion); life insurance companies (£1,610 billion); general insurance companies (£220 billion); unit trusts (£700 billion); hedge funds (£670 billion); private equity (£90 billion); exchange-traded funds (£90 billion); investment trusts (£90 billion); and a category designated other unauthorised funds, without a balance sheet statement. The vertical rectangles constituting the interstices consist of the Bank of England (£400 billion) and central counterparties (£160 billion). The UK financial system, having a value of about £20 trillion, is large compared to the UK's GDP of £1.8 trillion. The largest part is the banking system.

In this context, the financial system "is the sum of all the financial assets owned by banks and non-bank financial companies in the United Kingdom" (Burrows) While the "summary map" does not contain financial markets, the assets traded in these markets are included in the non-banks' side of the balance sheets. The "balance sheet" approach is used to "explore how the economy fits together" (Ibid.). Since "financial balance sheets represent the stock of financial contracts, they reveal the ties between agents through time. The primary agents of the financial systems are: households, non-financial firms, and the public sector (government). For example, when a household takes a mortgage from a bank to buy a house, the bank lends the funds "today" in exchange for a promise by the household to repay the debt over time. The "loan" is an asset for the bank and a liability for the household. Financial systems comprise a deep network of connections among agents in the economy. Knowledge of these connections provides insights into threats to financial stability. When commitments to pay exceed the ability or capacity of borrowers to meet obligations, the losses that cascade through the system potentially lead to a financial collapse if they are not backstopped by the government.

The following stylised illustration of agents and financial institutions transacting in the market shows the complexity of the network, at the simplest level (Fig. 3.2).

This figure shows six transactions between six agents: two households, two non-financial companies, and two financial companies. The transactions involve a series of sales and purchases. Household 1 borrowed money from Megabank to purchase real property from Household 2. Household 2 has proceeds from the sale of the real property. Household 2 uses the proceeds of the sale to purchase shares in Unit Trust. Household 2 has invested the proceeds to save for the future; the shares may rise or fall in value. Ed's Beds, a non-financial company, purchases a vehicle from Anne's Vans, a non-financial company. The purchase is funded when Unit Trust, a financial firm, takes an equity stake in Ed's Beds. In other words, Unit Trust purchases equity shares in a non-financial firm to expand its portfolio of investments. Anne's Vans deposits the proceeds of the sale of the vehicle in Megabank.

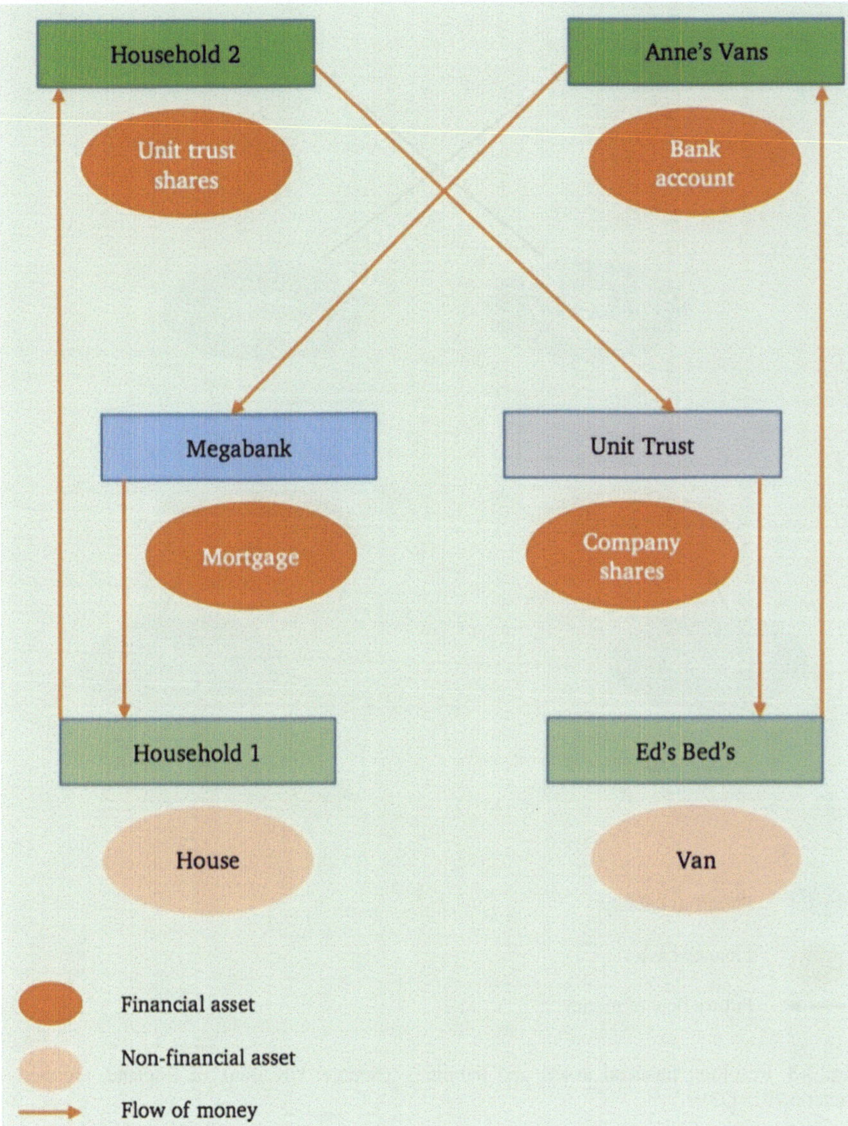

Fig. 3.2 Stylised transactions. (Source: UK Bank of England, Quarterly Bulletin 2015 Q2)

The next figure shows the results of the transactions in terms of assets and liabilities (Fig. 3.3).

Megabank has a new asset, a deposit account created for Household 1 to enable the purchase of the house. Household 1 has a liability (a mortgage) to Megabank to pay bank the amount borrowed. Megabank also incurred a new liability to Anne's Vans when she deposited the sales proceeds into a demand account. Anne's Vans has

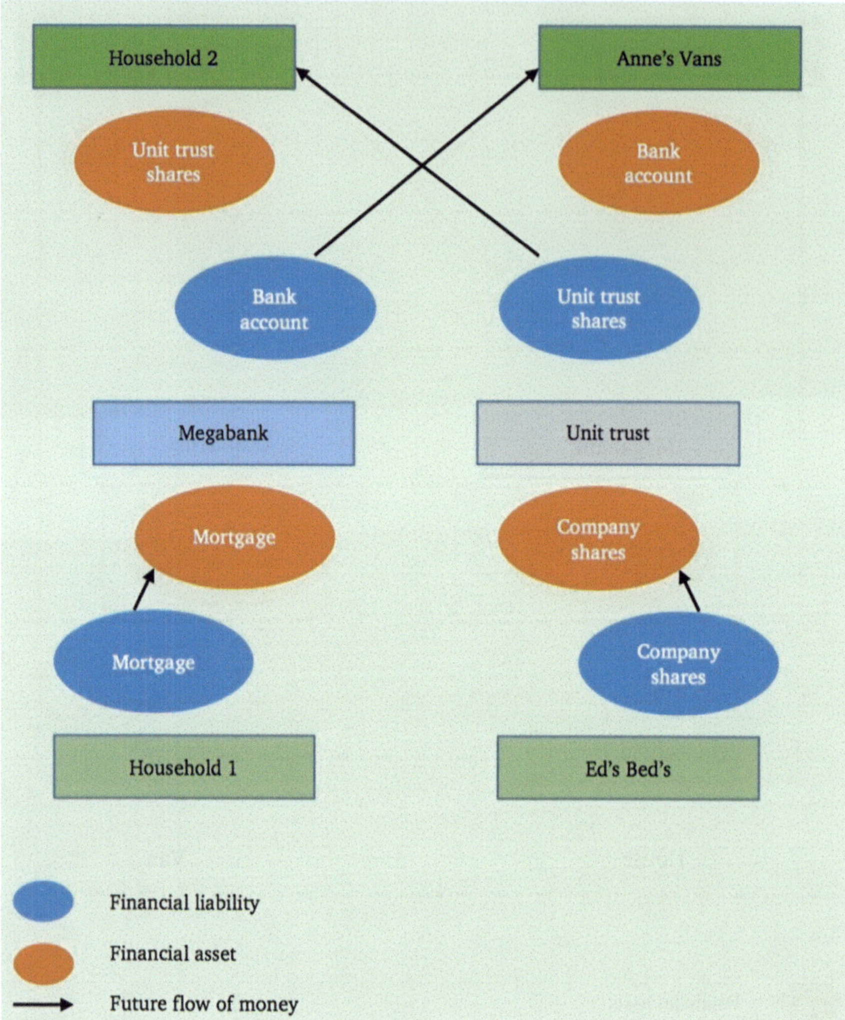

Fig. 3.3 Resulting financial assets and liabilities. (Source: UK Bank of England, Quarterly Bulletin 2015 Q2)

a new asset and a claim against Megabank. Unit Trust has a financial liability to Household 2, while the latter has an asset held by Unit Trust. Unit Trust purchased shares in Ed's Beds, so therefore may profit or not depending upon the performance of the company. Megabank distinctly differs from Unit Trust, though both are financial firms. As discussed in detail in a later chapter, banks have the capacity to create money. They do so by creating deposits through the act of lending in the absence of pre-existing funds to finance the loan. Unit Trust, a non-bank, cannot "create money" but must seek a source of funding to make investments. In our figure, Unit

Trust sold shares to Household 2 (receipt of funds) and bought shares from Ed's Beds, matching an existing saver to an existing buyer.

The stylised figure also shows how agents in the system become connected in the absence of direct transactions. For example, Household 1 and Anne's Vans now are connected through Megabank. The security of Anne's Vans' demand account depends upon the capacity of Household 1 to repay the loan when due. As more transactions are added to the network, agents in the economy become ever more connected. Mapping out the agents and interconnections is essential to understand the real economy and the financial system. These relations are key for the UK Central Bank to identify risk and to formulate policy. Without undertaking a study of monetary policy, the summary figure depicted the role of the central bank and central counterparty. The central bank is responsible for managing interest rates and for setting prudential policy. Using open market operations or quantitative easing, the bank may expand or contract the balance sheets of the financial sector. The central counterparty stands in the middle of the market between buyer and seller ready to step in to prevent default by one to the transaction.

The map shows, for example, that households have about £6 trillion of financial assets meaning that other sectors have a total of £6 trillion of liabilities to the household sector. In the UK, non-financial firms and households "hold deposits with banks, and banks largely lend to firms and households". Likewise, "firms and households hold insurance contracts and pensions, and insurance companies and pension funds in turn hold debt and equity of real economy and other financial institutions, sometimes directly and sometimes via collective investment schemes". The reference to the "real economy" raises an interesting question in the context of the UK. The bulletin states the total value of GDP was £1.4 trillion, of which £1 trillion was paid in wages or national income. Presumably, wages included those payments made to UK workers in the financial system. The interconnections implied by the map go well beyond the simple connections shown by the six transactions. "There is a large web of lending between different banks, and the links between banks and other financial institutions are also very important" (Burrows). The bulletin also excludes "the foreign assets and liabilities of foreign branches" (Fig. 3.4).

The vast network of institutions makes up the "financial intermediation system". This concept presumes that financial firms are essential to the economy as they move funds from those holding excessive savings to those needing finance to produce goods or services or promote the objectives of the economy. Without expert financial agents "in the middle", it is presumed that matching lenders and borrowers would be inefficient and ineffective. Expertise owned by the financial intermediaries is based on their access to information, ability to assess credit and other risks, and their capacity to absorb loss, without the spectre of bankruptcy or creation of systemic risk. "The bank uses its specialist expertise to acquire a diversified portfolio of investments. Without the existence of the bank, depositors would have neither the time nor the expertise to decide which of these loans or investments to make" (Begg et al. 2003).

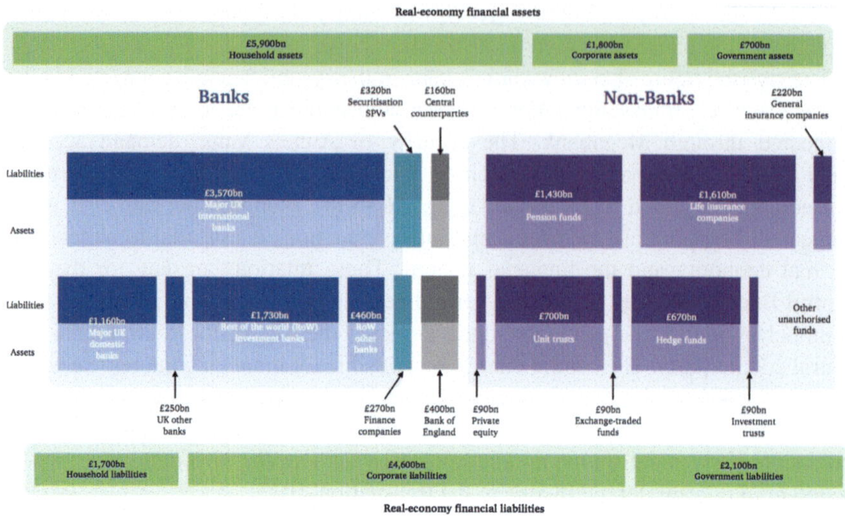

Fig. 3.4 The financial balance sheet of the UK economy in 2014—'the map'. Excludes cross-border exposures of foreign-owned bank branches and derivatives. (Source: UK Bank of England, Quarterly Bulletin 2015 Q2)

The bulletin mapped the UK financial system, a single domestic albeit international financial centre. To build a map of the "global financial system" would require construction of maps for individual Nation States, and then constructing the connections among all extant financial institutions and the underlying real economies of these Nation States, and off-shore financial havens. The financial galaxy, probably impossible to contextualise, would be practically unfathomable, and subject to perpetual modification because of the system's evolution. A complete map also would have to include the infrastructure supporting the flow of funds through the system and the diverse regulatory environments, as well as the contractual base of transactions.

Conclusion

The bulletin painted a picture of the financial system ecosystem in the UK. The description of institutions and transactions in this chapter is superficial but gives an accurate impression of select financial services and the institutions that provide them. The bulletin focused on the interdependence of financial institutions and economic agents to identify potential risks to the stability of the system. The sketch enables readers to question the rationale and necessity of the ornate financial system. The Bank of England publications failed to provide empirical data to support the hypothesis that a causal link exists between economic growth in the real economy and the financial system. This hypothesis is examined in subsequent chapters attempting to identify "drivers" of economic growth.

Questions

1. How do the authors explain the difference in size between the economy and the financial system?
2. What four factors does Bush speculate may be the reasons why the UK banking system is large relative to other Nation States and to the UK domestic economy?
3. What is financial intermediation?
4. The UK financial system is composed of many financial institutions. One institution is called the "hedge fund". In 2004, Timothy F. Geithner, President and CEO of the Federal Reserve Bank of New York, gave a speech entitled "Hedge Funds and Their Implications for the Financial System", reproduced here:

   https://www.newyorkfed.org/newsevents/speeches/2004/gei041117#:~:text=Hedge%20funds%20play%20a%20valuable,breadth%20to%20our%20capital%20markets.

   Read the article, and define a hedge fund and the role Geithner states it plays in the financial system. In retrospect, given the 2008 financial crisis, is it necessary to modify Geithner's comments? What does this article imply about the predictions of so-called "economic experts"?
5. In 1998, Long-Term Capital Management (LTCM), a hedge fund, failed and posed a risk to the financial system. Why did it fail and why does Geithner in 2004 support hedge funds?

Note

1. UK Office of National Statistics at https://www.ons.gov.uk

Bibliography

Oliver Burrows and Katie Low, Mapping the UK financial system, Bank of England Quarterly Bulletin 2015 Q2.

Office for National Statistics, Transforming the UK financial accounts: flow of funds, 26 November 2019.

David Begg, Stanley Fischer, Rudiger Dornbusch, Economics (7th ed. McGraw-Hill 2003).

Oliver Bush, Why is the UK banking system so big and is that a problem? Bank of England Quarterly Bulletin 2014 Q4 at https://www.bankofengland.co.uk/quarterly-bulletin/2014/q4/why-is-the-uk-banking-system-so-big-and-is-that-a-problem.that a problem?

European Parliament Briefing, Brexit: the United-Kingdom and EU Financial Services 2016 at https://www.europarl.europa.eu/RegData/etudes/BRIE/2016/587384/IPOL_BRI(2016)587384_EN.pdf.

Capital in the Twenty-First Century

4

Introduction

"Capital in the Twenty-First Century" is "an analytical historical narrative based upon" (Piketty 2015) a "relatively large historical database on the structure of national income and national wealth" (Ibid). The dataset to which Piketty refers was developed mainly in the twentieth century by pioneers like Kuznets and Solow. It therefore is a book about "distribution" of capital and income and the multiple causes of inequality of distribution set within a multi-century factual framework. A major result of the study finds: "The history of inequality is shaped by the way economic, social, and political actors view what is just and what is not, as well as by the relative power of those actors and the collective choices that result" (Piketty 2014). The question of what share of output should be allocated to labour (wages) and what share to profits (capital) is a conflict permeating history and is a central question today, given the rise of the "billionaire class", if not "trillionaire class."

Piketty's analytical historical narrative raises concepts central to understanding economics, finance, and money and therefore is a useful starting point from a student's perspective. Understanding Piketty requires knowledge of his definitional terms. We start with "national income": the "sum of all income available to the residents of a given country in a given year, regardless of the legal classification of that income" (Piketty 2014). National income is closely related, but not equivalent, to gross domestic product (GDP). GDP is the total of all goods and services produced in a country in a given year. Calculating national income requires us to deduct depreciation from GDP, that is, the wear and tear on physical assets used to produce the goods and services. In general, depreciation averages about 10% of GDP. When depreciation is subtracted from GDP, one obtains "net domestic output", or "domestic output", generally 90% of GDP. Next, one must add net income received from abroad or subtract net income paid to foreigners. This depends on a country's balance of payments. If residents of Country "A", firms and natural persons, own capital assets located in Country "B", then Country "A" receives a flow of profits and

J. JA Burke, *Financial Services in the Twenty-First Century*,
https://doi.org/10.1007/978-3-030-63967-9_4

rents from Country "B". Even if the latter has a high domestic product, it will have a lower national income. "To sum up, a country's national income may be greater or smaller than its domestic product, depending on whether net income from abroad is positive or negative" (Piketty 2014). It follows that "national income" = domestic output + net income from abroad.

At the global level, income received and paid from abroad must balance. Global output = global income. The equality of the two flows is an accounting identity. Yet, it reflects important facts. In a given year, it is impossible for total income to exceed the amount of new wealth produced in that period. Conversely, all production must be distributed as income in one form or another. Payments must be made to workers and others who contributed labour to the process of production. Profits, dividends, rents, and so on must be paid to owners of capital used in the production process. Whether we look at the accounts of a company, nation, or the global economy, output and income can be decomposed as the sum of income distributed to capital and income to labour, so that national income = capital income + labour income.

Before turning to the definition of "capital", a diversion is justified. The term "GDP" requires further precise definition, since it is widely used in economics and finance. "When the total value of final goods and services is calculated using current prices, the resulting GDP measure is referred to as *nominal* GDP" (Mishkin 2018). The word *nominal* indicates that values are measured using current prices. Nominal GDP may be deceptive. For example, assume that all prices doubled, but that the level of actual production remained the same, nominal GDP would double but no person would have benefited from twice as many goods and services. "A more reliable measure of economic production expresses values in terms of prices for an arbitrary base year, currently 2009" (Mishkin 2018). GDP measured in constant prices is called *real* GDP because price distortions are factored out of the equation and only actual changes in the quantity of goods and services are measured. This observation then leads to an account of measuring aggregate price levels, that is, average prices in an economy. We shall deal with only one measurement: the GDP deflator: defined as nominal GDP divided by real GDP. "Thus, if 2019 nominal GDP is $10 trillion but 2019 real GDP in 2009 prices is $9 trillion" (Mishkin 2018), then it follows that GDP deflator = $10 trillion/$9 trillion = 1.11. This illustration demonstrates that on average prices have risen 11% since 2009, the arbitrary base year.

Returning to Piketty, we now endeavour to define "capital", stressing that the term is mutable and ever changing in characteristics. First, Piketty excludes what economists call "human capital" since the term merely refers to an individual's labour power, training, skills, and abilities. Piketty states: "In this book, capital is defined as the sum total of nonhuman assets that can be owned and exchanged on some market" (Piketty 2014). He further states that capital includes "all forms of wealth that individuals (or groups of individuals) can own and that can be transferred or traded through the market on a permanent basis" (Piketty 2014). In practice, capital may be owned by private individuals called "private capital" or capital may be owned by governments or their agencies called "public capital". "Public wealth in most developed countries is currently insignificant (or even negative, where public debt exceeds public assets)" (Piketty 2014). Private wealth accounts for almost all national wealth throughout the world.

In his convention, Piketty does not distinguish between wealth and capital, and uses the terms interchangeably. He thus is able to define "national wealth or "national capital": "the total market value of everything owned by the residents and government of a given country at a given point in time, provided that it can be traded on some market" (Piketty 2014). Capital therefore is the "sum total of nonfinancial assets [land, plant, machinery, dwellings, patents, and other intellectual property] and financial assets [bank accounts, mutual funds, bonds, equity, financial investments of all kinds, insurance policies, pension funds], less the total amount of financial liabilities (debt)" (Piketty 2014). National wealth = private wealth + public wealth. Total national wealth can be decomposed into two parts: national wealth = national capital = domestic output + net foreign capital.

Building upon the definitions of "capital" and "national income", Piketty constructs the capital/income ratio that leads to his first "law of capitalism". Income is a flow of goods and services produced in a given period, usually measured annually. By contrast, capital is a "stock" where wealth is measured at a particular point in time and includes wealth accumulated in prior years. In most advanced countries, capital stock represents about six years of national income, and virtually all capital stock is privately held (Piketty 2014). The way to measure the capital stock of a given country is to divide that stock by the annual flow of income denoted by the beta sign, ß. Let us assume, following Piketty, that ß = 6 or 600%, that is, the accumulation of capital during the six-year period. Taking data from year 2010 for the countries France, Britain, Germany, Japan, and the United States, national income was roughly €30,000–35,000 per capita, while total private wealth (net of debt) was around €150,000–200,000 per capita. These figures, like all averages, hide enormous disparities. Some people own millions and millions of capital assets, while others own little or even none, especially if their debts exceed their assets. The same observation is true of income, wages range from a thousand or so per month to tens of thousands monthly for highly compensated managers.

Piketty then presents the first law of capitalism by linking capital stock to the flow of income. The capital/income ratio ß is related to the "share of income from capital in national income" denoted œ. The formula is œ = $r \times \beta$ where r is the rate of return on capital. For example, if ß = 600% (six years of accumulated capital stock) and r = 5%, then œ = 600% × 5% = 30%. "In other words, if national wealth represents the equivalent of six years of national income, and if the rate of return on capital is 5 percent per year, then capital's share in national income is 30 percent" (Piketty 2014). The rate of return measures the yield on capital and is a broader measure than "return on profits" or "rate of interest". Rates of return vary widely depending on the type of investment, and on the interaction of endogenous factors like "belief systems, institutions, and the dynamics of inequality" (Piketty 2015). The forces that drive income inequality and capital inequality are different. Although the three variables in the equation are not independent of one another, the equation does not explain how each of the variables is determined. Piketty states that additional ideas and relationships must be introduced such as savings and investment rates and the rate of economic growth, leading to the second fundamental law of capitalism.

The second fundamental law of capitalism is that if a country saves a substantial portion of its national income and the economy grows slowly over a long period, then the capital stock accumulates at an exponentially fast rate. Piketty states: "In the long run, the capital/income ratio ß is related in a simple and transparent way to the savings rate s and the growth rate g according to the following formula: $ß = s/g$. The example Piketty gives is: if $s = 12\%$ and $g = 2\%$, then $ß = s/g = 600\%$ (Piketty 2014). In other words, a country that saves a lot and grows slowly "will over the long run accumulate an enormous stock of capital (relative to its income), which can in turn have a significant effect on the social structure and distribution of wealth". It does not logically follow that the second law must lead to higher concentrations of wealth at the top and impoverishment of those at the bottom. These results also depend upon fiscal and a myriad of other endogenous factors effecting the ultimate distribution.

To follow Piketty's narrative, we must introduce two more concepts: the law of cumulative growth and the law of cumulative returns. The "law of cumulative growth" states that a low annual growth rate over a long period of time gives rise to large increases in population. For example, between years 1700 and 2012, the world grew at an annual growth rate of 0.8%, from 600 million inhabitants to more than 7 billion. If this pace of growth were to continue for the next three centuries, "the world's population would exceed 20 billion in 2300" (Piketty 2014). The law of cumulative growth is virtually equivalent to the law of cumulative returns, "which says that an annual rate of return of a few percent, compounded over several decades, automatically results in a very large increase of the initial capital, provided that the return is constantly reinvested" (Piketty 2014). These observations lead Piketty to conclude: "The central thesis of this book is precisely that an apparently small gap between the return on capital and the rate of growth can in the long run have powerful and destabilising effects on the structure and dynamics of social inequality" (Piketty 2014).

Equally important as demographic growth is economic growth per capita and the diffusion of knowledge. The historical record is illuminating. Prior to the Industrial Revolution, economic output per capita was zero, that is a duration of 1700 years. Between 1700 and 1913, average annual per capita world output remained under but close to 1%. From 1913 to 2012, average per capita world output surged to 1.6%, with astonishing periods of exceptional output: 1950–1970, 2.8% worldwide; during the same period in Europe, 3.8%; between 1990 and 2012 in Asia, 3.8%; and from 1980 to 2012 worldwide, 1.7%, with Asia at 3.1%. An annual growth rate of 1% implies major social changes.

We now are positioned to draw several conclusions. With risk of oversimplification, whenever "the rate of return on capital is significantly and durably higher than the growth rate of the economy, it is all but inevitable that inheritance (of fortunes accumulated in the past) predominates over saving (wealth accumulated in the present)" (Piketty 2014). Wealth is not merely a matter of merit. For example, during the period 1990–2010, the fortune of Bill Gates, the founder of Microsoft and the incarnation of entrepreneurial wealth, increased from \$4 billion to \$50 billion. At the same time, the fortune of Liliane Bettencourt, the heiress of L'Oréal, founded by her father in 1907, increased from $2 billion to $25 billion. "Both fortunes grew at an annual rate of more than 13%, equivalent to a real return on capital of 10 or 11 per cent after correcting from inflation". Hence, an heiress who never worked in her life saw her fortune grow exactly as fast as Bill Gates, whose wealth continues to grow just as rapidly after his retirement. "Money tends to reproduce itself" (Piketty 2014). Microfinance founder Muhammad Yunus states, "I sleep at night and I wake up in the morning and my wealth has doubled. I didn't do anything, I just slept. We have to undo the system that automatically gives me money without contribution from my side" (Financial Times 2019).

Further support for Piketty's thesis follows from his study of the return on the capital endowments of US universities, 1980–2010 as depicted in this table (Fig. 4.1).

Remarkable is the extremely high rates of returns, given the ups and downs of market performance in each decade, some with negative returns. Piketty notes, "we find extremely high returns of the same sort I examined for the billionaires in the *Forbes* rankings" (Piketty 448). The second conclusion is that returns increase rapidly with the size of endowment. Third, because of capital size, the universities deploy "alternative investment strategies" unavailable to the less wealthy. Fourth, the rates of return on sovereign wealth funds also display equally impressive returns even when investments in low-yielding debt like US Treasuries are made for political reasons (e.g. Saudi Arabia that invests in low-yielding US debt as a *quid pro quo* for military protection). While faster economic growth mitigates the divide between rich and poor, Piketty's work makes clear that "average labour" is no substitute for "capital".

All universities (850)	8.2 %
Harvard, Yale and Princeton	10.2 %
Endowments higher than $1 billion (60)	8.8 %
Endowments between $500 million and $1 billion (66)	7.8 %
Endowments between $100 and $500 million (226)	7.1 %
Endowments less than $100 million (498)	6.2 %

Fig. 4.1 Average real annual rate (after deduction of inflation and all administrative costs and financial fees). (Source: Piketty 2014)

Inequality of wealth is the product of a complex, social construct, not logical necessity. Nevertheless, it seems fitting to close our précis of Piketty by reproducing his report of global inequality in the early twenty-first century. "Global inequality of wealth in the early 2010s appears to be comparable in magnitude to that observed in Europe in 1900–1910", when concentrations of wealth were extremely high. "The top thousandth seems to own nearly 20 percent of total global wealth today, the top centile about 50 percent, and the top decile somewhere between 80 and 90 percent" (Piketty 2014). The bottom half owns less than 5% of total global wealth. In concrete terms, this means that 0.1% of the people on the planet—about 4.5 million out of an adult population of 4.5 billion—possess fortunes of €10 million on average, "or nearly 200 times average global wealth of 60,000 euros per adult, amounting to nearly 20 percent of total global wealth" (Piketty 2014).

Role of Financial Sector in Income Inequality

Implicit in our discussion is that "financial systems" do not always function in the benign fashion of the orthodox functional view. Rather, financial systems allocate concentrations of wealth in an exclusive minority of persons. In other words, financial systems are not necessarily "pass-through" entities funnelling excess savings to borrowers of capital for productive purposes as portrayed in conventional textbooks. Rather, financial systems have developed to serve their own ends, in a perverse reversal of their intended function. A substantial fraction of global financial assets is held in opaque tax havens. Gabriel Zucman, based on a study of Swiss bank data, found large amounts of unreported financial assets are held in tax havens, amounting to nearly 10% of global GDP.

Piketty does not let this twisted role of the financial sector go unnoticed. His narrative of inequality in the US after 1980 and his discussion of the 2008 financial crisis establishes a relationship, on the one side, between the financial sector: banks and capital markets, and on the other side, soaring income inequality in the United States. "The upper decile's share increased from 30–35 percent of national income in the 1970s to 45–50 percent in the 2000s – an increase of 15 points of national income" (Piketty 2014). Piketty acknowledges the shortcomings of the World Inequality Database that takes account only of information declared in tax returns and fails to account for assets held in tax havens.[1] He also notes that stock market euphoria and capital gains "can account for only part of the top decile's share" since 1980 (Piketty 2014), though capital gains between 2000 and 2007 "accounted for about five additional points of national income for the upper decile" (Piketty 2014). Exclusive of capital gains, the top decile's share of national income rose from 32% in 1970 to more than 46% in 2010. The financial crisis not only failed to end structural inequality but also exacerbated the level of income inequality.

In Piketty's view, "there is absolutely no doubt that the increase of inequality in the United States contributed to the nation's financial instability" (Piketty 2014). A consequence of increasing inequality was stagnation of purchasing power for the middle and lower classes making it more likely that these households would take on debt. The well-off had injected enormous savings into banks and financial institutions. These institutions, freed from regulation, exploited the opportunity to earn good yields on making loans cheap to acquire. In support of this statement, we find that "from 1977 to 2007, the richest 10 percent appropriated three-quarters of the growth" (Piketty 2014). In other words, the richest 1% took nearly 60% of the total increase of US national income in this period, leaving the bottom 90% with a rate of income growth less than 0.5% per year.

Conclusion

Piketty's "analytical historical narrative", based on evidence drawn from national accounts, is compelling. The stunning factual inequality of wealth and of income distribution is a political, economic, and financial problem. His sweeping historical narrative demonstrated the varying behaviour of capital and income, sometimes converging toward lesser inequality and sometimes morphing toward great degrees of inequality. Piketty also identified the main forces shaping these developments. His laws of capitalism are useful tools but, as he states, are not scientific certainties. The picture Piketty paints for democratic societies is not pretty as it challenges the meritocratic belief system used to justify very large inequalities. In the United States particularly, wealth and income inequalities are justified on grounds of merit, risk-taking, and hard work. However, "historical experience shows …that such immense inequalities of wealth have little to do with the entrepreneurial spirit and are of no use in promoting growth" (Piketty 2014). Nor are they of any "common utility" thereby conflicting with the nice statement in the Declaration of the Rights of Man and of the Citizen: "Social distinctions can be based only on common utility".

Questions

1. How does Piketty define the term "national income" and what is its relationship to GDP?
2. What is the difference between *nominal* GDP and *real* GDP?
3. What is Piketty's definition of capital?
4. What is the first law of capitalism? Explain how Piketty reaches this determination.
5. What is the second law of capitalism? How does the second law relate to the first law?
6. What is the relationship between the financial sector and inequality of wealth and income?

Appendix

This appendix provides more data supporting Piketty's hypothesis taken from the United States and the OXFAM database.

Income Inequality in the US

Piketty speaks to "capital". However, his claim of unequal distribution of capital applies with equal force to income distribution. The figure below shows that the top 10% of households in the United States take more than 50% of the income produced by the United States.

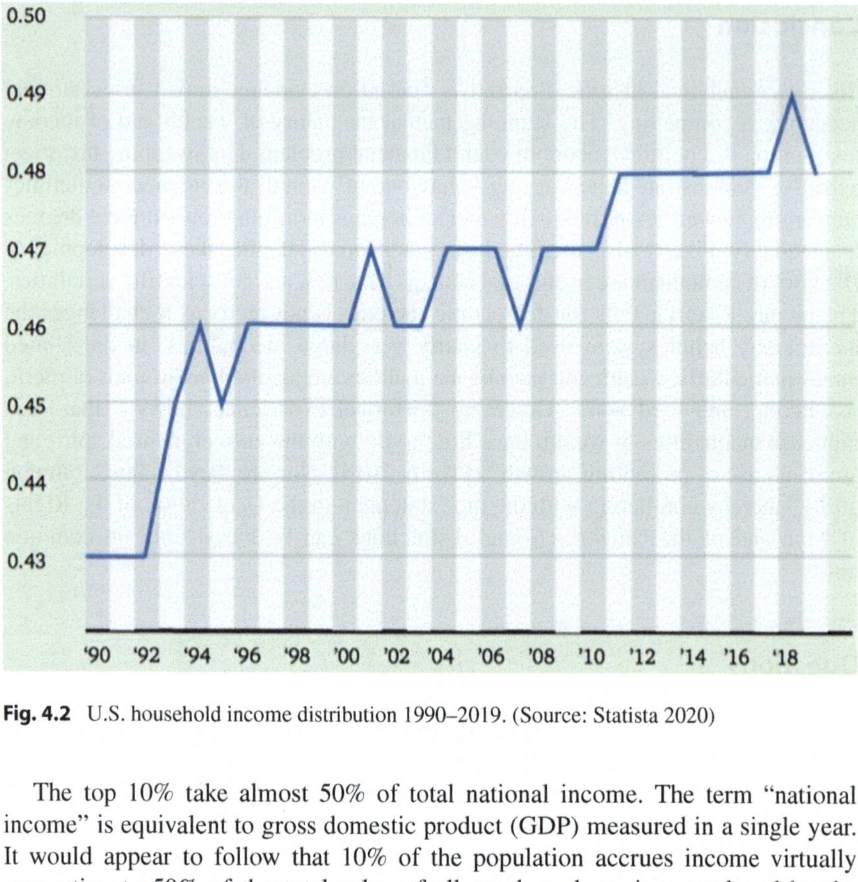

Fig. 4.2 U.S. household income distribution 1990–2019. (Source: Statista 2020)

The top 10% take almost 50% of total national income. The term "national income" is equivalent to gross domestic product (GDP) measured in a single year. It would appear to follow that 10% of the population accrues income virtually amounting to 50% of the total value of all goods and services produced by the United States in a calendar year. If that were true, then in 2017, the top 10% would take 50% of GDP ($19.4 trillion), or $9.7 trillion. However, in 2017, total household income equalled $14.6 trillion; leaving a $5 trillion sector gap, that requires accounting gymnastics to explain. Nevertheless, the point is well-taken: the rich are getting richer.

In 2018, the Congressional Budget Office published a report entitled "The Distribution of Household Income, 2015" consistent with the growing wage gap in the United States. In 2015, the average income for the top 20% was around $300,000 before taxes and transfers. By contrast, the average income of the fourth quintile amounted to around $100,000, while the average income of the lowest quintile was around $10,000. In the United States, ownership of wealth (i.e. capital) demonstrates similar disparities in allocation.

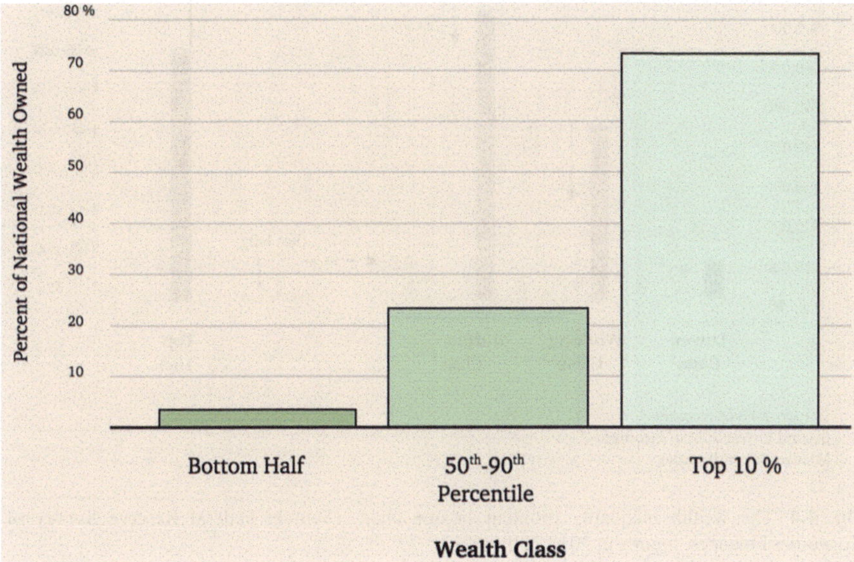

Fig. 4.3 Who owns all the stuff? (2013). (demos.org)

National wealth is defined as "the total monetary value of the capital, goods, and services, including net foreign balance and tangible assets, owned by a nation at a particular period of time" (Business Dictionary 2019). The figure indicates that the wealthiest top 10% of the US adult population own slightly less than 80% of national wealth.

The wealth of the lower, working, and middle classes is declining (negative percentages), while the wealth of the top 10% is expanding disproportionately. The lower-income 50% of the American population owned about 1.2% of the total wealth, while the 1% top-earners were in possession of about 38.6% of the wealth. However, nominal GDP per capita misleads not only because it is unadjusted for inflation but also because it tells the average allocation of wealth among households within a particular country. The United States has a GDP per capita of $59,500, ranked 17th in the world, according to statistics drawn from 2016 household data. An analysis of how that wealth is distributed tells a different story.

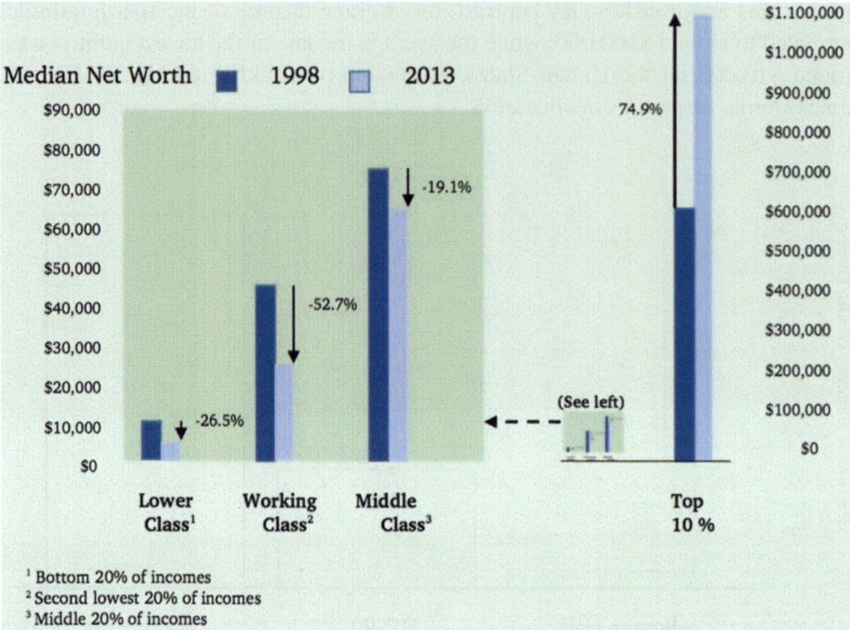

Fig. 4.4 The wealth inequality problem in one chart. (Source: Federal Reserve Survey of Consumer Finances, figures in 2013 dollars)

Without repeating Piketty and with due caution to journalist-acquired information, we end our survey of select indicators by identifying billionaire's total wealth and contrasting that wealth with the net worth of countries.

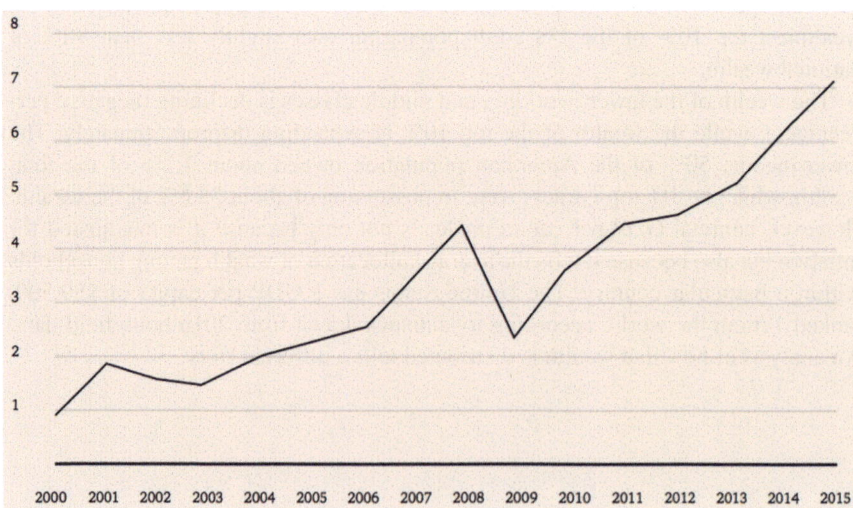

Fig. 4.5 Billionaires' net worth (in trillions of U.S. dollars). (Source: Forbes 2018)

According to *Forbes*, in 2018, there were 2,208 billionaires worldwide. The total net worth for the 2018 billionaires was $9.1 trillion. According to Bloomberg News, in 2017, 500 of the richest people in the world became richer by $1 trillion. The 2017 OXFAM report states that the top eight billionaires own a combined wealth exceeding the wealth held by the poorest half if the human race.

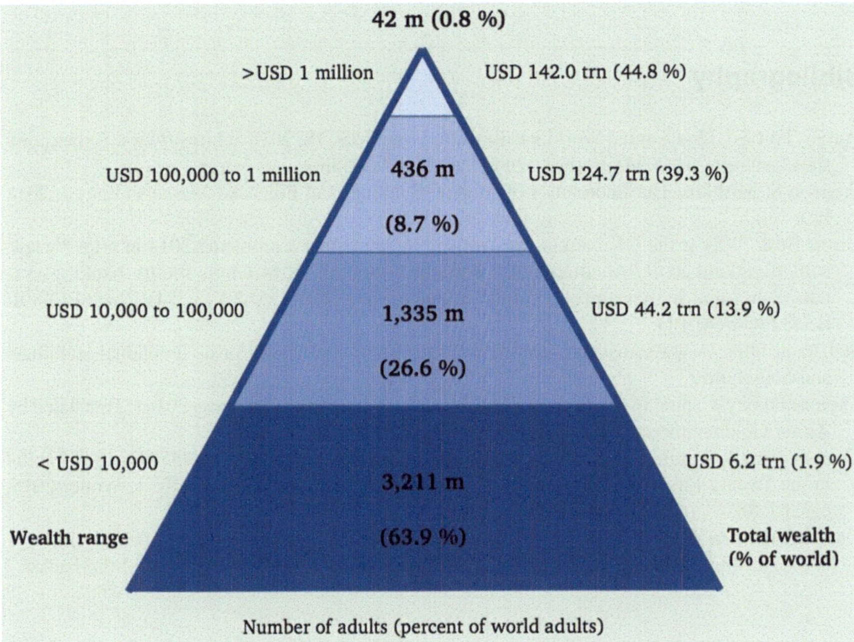

Fig. 4.6 The global wealth pyramid (2018). (Source: James Davies, Rodrigo Lluberas and Antony Shorrocks, Credit Suisse Global Wealth Databook 2018)

The distribution of wealth, though unrelated to the financial system *per se*, cannot be ignored as it refers to access of credit to pull populations out of poverty. The financial system operating with "eyes wide shut" does not bode well against this measure. The OXFAM 2019 Report entitled "Public Good or Private Wealth?" states that "26 individuals in the world hold as much wealth as the poorest 3.8 billion persons in the world".[2] Even proponents of capitalism, though fiercely contesting OXFAM's methodology, must question the sustainability of this statistic. Jeff Bezos, founder of Amazon, is the wealthiest individual in the world, though this position is inevitably ephemeral. Nevertheless, his reported wealth of $175.3 billion (2020 figure) represents the entire expense of the medical system of Somalia with a population of more than 14 million. The OXFAM Report remarks, that, given the inequality of wealth, Bezos "has decided to invest his fortune in space travel, as he can't think of anything else to spend his money on".[3] Meanwhile, Zay, a Vietnamese shrimp peeling worker, makes $15 per day while indirectly working for Whole Foods Market, a supermarket chain owned by Amazon.[4] A question arises: for whom then does the financial system toll? The question is immensely complicated but prosaic observations enlighten.

Notes

1. World Inequality Database at https://wid.world/
2. OXFAM Report 2019, Public Good or Private Wealth?, found at https://www.oxfam.org.nz/reports/public-good-or-private-wealth, last viewed 31 January 2019.
3. *Id.* at 10.
4. *Id.*

Bibliography

Forbes, Forbes' 32nd Annual World's Billionaire Issue, Mar. 18, 2018 at https://www.forbes.com/sites/forbespr/2018/03/06/forbes-32nd-annual-worlds-billionaires-issue/.

Frederic S. Mishkin, The Economics of Money, Banking, and Financial Markets (12th ed. 2018 Pearson).

Oliver Bush, Why is the UK banking system so big and is that a problem? 2014 at https://www.bankofengland.co.uk/-/media/boe/files/quarterly-bulletin/2014/whyis-the-uk-banking-system-so-big-and-is-that-a-problem.pdf?la=en&hash=F7DD8DA63A43C54BF1456EFF89EBA7117C6AAEBD

Statista at https://www.statista.com/statistics/219643/gini-coefficient-for-us-individuals-families-and-households/.

Thomas Piketty, Capital in the Twenty-First Century (Belknap Harvard Press 2014) (Translated by Arthur Goldhammer).

Thomas Piketty, Putting Distribution Back at the Center of Economics: Reflections on Capital in the Twenty-First Century, Journal of Economic Perspectives, Vol. 29, Nr. 1, Winter 2015, pgs. 67–88.

Daniel Carpenter, What Piketty Missed: The Banks, Washington Monthly Magazine (May 2015) at https://washingtonmonthly.com/magazine/maraprmay-2015/what-piketty-missed-the-banks/

Part II

The Conventional Paradigm: Questioned

5 The Conventional Narrative: Deconstructed

Introduction

Financial systems arguably promote greater economic efficiency and lead to higher economic growth. Ferguson states, "Credit and debt … are among the essential building blocks of economic development as vital to creating the wealth of nations as mining, manufacturing or mobile telephony" (Ferguson 2008). Conversely, poverty results from lack of financial institutions like banks: "only when savers can put their money in reliable banks that it can be channelled from the idle to the industrious"[1] (Ibid). Mishkin is equally sanguine, "Financial markets are critical for producing an efficient allocation of capital (wealth, either financial or physical, that is employed to produce more wealth), which contributes to higher production and efficiency for the overall economy" (Mishkin, Matthews and Giuliodori). John Maynard Keynes stated, "I think that capitalism, wisely managed, can probably be made more efficient for attaining economic ends than any alternative system yet in sight" (Keynes 1926).

The primary mechanism for achieving both goals (economic efficiency and economic growth) is that financial systems provide a mechanism to transfer funds from passive holders of excess "money" to active and productive users of these funds. The paradigmatic example found in the textbooks is householders' bank savings being transferred to companies that deploy the borrowed funds for investment purposes. The bank or other financial services institution serves as the "intermediary". This declaration about the virtues of financial markets is a foundational principle observed in virtually every textbook on the subject. Textbooks illustrate the orthodox function often by using a "circular flow" infographic (Fig. 5.1).

This flow-through model shows the source of funds, "lenders/net savers", for investment transferred through "financial intermediaries" or "financial markets", to be lent to borrowers/net spenders". The function of intermediation optimises the allocation of borrowed funds to enable their best and highest use. Markets provide

J. JA Burke, *Financial Services in the Twenty-First Century*,
https://doi.org/10.1007/978-3-030-63967-9_5

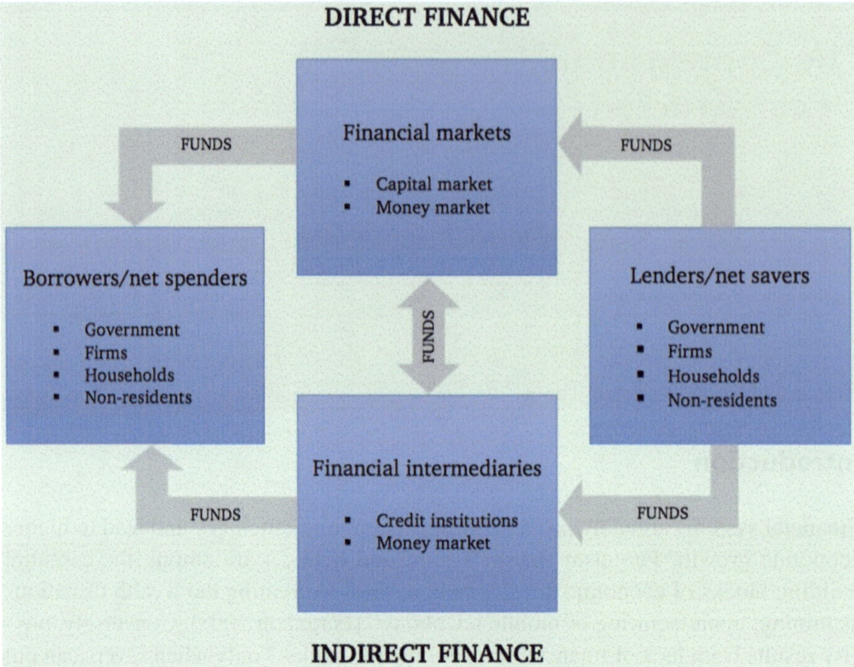

Fig. 5.1 Circular flow. (Source: Mishkin, Matthews, Guiliodori 2013)

direct finance by matching buyers and sellers, lenders and borrowers in organised and regulated marketplaces.[2]

The next chapter demonstrates that the "circular flow" model misleads. Primarily, it sanitizes the adverse effects of the financial services system. Secondarily, it provides a partially inaccurate description of banks. The source of funds lent by banks "for productive purposes" is not customer deposits, but the act of creating money by banks, money that did not previously exist as a savings instrument. Banks do not wait for customers to make deposits sufficient to meet demand of borrowers. Thirdly, the perfect "model" ignores studies showing that after a certain size relative to the economy, the financial system is detrimental to economic growth. Fourthly, the model presumes a return of value to its original source or "recycling" of value but does not account for distribution or outcomes. Thus, the model is incomplete.

Although the "circular flow" model is incomplete, private credit, subject to exceptions, tends to increase GDP growth. In 2012, Cecchetti and Kharroubi conducted a study of 50 advanced and emerging countries over the period 1980–2009. They constructed a histogram from the sample using measures of five-year periods correlating GDP-per-worker growth and private credit to GDP. The histogram was divided into four quartiles. The results of their research demonstrated that "GDP-per-worker growth increased from the first to the third private credit to GDP quartile, before declining in the final fourth quartile" (Cecchetti). Even taking into account that advanced economies tend to grow slowly, as opposed to emerging economies due to the "catch-up" factor, the researchers estimated that the ratio of private credit extended by banks to GDP is the gear that pushes growth. Cecchetti and Kharroubi found that private credit was most effective at increasing GDP when the private credit/GDP ratio was about 90% of GDP. In other words, additional private credit stops promoting real economic growth and impedes it.

Cecchetti and Kharroubi also examined the collateral effects of "oversized financial sectors" on the economy. They focused upon "financial sector employment as a measure of financial development". A gauge of financial sector size and financial development is based on inputs: "the financial sector's share in the economy's total employment". The results confirmed "that the relationship between growth and the financial sector's share in employment is an inverted U". At low levels, increases in the financial sector's share of total employment are associated with higher GDP-per-worker growth. But "there is a threshold beyond which a larger financial sector becomes a drag on productivity growth" (Cecchetti). For example, the financial sector uses rocket scientists and mathematicians to build financial algorithms, thereby diverting these exceptional resources from more productive use in other industries. In sum, the financial sector becomes a parasite on the real economy, and large and "fast growing financial sectors" are detrimental to growth at the aggregate level."

The "orthodox function of financial systems" also is unsupported, even contradicted, by empirical evidence. The industrial revolution in England in the manufacture of textiles and iron did not rely upon the financial system. Although the industrial revolution in other countries did rely upon the financial system to a significant degree, the only plausible statement that follows from these inconsistent facts is that economic development and the financial system are intertwined in a way that requires elaboration. History instructs that the financial system often is the cause of financial catastrophe and reversal of economic fortune. Illustrative are asset bubbles: the collapse in 1720 of Law's Mississippi Company that left French, Dutch, and other European investors in financial ruin; the British South Sea Bubble in 1720; the 1929 Wall Street crash; "Black Monday" of 1987; the bursting of "dot com" in 2000; and the 2008 financial crisis. Historically, finance served to support the conduct of war, as opposed to economic growth, by funding centres of power engaged in conflict: The Crusades, funded by the Medici, and the wars between England and France, funded by the Rothschilds, support this claim. In both cases, the bankers had one interest: personal profit.

"At the height of the financial crisis [2008], Adair Turner, then head of the UK's financial regulator, dared to suggest that the sector he oversaw had become 'swollen' and addicted to 'socially useless' activities. It was an extraordinary statement for a public official to make, especially one charged with understanding and watching over the finance sector. Fast forward a decade—past Too Big To Fail and misselling scandals and Occupy protests and $150bn of bank fines—and it is no longer so controversial." This view is shared by Nicholas Shaxson and Oliver Bullough, authors of arguably extreme but widely read and influential books on finance. Not only do they argue that the financial system is broken but also that the financial system actively damages society. Shaxson states, "In the era of financialization, the corporate bosses and their advisers, and the financial sector, have moved away from creating wealth *for* the economy, and towards extracting wealth *from* the economy, using financial techniques." Bullough states, "Moneyland" set wealth free, and it didn't care where that wealth came from: steal, hide, spend, in perpetuity. This is the dirty secret at the heart of eurobonds. It was all made possible by modern communications – the telegram, then the phone, then the telex, then the fax, then the email – and this is the dark side of the revolution of convenience that we call globalisation" (Bullough).

The Flawed "Principal Conclusion": Exceptions

Though distinct from the "circular flow" model, the following illustrations support the hypothesis that financial services promote economic growth and pull populations out of poverty: (1) Porter's Diamond Theory, (2) Muhammad Yunus' microfinance for which he won the Nobel Peace Prize, and (3) venture capital firms that invest in start-ups. These non-exhaustive illustrations demonstrate how funds may be deployed to stimulate economic growth and provide a qualified justification to the conventional view found in extant textbooks. We start with Porter's Diamond Theory providing indirect support for the principal conclusion of modern economics. The qualification "indirect" means that Porter's theory is based on product, process, or technical innovation, not finance.

Porter's Competitive Advantage of Nations

Michael E. Porter in his publication *The Competitive Advantage of Nations* demonstrated, contrary to the classical view, that a nation's competitiveness depends upon the capacity of its industry to innovate and upgrade. Innovation and upgrading require financial investment. Nations, *per se*, are abstract juridical entities and cannot be competitive; rather their firms are competitive, are innovative, and have the capacity to upgrade. "The only meaningful concept of competitiveness at the national level is productivity." "National prosperity is created, not inherited. It does not grow out of a country's natural endowments, its labour pool, its interest rates, or its currency's value, as classical economics insists" (Porter HBR 1990). Rather, a nation's competitiveness depends upon the capacity of its firms to innovate and upgrade continuously. "The principal goal of a nation is to produce a high and rising standard of living for its citizens" (*Ibid.*). Labour productivity measures the amount of output per employee. Firm profitability is correlated to labour productivity. The more output per employee the higher the level of labour productivity.

However, maximisation of labour productivity does not require harsh conditions and underpayment, but requires investment in fixed assets, employee education, and improved methods of production organisation. In other words, *increased labour productivity requires capital investment and therefore access to capital markets to raise funds*. Economic prosperity requires perpetual investment in labour. Without engaging in debate between Porter and Krugman regarding international trade theory, one thing is clear: without firm access to capital markets, competition is constrained, and innovation is stifled, if not impeded. Financial systems are not self-serving masters (at least supposedly) but are agents of commerce.

A review of what Porter calls the "determinants of national competitive advantage" suffices to introduce the theory's core concepts. Porter attempts to answer the question why "certain companies in certain nations" are capable of consistent innovation, ruthless improvement, development of competitive edge, and overcoming substantial barriers to change. Porter's answer: "The Diamond of National Advantage". The four constituents of the "diamond" establish the context a nation establishes and operates for its industries. The four attributes are: (1) Factor Conditions, (2) Demand Conditions, (3) Related and Supporting Industries, (4) and Firm Strategy, Structure, and Rivalry. "These determinants create the national environment in which companies are born and learn how to compete" and form a "Diamond" (Fig. 5.2).

While the four factors share complex interrelationships, our focus is "Factor Conditions". According to Porter, the most important factor conditions are skilled labour and infrastructure, a definition that runs counter to the classical definition of "land, labour, and capital". The most important factors of production are skilled

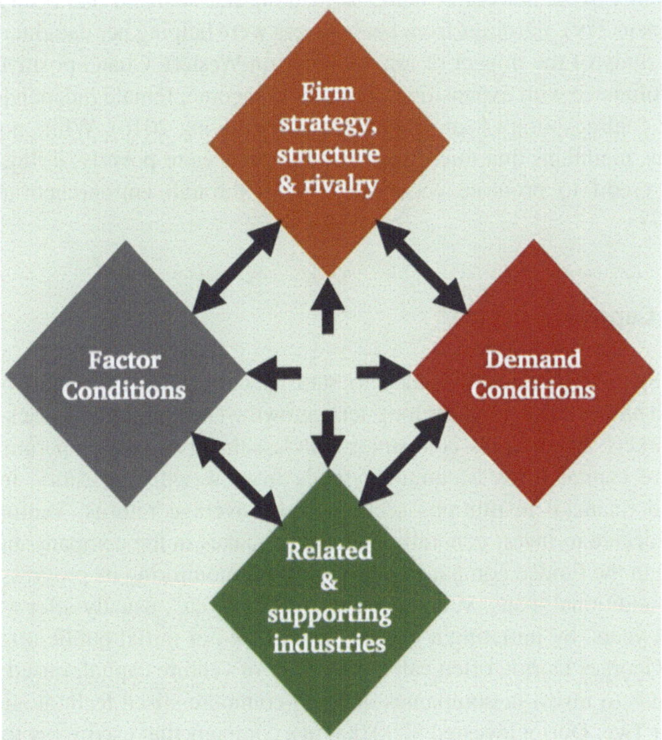

Fig. 5.2 Porter' diamond model. (Source: Porter 1990)

human resources and a scientific base. These factors require access to capital, including venture capital. An idealised financial system would deploy capital to create "factor conditions" and develop the three other points of the "Diamond". This conclusion supports the conventional view that financial systems promote economic growth. Further support is found in alternative methods to promote economic growth such as "microfinance".

Microfinance

In 2006, Muhammad Yunus and Grameen Bank were jointly awarded the Nobel Peace Prize by pioneering the concept of microcredit. Yunus founded Grameen Bank (a mutually owned institution) in 1983 in the village of Jobra, Bangladesh. Grameen provides small loans mainly to women, without collateral, to support entrepreneurial activity. "Since its inception, Grameen Bank has made microloans worth more than $3 billion" (Ferguson 280). The practice of microfinance has spread to other regions of the world, for example, India, Africa, and South America. The fundamental revelation is that women are a better credit risk than men. Ferguson provides a concrete example. Betty Flores, a customer of Pro Mujer in Bolivia took out a loan to expand her coffee stall, "something her husband had been unable to do" (Ferguson 279). Earnings from her business were helping her daughters through school. A study of the impact of microfinance on Western Ghana positively correlated microfinance with expansion of household income, female independence, and the use of contraception (Asare-Bediako and Frempong 2016). While no one, not even Yunus, maintains that microfinance is the panacea to poverty, it illustrates the power of credit to promote economic growth through entrepreneurial activity (PBS 2007).

Venture Capital

Venture capital is funding provided to start-up companies and small businesses believed to have the potential for long-term growth. These companies lack access to capital markets, as most new companies with less than two years' operating history do. Venture capital firms accumulate funds from wealthy investors, investment banks, and financial institutions seeking above-average returns. Venture capital firms that decide to invest generally take equity stakes in the company and take an active role in the funded company by advising and monitoring its progress and then providing additional loans. Venture capitalists "cash out", usually after a period of four to six years, by initiating a merger, acquisition, or initial public offering. For example, Georges Doriot, often called the father of venture capital, raised $3.5 million in funds to invest in companies that had commercialised technologies during World War Two. Doriot invested $200,000 in a company that used x-ray technology for cancer treatment. When the company went public in 1955, the $200,000 investment turned into a $1.8 million return. Venture capital played a critical role in

Silicon Valley funding the likes of Apple and Intel. Today, many venture capital firms back FinTech companies. While Porter's strategy, microfinance, and venture capital constitute non-exhaustive illustrations of financial systems promoting economic growth, we turn now to alternative uses and effects of financial systems. As the next sections explain, financial systems often fail to serve their intended purpose and serve their own ends, or the ends of their master Nation States.

Non-finance Factors of Economic Growth

The relationship between population growth and growth of economic output has been studied extensively though analysts have failed to reach any consensus (Peterson 2017). As already noted, Piketty maintains that, if the rate of economic growth as measured in GDP does not exceed the rate of return on capital, the result is a widening gap between the immensely wealthy and the remainder of the population. Certain theoretical models demonstrate a positive link between population growth and per capita economic growth. The rationale proceeds as follows: larger populations are likely to create a large stock of useful knowledge that fosters economic growth (Simon). But empirical data does not support these theoretical models. Rather the interface among population, economic growth, and technological innovation appears country specific. Nevertheless, looking through the lens of the role of population in economic growth is necessary to understand world economic development and provokes the need for critical assessment of this domain.

Overview and Data

Piketty observes that economic growth "always includes a purely demographic component and a purely economic component and only the latter allows for an improvement in the standard of living" (Piketty 2014). Economic growth is measured by changes in a country's gross domestic product (GDP). The latter is computed by multiplying population "x" GDP per capita. Economic growth is measured by adding changes in population growth plus changes in growth of GDP per capita. Piketty evidenced that "average annual world economic growth between 1700 and 2012 was 1.6% made up of equal parts population growth and per capita output growth of 0.8% each" (Peterson 2017). Population growth at an annual average of 0.8% over this extended period resulted in an increase of population from approximately 600 million in 1700 to more than 7.3 billion in 2015. Peterson has compiled data from various historical periods across a wide swath of regions to determine whether any relationship exists between population growth and per capita GDP. I take data from a category of countries Peterson calls "Western offshoots" comprising the United States, Canada, Australia, and New Zealand, and world-level data for the periods 1820–1913, 1913–2010, and 1820–2010. The data consists of three components: (1) Average Annual Growth Rates of Population, (2) Per Capita GDP, (3) and GDP, and is incorporated in the following tables: Figs. 5.3, 5.4, and 5.5.

Period from 1820 to 1913			
Region	Population	Per Capita GDP	GDP
Western offshoots	2.47	1.50	3.97
World	0.58	0.83	1.41

Fig. 5.3 Average Annual Growth Rates of Population, Per Capita GDP, and GDP for Three Time Periods. (Source: Peterson 2017)

Period from 1913 to 2010			
Region	Population	Per Capita GDP	GDP
Western offshoots	1.29	1.79	3.08
World	1.38	1.67	3.05

Fig. 5.4 Average Annual Growth Rates of Population, Per Capita GDP, and GDP for Three Time Periods. (Source: Peterson 2017)

Period from 1820 to 2010			
Region	Population	Per Capita GDP	GDP
Western offshoots	1.84	1.64	3.48
World	0.99	1.26	2.25

Fig. 5.5 Average Annual Growth Rates of Population, Per Capita GDP, and GDP for Three Time Periods. (Source: Peterson 2017)

Country Specific Data for Period from 1820 to 1913			
Country	Population	Per Capita GDP	GDP
Argentina	2.86	1.40	4.30
Canada	2.43	1.71	4.14
United States	2.45	1.46	3.91
Germany	1.03	1.31	2.34
South Africa	1.48	0.82	2.30
Norway	0.99	1.20	2.19
Iraq	0.42	0.57	0.99
India	0.4	0.25	0.65
Korea	0.13	0.40	0.53
World	0.54	0.83	1.37

Fig. 5.6 Country specific data for period from 1820 to 1913. (Source: Peterson 2017)

Average annual compound growth rates for population, real GDP, and real per capita GDP produced significantly higher numbers in every period, excepting the period from 1913 to 2010 where the world produced real per capita GDP and GDP that approximated the Western offshoots. Until 1913, world-level data was anaemic. Viewed in isolation, the data in Fig. 5.3 allows a crude observation: higher growth rate changes in population appear to be correlated with higher GDP and higher real per capital GDP. Figure 5.4 that contains country-specific, as well as world-level, data appears to confirm this observation (Fig. 5.6).

Country Specific Data for Period from 1960 to 2015			
Country	**Population**	**Per Capita GDP**	**GDP**
China	1.31	6.41	7.72
Korea	1.28	5.68	6.96
Indonesia	1.96	3.44	5.40
India	1.95	3.16	5.11
Kenya	3.16	1.36	4.52
Turkey	1.91	2.43	4.34
Brazil	1.91	2.16	4.07
France	0.65	2.10	2.75
Austria	0.37	2.35	2.72
Italy	0.35	2.06	2.41
World	1.61	1.85	3.46

Fig. 5.7 Country specific data for period from 1960 to 2015. (Source: Peterson 2017)

However, the apparent correlation does not withstand scrutiny for the period from 1960 to 2015, using select countries, and world aggregate data, and the period from 1990 to 2015 (Figs. 5.7 and 5.8).

The period from 1960 to 2015 shows the economic growth of emerging economies like China, India, Indonesia, and Brazil, for example. While the Western offshoots continued to perform very well, certain western European countries, and Japan in particular, exhibited substantial contraction of economic growth. The

Country Specific Data for Period from 1990 to 2015			
Country	**Population**	**Per Capita GDP**	**GDP**
China	0.76	8.72	9.48
India	1.64	4.69	6.33
Nigeria	2.58	2.48	5.06
Korea	0.66	4.18	4.84
Indonesia	1.40	3.37	4.77
Turkey	1.51	2.30	3.81
Argentina	1.13	2.68	3.81
Honduras	2.00	1.71	3.71
Kenya	2.71	0.80	3.51
Brazil	1.29	1.38	2.67
France	0.53	0.95	1.48
Austria	0.44	1.38	1.82
Italy	0.28	0.36	0.64
World	1.32	1.42	2.74

Fig. 5.8 Country specific data for period from 1990 to 2015. (Source: Peterson 2017)

question arises: is there a correlation between population growth and economic growth? The answer appears to be "no". "For the world as a whole, over the period 1990 to 2015, the correlation between population growth and real per capita GDP growth, based on World Bank (2017) data, was −0.1849 suggesting that these two variables were uncorrelated during this period" (Peterson 6–7). If this conclusion is correct, then economic growth is propelled by savings that increase capital stock and labour productivity, supplemented by what is deemed "multifactor productivity" (MFP), or in simple terms: technological innovation. However, correlation coefficients for per capita GDP and MFP growth for the period 1990–2014 based on OECD (2017) for OECD countries do not support the hypothesis that MFP growth leads ineluctably to economic growth. For example, MFP and per capita GDP are strongly correlated for Germany, Japan, and Sweden. But for countries like Ireland and Korea that had per capita GDP growth exceeding 4% during the period of study, the two factors were uncorrelated.

In conclusion, population growth appears to foster overall economic growth and may contribute to an increase in per capita GDP. But this conclusion is very country specific. Low-income countries with substantial increases in population are likely to have poor economic results as resources are shifted to the education and health care of young persons. However, this scenario may change as the new generation enters the workforce. By contrast, developed countries face a different demographic: slow or even negative population growth and aging populations. The burden of caring for a large number of retired people is likely to impede economic growth. Finally, world population is expected to exceed 10 billion by 2050 raising of the question of sustainable vital resources. Two contrary views prevail: exhaustion of farmland, water, and raw materials is unavoidable. The competing view is that human ingenuity and technological innovation will overcome potential resource constraints.

Misuse of the Financial System

In his book *Currency Wars: The Making of the Next Global Crisis*, James Rickards demonstrates how Nation States use their financial systems, particularly their currencies, to wage economic warfare against other Nation States. "Historically a currency war involves competitive devaluations by countries seeking to lower their cost structures, increase exports, create jobs and give their economies a boost at the expense of trading partners" (Rickards 145). Economic sanctions are another form of economic warfare generally intended to attain "regime change". The United States is the master *par excellence* at manipulating its currency to gain competitive international trade advantage and waging war by imposing economic sanctions on countries deemed hostile to its national interests that pervade every geo-political area of the world.

Rickards provides an excellent example of a currency war: the conflict between the United States and China. In 2009 at the Pittsburgh G20 summit, the participants decided there was a need to "rebalance growth". The plan was entitled "A Framework for Strong, Sustainable, and Balanced Growth". Though the language of the plan was written in "global-elite" speak, "rebalancing" meant increased consumption by China and increased exports by the United States, with the IMF deputised as a type of cop to enforce member obligations. The United States' financial weapon was "quantitative easing" or "QE", that "essentially consists of increasing the money supply to inflate asset prices". By using "QE" to generate inflation abroad, the United States "increased the cost structure of almost every major exporting nation and fastest growing economies" (Rickards 134).

Quantitative easing is printing money.[3] The instrument works as follows. The Federal Reserve creates money from thin air by purchasing Treasury debt securities from a select group of banks called "primary dealers". The dealers that have a global base of institutional customers and high-net-worth individuals underwrite the Treasury auction of new debt and make a market in existing debt (Rickards 134). When the Federal Reserve wants to increase the money supply, it buys securities from the dealers and pays the dealers with freshly printed money. Quantitative easing worked to "rebalance growth" vis-à-vis China because of the dollar-yuan peg maintained by the People's Bank of China. As the Federal Reserve printed more money, that money found its way into China as investors looked for higher rates of return than available in the United States. The more money the Federal Reserve printed the more money China had to print to maintain the peg. The Federal Reserve "was printing with a vengeance" (Rickards 135).

The result: The United States exported inflation to China at a time when China was a booming economy and lacked capacity to absorb new money without causing domestic inflation. "China was now importing inflation from the United States through the exchange-rate peg after previously having exported its deflation to the United States in the same way" (Rickards 135). Revaluation of the yuan and inflation increased the cost of Chinese exports and made the United States more competitive. In early 2011, inflation in China passed 5% on an annualised basis, and the yuan revaluation was moving at about 4% thereby increasing the Chinese cost structure by 9%. The United States had achieved its objective against China.

However, QE found victims around the world. The inflation the US desperately sought in China found its way to emerging markets generally: South Korea, Brazil, Indonesia, Thailand, Vietnam, and elsewhere. The US policy ignored the fact that many commodities, such as wheat, corn, oil, soybeans, lumber, coffee, and sugar are priced on "world, not local, markets". As consumers bid up prices in commodities, the effects of QE were felt in poorer parts of Africa and the Middle East. The situation became so dire that the G8 arranged a $20 billion pledge to Tunisia and Egypt to prevent additional civil unrest. What started as an attack on China ended up flooding the world with dollars and causing inflation on a global level in food and energy prices thereby demonstrating the unintended consequences of unleashing an arguably reckless policy of QE.

Economic sanctions are the province of the largest economies in the world. Sanctions are used by one Nation State, or a collective group, to destabilise another Nation State and attain a regime change. Nation States justify economic sanctions on dubious grounds often invoking threats to internal national security. Sanctions cover a wide range of actions from list-based economic sanctions to full economic embargo. While numerous studies demonstrate that economic sanctions do not achieve their intended purposes, the collateral effects of the target Nation State's population are devastating.

Exacerbating the attacks on the "neutrality" of the financial system is the willingness of financial institutions to ignore unexplained wealth. KYC (know your client) and AML (anti–money laundering) rules of the Financial Conduct Authority of the United Kingdom (FCA) require financial institutions to conduct due diligence before opening an account. However, KYC and related rules are subordinated to profit. If financial institutions can benefit, they disregard the origin of funds. Take, for example, Nursultan Nazarbayev, the president of Kazakhstan since the late 1980s. His estimated wealth exceeds $1 billion. The salary of his position is $20,000 annually. His total wealth and source of income do not square. Plus, he is a politically exposed person (PEP), whom financial institutions purportedly are required to subject to special scrutiny. Other individuals with substantial investments are no exception to the general rule of disregarding the origin of funds, if the funds are large enough in value to make profits.

Conclusion

This chapter identified flaws in the fundamental precept underlying textbooks on financial services. Financial systems do not necessarily promote economic growth in the strong form. Although the chapter breaks the link between lending and economic growth, it does not deny that finance is needed for economic expansion, though the use of financial services to achieve its intended objective is qualified. This chapter also has shown that factors unrelated to finance expand GDP and the real economy. Finally, the chapter explained how Nation States use the financial system for nefarious ends based on political agenda.

Questions

1. Explain the orthodox function of financial systems and financial markets to promote economic growth. Conduct research to support this fundamental precept of explaining the purpose of financial institutions.
2. How do you square Porter's theory of national competition with the global multinational corporation whose relationship to its nation of incorporation seems notional at best? Explain the difference in approach between Krugman and Porter theories of international trade.
3. Define Piketty's "laws of capitalism" and apply them to a specific example.

4. Rickards maintains that a Nation States' Achilles heel is its currency: destroy its currency and the economy is destroyed. Explain his rationale and provide your opinion.
5. Rickards raises the question of the size of the global financial system, by claiming it is larger than required. Explain his reasoning and provide your view.

Appendix

The following material provides factual data related to country population, economic size, GDP, and per capita GDP, and supplements the foregoing discussion. The chart below depicts the world's top ten most populated countries:

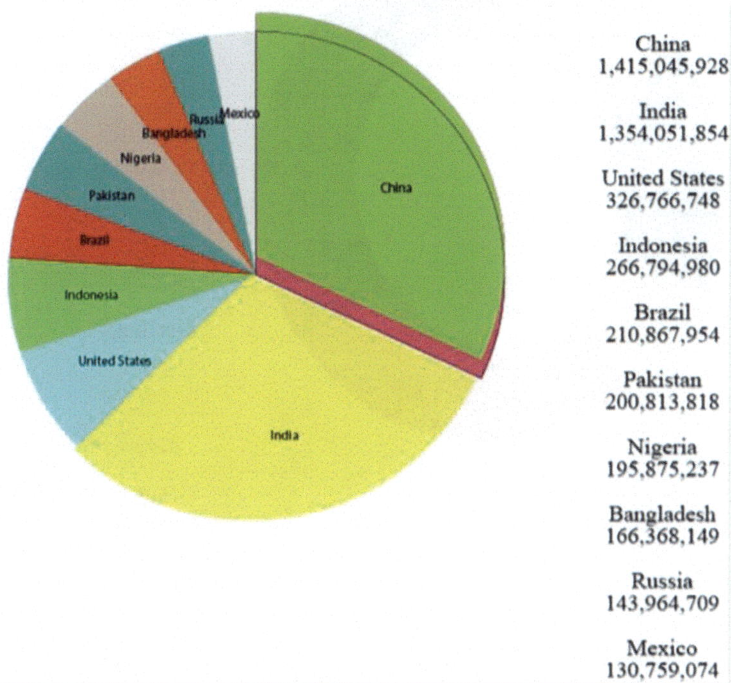

Fig. 5.9 World population top ten countries. (Source: Author)

China and India unremarkably are the most populated countries in the world, each with a population exceeding one billion. Remarkable is the fact that the United States is placed third with a population of approximately 326 million, or less than 60% of the two most populated countries. The remaining seven countries have comparably sized populations to the United States and to each other, but with extreme differences in forecasted population growth rates. For example, Nigeria's expected population in 2050 is 391,296,754 that would then alter its rank to the fourth most populous nation in the world.

The next chart depicts the top ten countries by economic size. The United States is the largest economy in the world followed closely by China. Noteworthy is that the population of the United States is 60% smaller than the population of China, the country with the largest population in the world. Except for China, its economic size is 75% larger than Japan, the country with the third largest economy, and is larger than the economic size of the next seven countries in the list taken together.

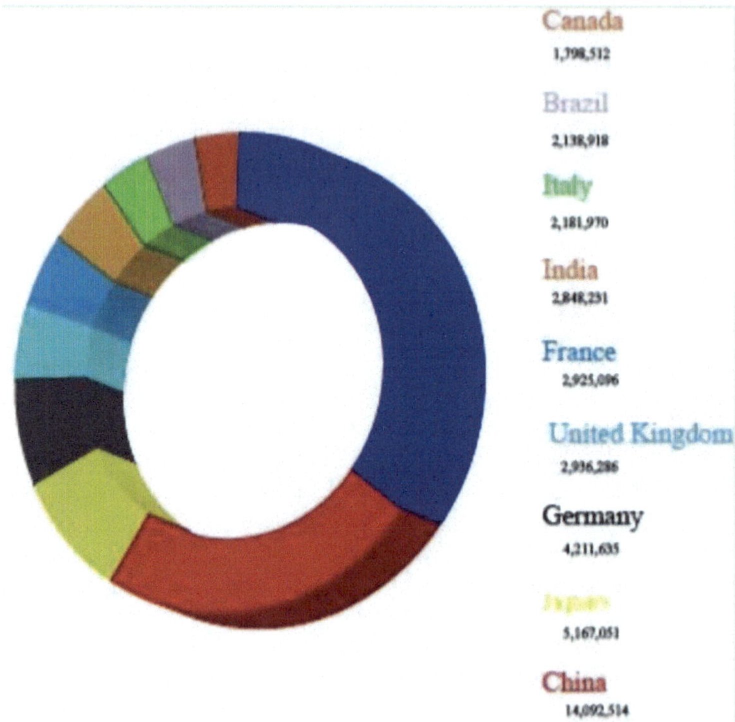

Fig. 5.10 Top ten countries ranked by economy size. (Source: Author)

The charts suggest that population size and economic size are not correlated. The United States with a population of less than 400 million is the largest economy in the world. Though China with the largest population in the world ranks second in economic size, India with a comparatively equal population to China has a smaller economic size than most countries in the top ten. The observation is important for the study of financial systems, since Part Two of the book questions the conventional view that the purpose of financial systems is to augment economic growth. The disparity between population and economic size of respective countries is ground for seeking a model to explain the data.

Except for the United States, the third chart showing the top ten countries by gross domestic product per capita is explained by individual characteristics of small-population countries.

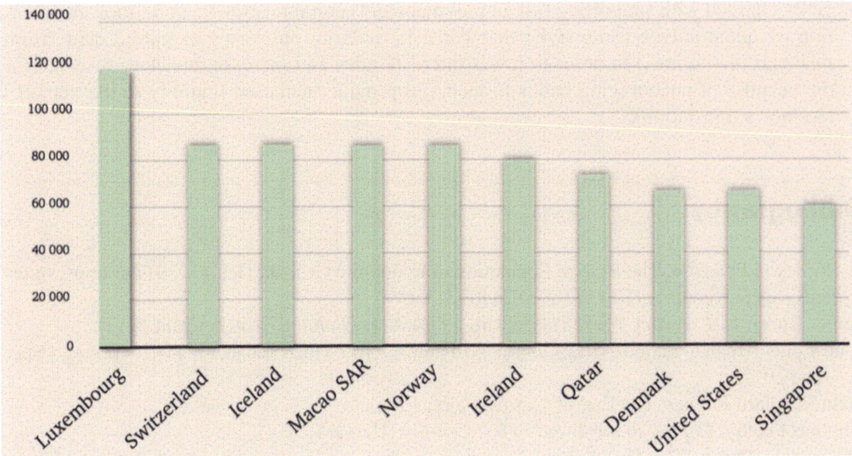

Fig. 5.11 GDP PC Nominal$ [IMF Projected 2018]. (Source: IMF Database)

This chart demonstrates that the richest countries measured by GDP per capita have small, if not tiny, populations compared to the countries listed in Chart 1: for example, Liechtenstein has a population of 38,547, Monaco 30,727, Macau 606,340, and Luxembourg 605,764. Common denominators among all the ten countries are difficult to identify. However, the economies of Monaco and Macau rely heavily upon the casino and tourist industries. Both countries face regulatory risk of money laundering. Luxembourg and Liechtenstein are financial powerhouses. In Luxembourg, the financial sector accounts for 35% of GDP, due primarily to assets under management derived from investment funds. In Liechtenstein, low business taxes, a 12.5% flat tax on income, and easy incorporation rules induce foreign corporations to establish holding companies, providing 30% of state revenues. Qatar's source of wealth derives from its oil and gas industry. Norway's wealth depends upon natural resources and has little to do with innovation other than expertise in sovereign wealth management. While these factors are insufficient to support generalisations, they raise questions as to the underlying reasons and the role of financial systems, and the distribution of wealth.

Notes

1. This statement is not entirely accurate as demonstrated by M-Pesa.
2. For example, investors hold equity and debt, though these instruments cannot be bought directly from issuing entities but require the services of a broker intermediary. The concept of "direct" arises when the investor does not rely upon the intermediary to make the investment choice.
3. La Fed, officiellement mandatée pour soutenir l'emploi et la croissance, s'est lancée dans une opération de quantitative easing (QE) qui consiste en l'achat massif de titres publics afin de faire baisser les taux d'intérêt et d'augmenter les réserves monétaires pour encourager les banques à prêter et augmenter la liquidité. Ugeux, Georges. La Descente aux enfers de la finance (OJ.ECONOMIE) (French Edition) (p. 17). (The Federal Reserve, offi-

cially charged with supporting full employment and economic growth, undertook an operation of quantitative easing (QE) that consists of large purchases of public debt (from financial institutions) in order to lower interests rates and increase monetary reserves for the purpose of encouraging banks to lend and provide increased liquidity to the market.) (Author's translation).

Bibliography

E. Wesley F. Peterson, The Role of Population in Economic Growth, Oct. 11, 2017 at https://journals.sagepub.com/doi/10.1177/2158244017736094.

James Rickards. *Currency Wars: The Making of the Next Global Crisis* (Penguin 2012).

Jean-Louis Arcand, Enrico Berkes, and Ugo Panizza, Too Much Finance?, IMF Working Paper June 2012.

John Maynard Keynes, The End of Laissez-Faire, 1926.

Thomas Piketty, *Capital in the Twenty-First Century* (Harvard 2014).

Michael E. Porter, *The Competitive Advantage of Nations* (Harvard Business Review March–April 1990).

Bureau of Labor Statistics, Monthly Labor Review, *Estimating the U.S. Share* February 2017.

Congressional Budget Office, The Distribution of Household Income, 2015 November 2018 retrieved https://www.cbo.gov/system/files/2018-11/54646-Distribution_of_Household_Income_2015_0.pdf

Federic S. Mishkin, Kent Matthews and Massimo Giuliodari, The Economics of Money, Banking and Financial Markets (2013 Pearson).

R.W. Goldsmith, Financial Structure and Development, The Economic Journal V. 80, No. 318 (June 1969).

Niall Ferguson, The Ascent of Money: A Financial History of the World (2008, 2009 Penguin Books).

Stephen G. Cecchetti and Enisse Kharoubi, Reassessing the Impact of Finance and Growth, July 2012, BIS Working Papers No. 381, Monetary and Economic Devlopment.

Steve Roth, Capital's Share of Income is Way Higher than You Think, 18 May 2018 retrieved http://evonomics.com/capitals-share-of-income-is-way-higher-than-you-think/

Caroline Binham, Is the financial system broken? Financial Times, 9 November 2018 available at: https://www.ft.com/content/39598462-ba64-11e8-94b2-17176fbf93f5, last viewed 16 January 2019.

Nicholas Shaxson, *The Finance Curse: How Global Finance Is Making Us All Poorer*, Vintage 2018, p. 87.

OECD at https://data.oecd.org/lprdty/multifactor-productivity.htm.

Oliver Bullough, *Moneyland*, Profile Books LTD 2018, p. 42.

6 Commercial Banks Create Money Out of Nothing

Introduction

Three competing theories of how banks operate in the economy are: (McLeay et al. 2014) financial intermediation, fractional reserve, and (Tobin 1963) credit creation. As previously noted but worth reiterating, most current textbooks assert the validity of the financial intermediation theory. The primary mechanism for achieving economic efficiency and economic growth is that financial systems provide a mechanism to transfer funds from passive holders of excess "money" to active and productive users of these funds. The *paradigmatic example found in the textbooks is householders' bank savings being transferred to companies that deploy the borrowed funds for investment purposes*. The bank or other financial services institution serves as the "intermediary", disbursing funding to its most productive and optimal use. This declaration about the virtues of financial markets is a foundational principle found in virtually every textbook. This quotation aptly expresses the view: "Banks take deposits from those who have money to save and bundle it up in various ways so that it can be lent to those who wish to borrow" (Valdez 2003). The "intermediation" model is depicted as follows (Fig. 6.1):

The model presumes that commercial banks use pre-existing funds drawn from a pool of aggregated funds to lend to competing users of those funds.

The second theory, the fractional reserve, asserts that banks draw down their reserves held at Central Banks to support their lending practices, implying that reserves are a binding restraint on lending. The fractional reserve theory relies upon a "common misconception … that the central bank determines the quantity of loans and deposits in the economy by controlling the quantity of central bank money" (McLeay et al. 2014). Rather than "controlling the quantity of reserves, central banks today typically implement monetary policy by setting the price of reserves – that is, interest rates" (McLeay et al. 2014). Hence, the activity of commercial bank lending does not depend upon the quantity of reserves, but turns on "profitable lending opportunities" available to commercial banks. Interest rates set by central banks

J. JA Burke, *Financial Services in the Twenty-First Century*,
https://doi.org/10.1007/978-3-030-63967-9_6

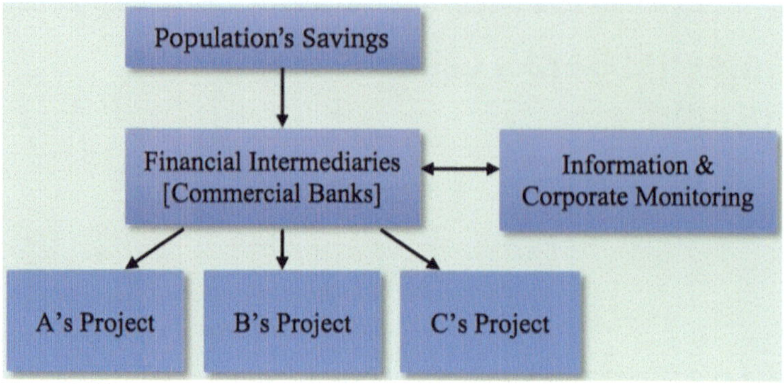

Fig. 6.1 Role of financial intermediaries. (Source: Werner 2014)

effect the perceived profitability of extending credit. Both the financial intermediation and fractional reserve theories are demonstrably false.

Empirical data is "consistent only with the credit creation theory of banking" (Werner 2014). Under this theory, banks individually create credit and money out of nothing, when they extend credit. Werner (2014) argued: "Bank credit creation does not channel existing money to new uses. It creates new money that did not exist beforehand and channels it to some use". The Bank of England supports the credit creation theory (McLeay et al. 2014). Why commercial banks can create money out of nothing while other companies cannot requires a "comparative analysis of the accounting treatment of lending by different types of corporate lenders" (Werner 2014).

Following Werner's explanation, and consistent with the Bank of England's view, we compare the accounting of a loan extended by (McLeay et al. 2014) a non-financial corporation (NFC), such as a manufacturer, (McCann et al. 2017) a non-bank financial institution (NBFI), such as a stock broker, (Tobin 1963) and a bank. We assume that each entity makes a €1,000 loan and look at the effects of each entity's balance sheet. Using T-accounts, the new loan effects the balance sheets as follows (Fig. 6.2):

Both the NFC and NBFI loan contracts increase assets, as the institutions have a claim on the borrower for repayment of the loan. In addition, both the NFC and NBFI record a negative entry on the asset side of the balance sheet to show that the firm used cash reserves or an equivalent to make payment to the borrower. The total impact of the transaction does not enlarge or contract the balance sheet. However, the bank's accounting treatment of the loan contract differs distinctly from the two non-bank corporations. The bank also records the loan as an asset but then enters a positive entry on the liability side of the balance sheet. It does not counter-balance the increased gross assets. Both sides of the balance sheet expand by the amount of the loan.

The question arises what enables a commercial bank to discharge its loan without drawing down any asset, as both the financial intermediation and fractional reserve theories maintain erroneously. Werner advises breaking down the lending

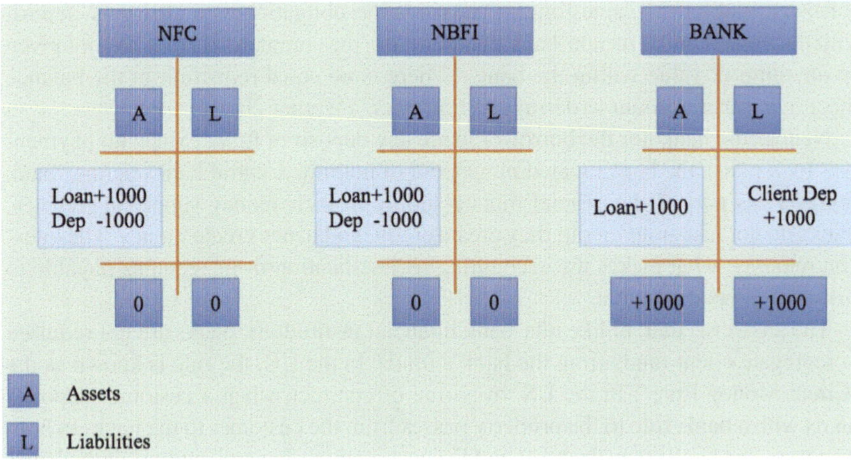

Fig. 6.2 The balance sheet of the new loan effects. (Source: Werner 2014)

process into two separate steps, first the borrower executes the loan contract with the bank but the borrower asks the bank to defer disbursement of the loan until a later date. Step one involves the bank and borrower expressing respective obligations to a written agreement: the loan contract or promissory note. At this stage of the disaggregated lending process, the NFC, the NBFI, and the bank make the following entries in their balance sheets: the loan is recorded as an asset and an "accounts payable" is recorded as a positive liability. All lenders have an open liability to pay an amount of €1,000 to the borrower at some future date. In step one, the balance sheets of all three entities expand. It may be concluded therefore that the decision to enter into a legally binding agreement to make a loan fails to explain the distinction between banks and non-banks. In general, the act of granting a loan from one legal person to another is an unregulated activity. Consequently, what makes a bank able to create money out of nothing happens in the act of making the loan proceeds available to the borrower.

In step two when the NFC and the NBFI make funds available to the borrower, each entity must draw down its cash or withdraw deposit balances with a bank. In other words, the lender uses an existing asset to discharge its liability arising from this accounts payable. Werner clarifies: "For firms without a bank license, the disbursement of the loan is from funds elsewhere within the firm. Thus there is an equal reduction in balance from another account from which the lent funds came from" (Werner 2014). Step two causes the balance sheet to shrink; there is no overall change in its size. The accounts payable is reduced to zero and the recording of the loan as an asset is offset in an identical amount by the disbursement. However, the story is quite different for the bank. After the bank makes the proceeds available to the borrower, the bank's balance sheet does not shrink, rather it remains at a standstill. The bank reduces its "accounts payable" on the liability side of the balance sheet by the amount of the loan, acting as if the loan has been made to the borrower, and, at the same time, reclassifies the obligation as a customer deposit with the bank. Unlike its non-bank counterparts, the commercial bank has not given up anything of value within the bank. "There is no equal reduction in the balance sheet of another account to defray the borrower" (Werner 2014).

Neither the bank nor the borrower made any deposit of funds. Since no payment ever took place, the bank created money out of nothing. Central banks define "bank deposits" as part of the official money supply in their money supply aggregates. Banks do not just grant credit; they create credit, and hence create money. The question remains: what makes the accounting reclassification from accounts payable to customer deposit possible.

The answer is that, unlike non-bank financial institutions, banks are not required to segregate client funds from the bank's funds. In the UK, the rule is known as the "Client Money Rule". In the US, by virtue of contract, when a customer deposits funds with a bank, title to the property passes from the customer to the bank. In both scenarios, the bank owns the asset and the customer is a general creditor of the bank, able to require repayment on demand when the bank is solvent.

The authority to create money has implications for bank regulation. The Bank of International Settlements has emphasised capital adequacy requirements, referred to as the Basel Accords, and implemented as law in virtually all major economies. History has not vindicated the effectiveness of the Accords. Issued in 1998, the Basel I Accord "called for a minimum ratio of capital to risk-weighted assets of 8%. Less than 10 years later, finding the original accords inadequate, the Basle Committee on Banking Supervision (BCBS) issued Basel II: the new capital framework, and shortly thereafter in 2009 Basel III, responding to the 2008 financial crisis. While empirical study is needed to conclude that the Basel Accords are ineffective at stemming financial risk, it may be validly observed that, since their inception, several banking crises have taken place. If the financial intermediation theory is false, as the evidence demonstrates, then regulation aimed at capital requirements is unworkable, since banks can generate money to purchase new capital. Werner's case study of Barclays Bank in 2008 illustrates this workaround. To avoid a taxpayer bailout, "Barclays Bank raised £5.8 bn in new equity from Gulf sovereign wealth investors – by lending them money" (Werner 2014). Barclays entered into a standard loan agreement with the sovereign fund thereby inventing the funds lent to the investor. The deposit then was used to purchase newly issued Barclays shares.

Werner observes: "Thus in this case the bank liability originating from the bank loan to the Gulf investor transmuted from (McLeay et al. 2014) an accounts payable liability to (McCann et al. 2017) a customer deposit liability, to finally end up as (Tobin 1963) equity, another category on the liability side of the bank's balance sheet" (Werner 2014). What matters more than regulating "capital" is regulating the different consequences of commercial bank's lending practices. For example, bank credit used to support financial transactions increases asset prices, without necessarily conferring any benefit on the real economy; bank credit used to finance consumer purchases affects consumer prices and imposes unsustainable household debt levels; bank credit used to facilitate productive investment purposes is sustainable and non-inflationary.

Restraints on Money Creation

The Bank of England identifies the following three mechanisms to restrain unlimited "money creation": (McLeay et al. 2014) self-imposed restraint, (McCann et al. 2017) behaviour of households and businesses, and (Tobin 1963) monetary policy (McLeay et al. 2014). The first restraint reposes upon market forces. In a competitive market, banks must lend profitably and reduce risks associated with making loans. Conventional wisdom, a view questioned later, depicts a bank's business model as dependent upon the receipt of interest payments exceeding the rate of interest paid on deposits and other liabilities. The "spread" covers operating costs and provides profits (McLeay et al. 2014). Under this simplified view, banks wanting to make additional loans reduce interest rates, relative to competitors, charged to households to induce the latter to borrow more. If this tactic works, the bank may lose the "customer deposit" to a competitor, and this risk influences the bank's decision to expand its lending portfolio.

An example illustrates this point. Assume Household "A" takes a loan from Bank "ABC" to purchase a house from Seller "B". Bank "ABC" creates a new deposit for Household "A" that is immediately disbursed to Seller "B". The result: Household "A" has real property and Seller "B" has money. It is likely that Household "A" and Seller "B" have accounts at different banks. In that case, the new deposit is transferred to the bank of Seller "B", leaving Bank "ABC" with fewer assets. The banks settle using reserves held by the Central Bank, leaving Bank "ABC" with less reserves relative to customer deposits. A bank cannot make more loans than its reserves required to settle interbank transfers and to meet demands for cash withdrawals. Hence, expanding its loan portfolio requires Bank "ABC" to attract new deposits, additional liabilities, or borrow from other institutions. These efforts require the bank to consider the cost, quality, and stability of new funds. "Competition for loans and deposits, and the desire to make a profit, therefore limit money creation by banks."

A second constraint arises from the response of households and companies. The behaviour of the non-bank private sector influences credit creation by the commercial banking sector because the non-bank private sector may wish to hold other assets, such as property or shares, or pay off existing liabilities held by the banks. As suggested by Tobin, money may be as quickly destroyed as it is created, when, for example, a debtor pays off an outstanding loan (Tobin 1963). Alternatively, the non-bank private sector may spend the extra bank-created money in the economy on goods and services, or higher-yielding assets, and increase inflationary pressure on the economy thereby slowing down money destruction.

The third instrument of constraint is monetary policy. Central banks are tasked with keeping inflation low, within a target set by the government or by treaty as in the European Union. Setting interest rates on reserves "should ultimately ensure a stable rate of credit and money creation consistent with meeting the target" (McLeay et al. 2014). Reserves are central bank money, money distinguished from "broad money" circulating in the open market. Reserves are used by commercial banks for interbank settlement. The price of reserves arguably "has a meaningful impact on other rates in the economy". The explanation proceeds as follows: commercial banks earn interest on their reserves; by manipulating these rates, central banks effect the interest rates "banks are willing to lend on similar terms in, for example, sterling money markets (the markets in which the central bank and commercial banks lend to each other and other financial institutions). It is argued that changes in interbank rates subsequently affect interest rates in different markets, including rates banks charge borrowers for loans and offer savers for deposits (McLeay et al. 2014).

Contrary to many textbooks, central banks do not determine or vary quantities of reserves to control commercial bank "money creation". "Rather, they focus on prices – setting interest rates" (McLeay et al. 2014). Supply of reserves therefore is linked to demand for reserves. The demand for reserves is a consequence, not a cause, of banks making loans and creating broad money. As stated earlier, banks' decisions to extend credit are based on profitable lending opportunities. A factor in the determination of profitability is the interest rate paid on reserves. A "loose" monetary policy is likely to increase the supply of broad money by reducing rates at which money may be borrowed and hence increase the volume of loans. It follows logically, that demand for reserves rise.

Seigniorage or Making Money from Money

Seigniorage has historically been defined as the difference between the cost of physically producing money and its purchasing power in the economy. For example, the cost of producing a £10 note is miniscule; therefore the seigniorage profits are equal to about £10. Historically, the sovereign state had the exclusive power to create and spend money. However, as we have just learned, commercial banks, not the sovereign state, are responsible for the money supply, through the creation of customer deposits. In the UK, it is estimated that physical cash represents only about 3% of the total money supply. The remaining 97% "is lent to economies as the digital IOUs of commercial banks – the deposits that are entered in to our bank accounts when banks make new loans" (McCann et al. 2017). The 2017 study calculates that this privilege has provided commercial banks with "seigniorage" profits amounting to an annual average of £23 billion per year in the 1998–2016 period (McCann et al. 2017). Hence, creating money is a profitable business. "The result is a government supported monopoly that drains resources from the productive economy and gives a megalithic international banking empire enormous power over people and governments" (Brown 2019).

Conclusion

We have shown that of the three competing theories of money that the only theory consistent with empirical data is the credit creation theory. Efforts to explain money by the financial intermediation or fractional reserve theories are demonstrably false.

This fact has implications for bank regulatory reform. We also have shown that central banks do not fix quantity of "reserves"—an elusive term referring to central bank money as opposed to broad money—but rather set the price of reserves to determine quantity required by demand. We have referred to a simplified, and misleading, model of how banks make money. This matter is dealt with later. Finally, we broached the subject of seigniorage and learned that commercial banks reap substantial profits from doing nothing that serves the public good.

Questions

1. What is a central bank and why is it deemed essential to modern economies?
2. Summarise the findings in the publication: New Economics Foundation, "Making Money from Making Money: Seigniorage in the Modern Economy", Copenhagen Business School 2017.
3. Using the example provided to show marketplace constraints upon commercial credit creation, create a stylised balance sheet showing the effects of the transactions upon Bank "ABC" and the seller's bank.

Bibliography

Duncan McCann, Josh Ryan-Collins, Laurie MacFarlane, Ole Berg, Rasmus Nielsen, Making Money from Money, 31 January 2017, New Economics Foundation.

Ellen Brown, Banking on the People: Democratizing Money in the Digital Age, (2019 Ellen Brown & the Democracy Collaborative).

Frederic. S. Mishkin, The Economics of Money, Banking, and Financial Markets (12th ed. 2018 Pearson).

Michael McLeay, Amar Radia, and Ryland Thomas, Money Creation in the Modern Economy, Bank of England Quarterly Bulletin 2014 Q1, 27 Mar. 2014 at https://papers.ssrn.com/sol3/papers.cfm?abstract_id=2416234

James Tobin, Commercial Banks as Creators of 'Money' (Cowles Foundation Yale University 1963).

Stephen Valdez, An Introduction to Global Financial Markets (4th ed. Palgrave Macmillan), 2003.

Stephen Valdez and Philip Molyneux, An Introduction to Global Financial Markets (Red Globe Press 2017).

Richard A. Werner, *How do banks create money, and why can other firms not do the same? An explanation for the coexistence of lending and deposit taking*, International Review of Financial Analysis 36 (2014).

Money

7

Introduction

Economics instructs that money possesses three mandatory characteristics. First, "money is any generally accepted means of payment for delivery of goods [and services] or settlement of debt, that is, it is a medium of exchange".[1] This definition is important for one reason: money allows the purchase and sale of goods and services quickly, mitigating transaction costs, that is, the time spent haggling over the transfer of products and services between sellers and buyers. A system without money increases transaction costs to acquire goods and services.

To see why, textbooks speak of a barter economy. A barter economy is a system without money where goods and services are exchanged directly for other goods and services.[2] The reality TV show called *The Alaskan Bush People* is illustrative. The Brown family live completely outside conventional society and lack regular employment to earn money. In one episode, their daughter requires dental care. The Brown family neither has health insurance nor money sufficient to pay the dentist in Alaska. However, the Browns' son has an uncanny ability to catch salmon. The dentist agrees to provide dental care in exchange for freshly caught fish thereby illustrating the double coincidence of wants required by the barter system. The Brown family needs dental care and the dentist needs or wants Alaskan salmon. Money obviates the "double coincidence of wants" and provides a common unit to permit a frictionless method to purchase and sell goods and services, thereby promoting efficiency.

Second, money serves as a "unit of account" that is, the unit in which prices are quoted and accounts kept. In other words, money serves as a means to "price" a good or service in specific units of a single currency. Hence, if there are 100 different goods, we have 100 prices. Money also is mathematically divisible; for example, €1 is divisible into 100 centimes. So, if I go to a café, and I order a latte at a price of €1, I can pay by exchanging a €1 coin, or I can give a €5 note and receive €4 in change. By contrast in a barter system, a single item cannot be stated in one price.

J. JA Burke, *Financial Services in the Twenty-First Century*,
https://doi.org/10.1007/978-3-030-63967-9_7

Mishkin observes, in a barter system, if a supermarket sells "1000 goods, we need 499,500 prices".[3]

Third, money is a "store of value", that is, money must retain a predictable value over time. This aspect of money is retention of purchasing power. We would like to think that our €20 note today, with which we can purchase a certain quantity of goods or services, can, one year from now, purchase approximately the same basket of goods or services. In the modern economy, the third characteristic of money refers to price stability, the objective of constraining inflation. The third function of money as a "store of value" arguably is the most important function and the most difficult to attain as future prices are subject to "profound uncertainty". A fourth factor is often added: money is a standard of deferred payment—a means of relating current and future values in contracts.

The Sovereign Definition

Sovereign states impose an additional criterion upon the economists' definition of money by dictating what constitutes "legal tender". "Legal tender is what the law of the country states is acceptable as means of payment".[4] Legal tender thus is defined in domestic legislation; legal tender must be accepted in payment of goods, services, debts and taxes. Examples of laws defining legal tender are those of the United States and the European Union.[5] Central banks issue legal tender in the form of notes and coin. Commercial bank deposits also are legal tender if these deposits are regarded as a component of monetary aggregates, an arbitrary method of measuring money. Placing control of money within government institutions is not without legal accountability. Central banks pledge to maintain price stability, but no currency maintains its value. Deane and Pringle note, "airlines or chemical companies that pollute the environment are liable for damages". But the economic pollution caused by deprecating money is more damaging to the economy than private liabilities.

The Metallic Definition

Gold, silver, and bronze coins served as money for millennia dating back at least to 600 BCE when archaeologists found Lydian coins in what is now modern-day Turkey.[6] The use of metal as money continued for more than a thousand years. In the time of King Charlemagne [768–814], prices were quoted in silver denarii, the Roman system of coinage. In the –fourteenth century, multiple systems of coinage circulated throughout Europe—gold, silver, and base metal, making long-distance trade or payment of taxes complicated by the need to convert from one currency to the other.

The Medici of Venice seized upon this difficulty by becoming foreign exchange dealers and bankers. They used "bills of exchange" to finance trade. For example, if one merchant owed money—in metallic form—to another merchant to be paid in the future, the creditor drew a bill of exchange on the debtor for the sum outstanding. The bill of exchange obliged the debtor to pay the drawer of the bill, or a third party properly holding the bill of exchange, a sum certain at a time specified in the bill. A bill of exchange therefore was a negotiable instrument, that is, the creditor could transfer the bill of exchange to another merchant as a means of payment or transfer the bill to a banker for cash at a discount, though ultimately settlement was made in coin. The bill of exchange facilitated international trade as metal is heavy and transport costly.

The formal transition from metal to paper notes as a form of money reportedly took place in 1661 when Sweden issued banknotes. Not all European countries adopted this practice. Spain, to its detriment, held to silver, importing vast quantities from South America, causing inflation in Europe thereby devaluing the very currency it sought to augment. The rise of paper-based banknotes did not displace the role of gold as the indisputable king of currency. Banknotes were convertible into gold until President Nixon cancelled the Bretton Woods system in 1971.[7]

The Trust Definition

The "Trust" Model is best explained by Mervyn King, the former Governor of the Bank of England.[8] King stated that money is an IOU, that is a debt. Assume the Bank of England mints coin and prints banknotes. Under King's view, these coins and notes are debts of the Central Bank of England; in other words, the government of the United Kingdom. But this debt is never repaid. If you hold a £50 note, you cannot go to the Central Bank of England and say, "repay me". The "base money" issued by central banks is a curious form of debt. Nevertheless, with that £50 note, you can buy commodities, pay off debt obligations, or open a current account in a commercial bank.

According to King, the whole enterprise is held together by "trust". In his view, "trust" constitutes protection of purchasing power: the £50 note I hold today can buy the same basket of commodities in the future, for example, one year from now. The "trust" King speaks of is trust in the central bank's ability to maintain price stability. King succinctly states, "Trust is fundamental to the acceptability and so the value, of money. But it is not trust in God but trust in the issuer of money, usually governments, that determines its value."

That explains why all central banks today, and parenthetically central banks are a recent phenomenon no more than a hundred years, have as their main objective containment of inflation. However, history does not vindicate the central bankers. As Deane and Pringle note the deutsche mark, the so-called unquestioned standard of currencies, between the period 1951 and 1994, lost more than 50% of its value. There is much room for thought in understanding what we now call "fiat" money, that is, money by command of the sovereign. King adds, "Much of the financial history of the past 150 years is the story of unsuccessful attempts to maintain the value of money."

The Fiat Definition

Fiat money comprises notes, coins, and electronic entries of "money" issued by a sovereign, unbacked by any physical asset. Fiat money is "legal tender" as it is issued by the sovereign and must be accepted in payment of debt and taxes in the jurisdiction where issued. By definition, fiat money cannot be exchanged for anything vis-à-vis the sovereign. Most national currencies are fiat currencies: for example, US dollar, euro, BPS, Yen, and SDR. The special feature of "fiat money" is that it is printed at will by the sovereign; the currency lacks any link to a reference asset to restrain the quantity produced. In international trade, the value of the currency is set in the international foreign exchange market based on supply and demand and primarily the credit standing of the issuer of the currency.

Special Drawing Rights are a special type of fiat currency. "The SDR is world money, controlled by the IMF, backed by nothing and printed at will" (Rickards 229). The International Monetary Fund created the SDR in 1969. An SDR is defined by a basket of currencies defined and adjusted by the IMF every five years or as deemed necessary by the IMF. Although individual persons and firms cannot use SDRs in private transactions, the SDR meets the economist's definition of money, though the IMF denies that the SDR is a currency. The IMF can issue an unlimited quantity of SDRs. Presently, the SDR is a significant reserve currency held by central banks. As of 2009, the IMF had issued approximately 204 billion SDRs. The IMF has the potential to become a global central bank and the SDR a global currency.

The Electronic Definition

Most money in a modern economy is a liability or asset recorded on a bank's balance sheet.[9] Liabilities are represented by deposits and like accounts (e.g., checking accounts, time deposits). A customer who deposits money in a bank is a creditor of the bank. The customer has a claim against the bank for the amount of the deposit, though, by reason of contract, the bank owns the deposit. Since ownership in property is transferred, the bank invests this money as it sees fit. The bank records a deposit of funds on its balance sheet as a liability. Conversely, when a bank lends money to a borrower, the bank creates a new deposit thereby creating money that never existed before. The bank is the creditor and the borrower is the debtor. The bank records the loan on its balance sheet as an asset. In both cases, money has no tangible form. Money is represented as an electronic record on a bank's balance sheet, a financial statement. While financial ledgers have roots in Mesopotamian clay tablets, the modern financial accounting system has rendered money simply as an electronic record.

The Digital Definition

This sub-section discusses P2P cashless payment systems using cryptocurrency. Cryptocurrency is privately issued money, often referred to as digital currency, unbacked by any physical asset to support its value, and unregulated by any single, central authority. It goes beyond fiat money created by Nation States, as cryptocurrency is not issued by any governmental authority, does not rely upon central banks to manage quantity, and "trust" is placed in mathematics, not the rationale of central banks or governments. Payments are not settled ultimately by adjusting reserve accounts of commercial banks held by the central bank of a sovereign. Payments are settled through a consensus system of nodes that comprise the network holding the ledger of accounts and verifying transactions. Any other system of payment, whether PayPal, mobile telephone, electronic wallets, and the like, relies upon the infrastructure of the banking system and therefore is beholden to the monopoly exerted by the sovereign and large financial institutions.

Nation States pose substantial threats to cryptocurrency precisely because Nation States have not yet agreed upon a uniform system of regulation. Governments categorise cryptocurrency or cryptoassets for purposes of regulation, ostensibly consumer protection. Take for example the case of the FCA. In its January 2019 Consultation Paper, the FCA found that Bitcoin, Litecoin, and the like are "exchange tokens", meaning that they are not issued by a central authority, but can be used directly as a means of exchange. The tokens can be used to pay for goods or services without going through an "intermediary" such as a bank. In spite of their use as a means of exchange, the FCA recognises exchange tokens neither as legal tender nor as currency or money. The question arises why not? The answer provided is that the value of exchange tokens is more volatile than traditional fiat currency, and that they are not widely accepted as a means of payment in the UK.

However, these conclusions beg the question. First, like money held in electronic records, one does not carry Bitcoin, Litecoin, or the like in his/her pocket. Arguably, it is the purest form of electronic cash recorded in a decentralised ledger known as blockchain. Consequently, exchange tokens do not differ from fiat currency in that both currencies have electronic forms. Second, all currencies are volatile. If the degree of volatility of exchange tokens is the differentiating factor, empirical study is needed to support the claim. Third, exchange tokens are units of account. For example, prices may be stated in Bitcoin and Bitcoin is divisible to eight decimal places. Fourth, the fact that a majority of merchants do not yet accept payment in cryptocurrency has nothing to do with the tokens *per se*, but the delay and cost of implementing technology needed for merchants to accept them in payment of goods and services. Hence, conclusions that exchange tokens are not money may be premature, as they fit the economists' three-function definition.

"Money as Energy Model"

Eric J. Chaisson, an astrophysicist, is a "leading theorist of complexity in evolution" (Rickards 216). Chaisson observes that the "universe is best understood as the constant flow of energy between radiation and matter". Applied to macroeconomics and capital markets, Rickards states that money may best be understood as "stored energy". Rickards begins his argument by noting that a fundamental characteristic of money is its "store of value". We have seen that King thinks that what is being stored is trust in the central bank to maintain the purchasing power of money. Rickards' analysis is more compelling. He asks exactly what is being stored, and notes that "value" is typically defined as the output of labour and capital, "both of which are energy intensive" (*Ibid.* 218). Assume a baker makes a loaf of bread using ingredients such as flour and wheat, equipment such as an oven, and the baker's labour. Each factor either uses energy, the oven, and baker, or is a product of energy and the agricultural ingredients. When the baker sells the bread for money, "the money represents the stored energy that went into making the bread" (*Ibid.* 219). The energy in the money is unlocked when the baker purchases a good or service that constitutes another store of energy. "Money works exactly like a battery". Money takes a charge of energy and stores it, for a period of time, for purposes of Rickards' illustration in the form of "money". The energy is released by exchange of money for some good, service, or other intangible that in itself is a fusion of energy. Unlike alternative definitions, the "money as energy model" is based in science though empirical study is required to provide further support for this concept. Nevertheless, this model is the most compelling of all definitions, except for gold.

The Rise of Digital Money: A Consolidated Construct and Taxonomy

In 2019, Adrian and Mancini-Griffoli published a paper "The Rise of Digital Money" under the auspices of the International Monetary Fund (Adrian and Mancini-Griffoli 2019). The paper speaks to new digital forms of money, considers their implications for the banking sector, still dependant primarily on two forms of money, creates a useful taxonomy of traditional payment instruments and digital money, and talks about possible central bank reactions. The authors challenge the economist's view of payments, that evolved, and was defined prior to social media platforms and applications.

An example suffices to set the stage. You walk into Starbucks and order a coffee. You pay by taping a smartcard near a reader or waving your mobile device. Payment by digital money seems easy at the level of sight. The liability to the vendor is extinguished virtually instantaneously, but the process is extraordinarily complex, "involving information exchange, legal and regulatory structures, and back-end settlement of funds" (Adrian). A second person walks into Starbucks and orders a coffee. The second person pays using a stablecoin, so called because its value is managed, by a social messaging app, or by a digital token backed by gold or another asset considered liquid and safe. "Cash and bank deposits will battle with e-money" (Adrian).

The paper is organised into four parts. The first part, most important for our purposes, reviews the "different models of digital money and offers a simple conceptual framework to compare and contrast them." The second part argues that, in spite of the problem of storing value, new currencies may be adopted quickly, due to network effects and online integration. The third part discusses the impact of these developments upon the extant banking sector, by considering several scenarios. The fourth part considers the response of central banks. The authors are sanguine in their outlook, implying that central banks will recognise the potential benefits of new models of payment, and adopt a form of Central Bank Digital Currency (CBDC).

The taxonomy is the "Money Tree", a structure borrowed from Bech and Garratt's "use of botanical analogies in monetary economics", that looks at "four attributes of means of payment: type, value, backstops, and technology" (Adrian). The first attribute to define a means of payment is "type—either a claim or an object" (Adrian). Cash is the classic example of payment by an object. Each party accepts the physical object and further information exchange is unnecessary. When payment is made by using a credit card for example, then payment is made by transferring ownership of a claim. The credit card holder has a claim on an account for the amount of the purchase and has the right to transfer that claim to the vendor. The infrastructure behind the payment by claim is complex, involving a card network system, and multiple banks (Fig. 7.1).

The second attribute to define a means of payment is value. It is customary to pay by an instrument of fixed value. In this way, both buyer and seller are assured that the value of the claim or currency is fixed and may be redeemed at face value. Payment by an instrument having a variable value contain an element of risk. For example, if payment is made by a claim and the value of that claim is tied to "going market prices", then the vendor takes the instrument with an "upside" and a "downside". Assume payment is made by Bitcoin, then the vendor assumes the risk of its volatility.

The third attribute to define a means of payment is whether its redemption value is "backstopped", that is, guaranteed by the government or relies solely upon prudent business practice and applicable legal structures. This attribute matters if trust is an essential component of the payment. The final attribute is the technical means of settlement, whether it is centralised or decentralised. In a decentralised system, a network of nodes, using an agreed-upon consensus, clear and settle the payments, for example Bitcoin or Ether. In a centralised system, transactions are cleared and settled by a central proprietary server.

The five attributes enable help to distinguish characteristics among five different means of payment: (1) central bank money; (2) cryptocurrency; (3) b-money, currently issued by banks; (4) electronic money or e-money, issued by "new private sector providers", and (5) i-money or investment money issued by private investment funds.[10] Central bank money is defined as cash. The authors reference debates concerning the development of "central bank digital currency" or CBDC (Adrian). Cryptocurrency also is deemed an object-based means of payment. It is created

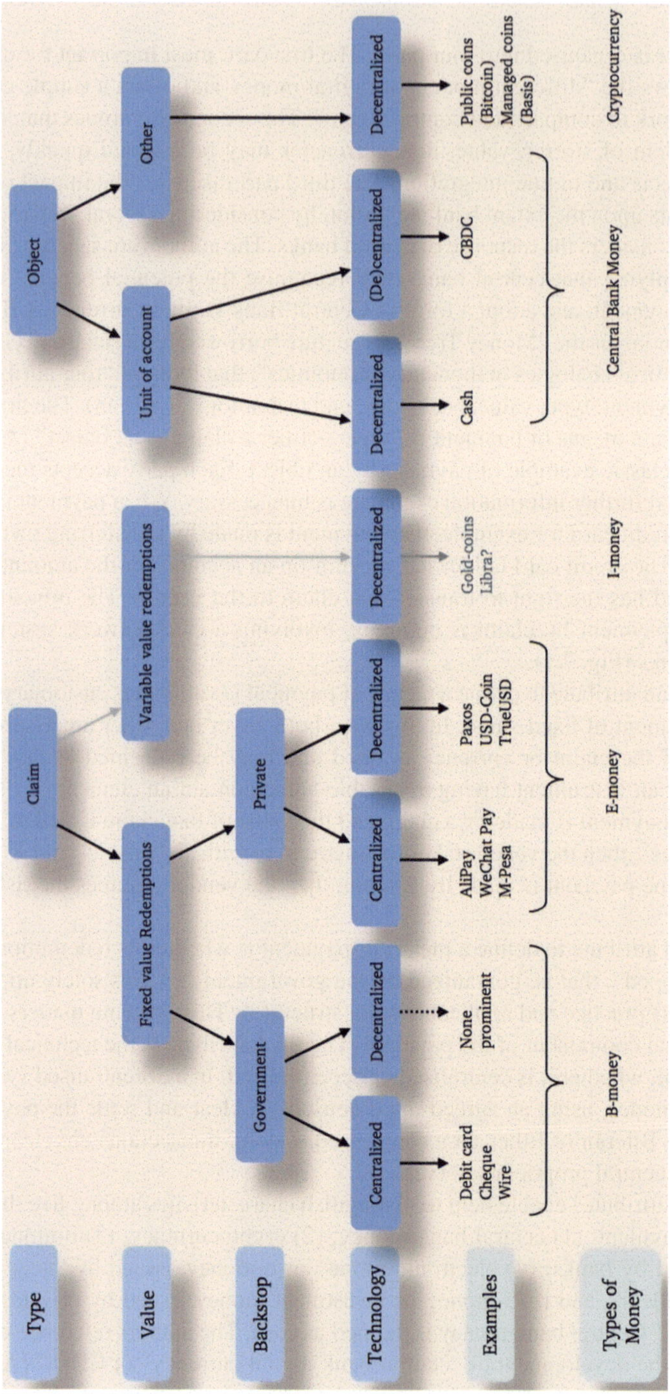

Fig. 7.1 Money trees. (Source: IMF Staff, 2019. Note: CBDC—central bank digital currency)

(issued or brought into existence) by solving mathematical problems; it is a unit of account, and payments are cleared and settled by distributed ledger technology, either permission-less or permissioned. However, the authors distinguish between "managed coins" and "public coins". The algorithm underlying "managed coins" contains rules to stabilise its value. For example, if managed coins are tied to fiat currency or a basket of currencies, the system automatically increases quantity when the value of the managed coin relative to its peg is too high. Conversely, when too low in value, more currency is issued.

"B-money" is claim-based money consisting primarily of commercial bank deposits. The authors argue that the claims function as debt instruments. Intuitively this is correct as the commercial bank holding the deposit has a liability to redeem the "instrument" in its unit of account at face value. Most b-money payments are executed by using debit and credit cards, ordering a transfer of funds, or issuing a cheque. The individual method of payment relies upon an unseen but complex and different infrastructure. A distinguishing feature of b-money is government guarantee; for example, deposits are insured up to a certain amount. In the United States, the standard insurance amount is $250,000 per depositor, per insured bank, for each account ownership category. E-money is deemed a "prominent new player in the payment landscape" (Adrian). "Borrowing from our earlier analogy, it is a debt like instrument … except that it is not backstopped by governments" (Adrian). In this author's view, the most novel aspect of e-money is that payments are made with mobile technology. The only difference between b-money and e-money is the technology connecting the payment to the bank backbone. For example, payment by Visa goes through a proprietary network eventually drilling down to the buyer's and seller's respective commercial bank accounts. Payment by Alipay with a mobile device is a similar means of payment except that the connection to the bank backbone is made using mobile technology. Finally, "i-money is a potential new means of payment" (Adrian). The "i" in "i-money" derives from its source: private investment funds, like money-market funds and exchange-traded funds, because these funds tend to be relatively safe and liquid. Because the value of "i-money" is tied to an investment vehicle, the value of the means of payment fluctuates leading the authors to conclude that, unlike b-money, i-money functions as an equity share. At present, "i-money" is a concept. Investment funds could become money if they are "tokenised", that is represented by a coin of any amount recorded on a digital ledger. Its potential to serve as a means of payment requires that the underlying fund is stable and liquid so that users can track its value.[11]

The biggest "takeaway" from the "The Rise of Digital Money" is the recognition that novel types of means of payment may quickly overtake traditional means of payments and that the payment system is quickly evolving, so that the most widely accepted form of money may yet be unknown. The most dynamic changes are taking place not in traditional money centres but in Asia, Africa, and South America.

Conclusion

The short discourse on money has crossed broad historical periods and touched upon the nature of money. We are told that money is sovereign debt but a debt that the sovereign never intends to pay. We are told that money is "trust", but, until the advent of blockchain, "trust" was faith in central bank policy. If money is "trust" then a deeper analysis of central bank policy is required. King aptly observes, "The crises of 2007–9 is evidence of the continuing folly of central banks and the attractions of an automatic standard for the value of money."[12] Money as stored energy is the most fascinating and compelling definition. We are told that banks create money by lending, but simultaneously we are told that money comprises only coin, banknotes, and bank reserves.[13] This conundrum cannot stand. Finally, we are told that money is recorded data in an electronic blockchain. It is no wonder that "money is surely one of the most perplexing inventions of human society".

Questions

1. Economists insist that money must be a widely accepted means of payment, a store of value, and a unit of account. Given this definition, what "novel" means of payment are able to meet this criteria?
2. Are cryptocurrencies money *per se*, as markets are needed to provide a ramp to convert them into fiat currency? Are statements made about cryptocurrency flawed by the fallacy of "circular reasoning"?
3. Visit the site https://coinmarketcap.com/ and explain how to purchase cryptocurrencies; identify how many cryptocurrencies have been issued; and explain Bitcoin futures.

Notes

1. David Begg, Stanley Fischer, and Rudiger Dornbusch, *Economics* 313 [McGraw-Hill 7th ed. 2003].
2. Frederic S. Mishkin, *The Economics of Money, Banking, and Financial Markets* 95 [Pearson 10th ed. 2013].
3. *Id.* at 97. The formula is that used to calculate the number of pairs if we have "N" items: N(N−1)/2, or 1000 (1000–1) divided by 2 equals 499,500.
4. Marjorie Deane and Robert Pringle, *The Central Banks* 115 [Penguin Group 1994].
5. United States coins and currency (including Federal Reserve notes and circulating notes of Federal Reserve banks and national banks) are legal tender for all debts, public charges, taxes, and dues. Foreign gold or silver coins are not legal tender for debts. 31 U.S. Code § 5103 [1983]. Article 128(1) of the Treaty on the Functioning of the European Union states, "The banknotes issued by the European Central Bank and the national central banks shall be the only such notes to have the status of legal tender within the Union". The legal status of euro coins is granted under secondary legislation (Article 11 Regulation EC/974.98); their existence is recognised by the TFEU Article 128(2) but that article does not speak to their legal status.

6. Niall Ferguson, *The Ascent of Money: A Financial History of the World* 25 [2008 Penguin Books]. The Ferguson book arguably is the best account of money.
7. Bretton Woods and the gold standard system are explained later, as they pertain to monetary policy and not money *per se*.
8. Mervyn King, The End of Alchemy 68 [W.W. Norton & Co. 2016].
9. Nathan Lewis maintains that money comprises only paper, coins, and bank reserves. The remainder is credit. His assertion is fascinating. However, convention dictates that money is defined to include a wider category of instruments.
10. The authors' categorisation is somewhat arbitrary and duplicative. For example, the authors make a distinction between cryptocurrency and e-money. Cryptocurrency is deemed an object form of payment like cash, except that cryptocurrencies are intangible and behave like digital assets. By contrast, for the authors, e-money is not an object; but e-money is tied to a bank account, and therefore functions more like a traditional payment by claim than as something novel.
11. The authors cite "Libra" as a tangible example of i-money backed by a portfolio of assets. However, due to negative signals generated in the US government, Libra as initially conceived is already dead.
12. Mervyn King, *supra* note 11 at 76.
13. Nathan K. Lewis, *Gold: The Monetary Polaris* 32 [Canyon Maple Publishing 2013].

Bibliography

Mervyn King, The End of Alchemy [W.W. Norton & Co. 2016]

James Rickards, Currency Wars: The Making of the Next Global Crisis [Penguin Books 2012]

Nathan K. Lewis, *Gold: The Monetary Polaris* [Canyon Maple Publishing 2013]

Niall Ferguson, *The Ascent of Money: A Financial History of the World* [2008 Penguin Books]

Marjorie Deane and Robert Pringle, *The Central Banks* [Penguin Group 1994]

Robert L. Heilbroner and James K. Galbraith, *The Economic Problem* [Prentice Hall 9th ed. 1990]

Angela Redish, *The Evolution of the Gold Standard in England*, The Journal of Economic History, Vol. 50, No. 4 (Dec. 1990) retrieved http://www.jstor.org/stable/2122455

Michael McLeay, Amar Radia and Ryland Thomas, Money in the modern economy: an introduction, Central Bank of England, Quarterly Bulletin, 2014 Q1

Financial Conduct Authority, Guidance on Cryptoassets, Consultation Paper, CP 19/3*, January 2019

Part III

Technologies Influencing Financial Services

The Genesis Files

8

Introduction

Timothy May was a computer scientist known for his work at Intel where he solved the "alpha particle problem" by noting that the ceramic covering the circuit was slightly radioactive allowing a single alpha particle to cause a "single event upset". However, he arguably is best known as the founder of the crypto-anarchist movement and the establishment of the Cypherpunks electronic mailing list. In 1988, he authored "The Crypto Anarchist Manifesto" where he stated "A spectre is haunting the modern world, the spectre of crypto anarchy" (May 1988).

May believed that computer technology would "alter completely the nature of government regulation, the ability to tax and control economic interactions, the ability to keep information secret, and will even alter the nature of trust and reputation" (May). He envisioned a CryptoNet, a marketplace for the purchase and sale of everything, including national secrets, and illicit and stolen material. Referring to how barbed wire used to fence land altered the concepts of property rights in the frontier West, May said an innocuous mathematical discovery would come to act like wire clippers to "dismantle the barbed wire around intellectual property". May's vision of a realm of anarchy in cyberspace and his stress upon developing a cashless encrypted payment system spawned the prolific output of the cypherpunks. May retired from Intel at the age of 34 and died in 2018.

David Chaum

David Chaum started his career as a computer science professor at the University of Berkeley pursuing solutions to achieve digital privacy and untraceable payment systems. In 1994, he invented digital cash but earlier works, such as untraceable email systems in 1981, and subsequent work, such as Praxxis and Elixxir, current as of 2020, are equally important achievements. Chaum consistently produced practical

J. JA Burke, *Financial Services in the Twenty-First Century*,
https://doi.org/10.1007/978-3-030-63967-9_8

cryptographic tools to provide secret communication. A common denominator in his early publications, "Untraceable Electronic Mail, Return Addresses, and Digital Pseudonyms" (1981), "Blind Signatures for Untraceable Payments" (1982), and "Achieving Electronic Privacy" (1992), was the modification of public key cryptography to blind both origin and destination as well as encrypt data. He developed an extension of digital signatures called "blind signatures".

Chaum explained the "extension" in his early work, but the 1992 *Scientific American* publication provides arguably the best and clearest explanation, within the context of a digital payment system. In the article, Chaum starts with traditional digital signatures and, using a bank as a "backbone", describes a payment system whereby clients generate digital cash and use them to make payments for goods.

The "Non-private" Digital Signature Scheme

Alice, a bank client whose account is funded with fiat money, generates a note number, with a serial number long enough to deter duplication, and signs the note number with her private key, corresponding to her public key held by the bank. When the bank receives the note number, the bank verifies Alice's signature, removes her signature from the note number, and replaces Alice's signature with the digital signature of the bank indicating the monetary value of the note, and deducts a corresponding value of fiat money from her account. The bank then returns the signed notes to Alice and gives her a withdrawal receipt. Alice then uses these note numbers to make a purchase from Bob. In practice, the payment is made through Alice's card computer and Bob's card reader. Bob transmits the notes to the bank. The bank verifies that the notes have not been spent and credits Bob's account with fiat money. While this system is secure, it lacks privacy.

The Solution: "Blind Signatures" and "DigiCash"

In 1990, Chaum founded the company "*DigiCash*" based in Amsterdam. The flagship product was "eCash". Prior to sending a note number to the bank, Alice multiplies that number by a random factor, thereby scrambling the data. The note number carries Alice's digital signature ("her private key corresponding to her digital pseudonym (the public key that she has previously established for use with her account)"). Chaum calls this data "the blinded note" (Chaum 1992). When the bank receives the signed notes, the bank applies its digital signature to the notes, but the bank has no idea of what it is signing. When Alice receives the blinded note signed by the bank, she strips out the "blinding factor" and can use the notes. The "blinded note" numbers are unconditionally untraceable. Neither the bank nor Bob has any method to trace the note numbers that Bob deposits with the bank to Alice. "The anonymity of blinded notes is limited only by the unpredictability of Alice's random numbers". To solve "double spending", Chaum and his colleagues Amos Fiat and Moni Naor, presaging "proof of work", required the payor to solve a random numeric query. Spending a note, submitted to this process, twice reveals information sufficient to trace the payor's account.

The Mechanics of eCash

"eCash" operates through a smartcard, a mini-computer containing memory, a processor, and a keypad. The smartcard functions as the owner's "representative". Chaum states, "The prototypical representative is a smart credit-card-size computer. In addition, each "personal representative" contains an "embedded observer". The "representative" and the "observer" generate the numbers that "the observer uses to produce a set of blinded digital pseudonyms" (Chaum 1992). "The observer signs the pseudonyms with a special built-in key". The representative then checks the pseudonyms—blinded public keys—to make certain they do not contain any compromising data.

Understanding "e*Cash*" requires precise definitions of the terms "observer", "representative", and "validating authority". According to Chaum, the observer is "a tamper resistant computer chip issued by some entity that organisations can trust" (Chaum 1992). The observer "acts like a notary and certifies the behaviour of the representative in which it is embedded." Alice acquires her "observer" from a company like Philips or Siemens, and the observer is placed in her smartcard representative. Alice then takes her smartcard to a validating authority. Neither the observer nor the representative trusts one another. The observer's function is to generate a batch of public and private key pairs based on random numbers and numbers supplied by the card. The representative "produces random data that the observer may use to blind each key" (Chaum 1992). The scheme works as follows: the observer blinds the public keys, signs them, and transmits them to the representative. The representative verifies the "blinding", the signature, and the validity of the keys. The blinded signed keys are passed to the validating authority, "which recognizes the observer's built-in signature, removes it and signs the blinded keys with its own key". The validating authority "then passes the keys back to the card, which unblinds them." Chaum concludes: "These keys, bearing the signature of the validating authority, serve as digital pseudonyms for future transactions; Alice can draw on them as needed." The following flow chart depicts the process secure digital pseudonyms (Fig. 8.1):

The observer matches fiat currency in Alice's bank account with its notes. Hence when Alice, for example, makes a purchase from Bob, using her smartcard, the transaction protects her identity while providing proof of payment.

Van Wirdum states that "*DigiCash*" received lucrative offers from several large and well-known companies, including Microsoft. Chaum's company never finalised a deal to implement its product. "*DigiCash*" failed and "*eCash*" with it (van Wirdum 2018). But, the "cypherpunk" movement it inspired kept the dream of an electronic cash system alive.

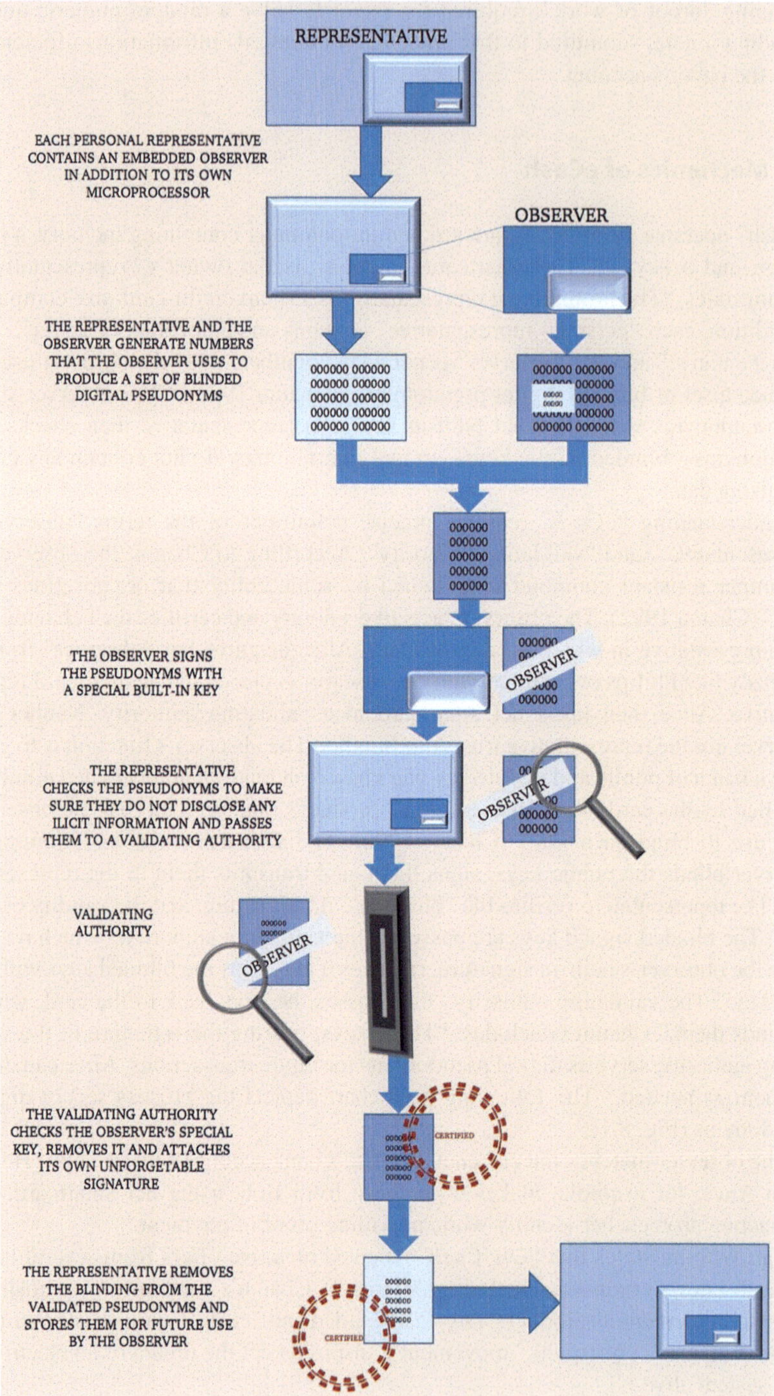

Fig. 8.1 Secure digital pseudonyms. (Source: Chaum 1992)

Adam Back

Dr Adam Back is the next legendary figure in the development of an electronic cashless payment system. He, along with Dwork and Naor, independently developed the consensus of "proof of work" that Nakamoto would modify and use in Bitcoin (van Wirdum June 4 2018). In 1990, IBM researchers Cynthia Dwork and Moni Naor addressed the problem of spam email. The two researchers proposed attaching "some data to any email" sent over the Internet. The data consisted of the solution to a mathematical problem, "unique to the email in question". The three solutions proposed relied upon "public-key cryptography and signature schemes." The solution to the mathematical problem would not be difficult to solve. It would require a few seconds of computing power, on the part of the recipient, to check the validity of the message. But, for persons who wanted to send thousands or millions of messages, the cost of computing power would be made expensive and therefore unprofitable. This solution would come to be known as "proof of work".

Unaware of the work of Dwork and Naor, Back proposed his own anti-spam solution: "hashcash." As the name implies, Back's solution to spam did not rely upon cryptographic puzzles, but upon hashing (van Wirdum 2018). Hashing "takes any data – whether a single letter or entire book – and turns it into a seemingly random number of predetermined length" (Ibid.). Take the example of an SHA-256 hash of the sentence: "This is a sentence." The textual statement is converted into this hexadecimal number: "B9AF3370F5913AF2C76D325868E202733353CD773 FDC29F9F1F0BA923F73B145F". This number may be translated to a regular decimal number or a binary number. However, the slightest alteration to the original sentence produces an entirely different hash, and, importantly, the hash cannot be reverse engineered to reveal the original sentence.

Hashcash worked as follows. The metadata of an email (the "from" address, the "to" address, time, and so on) "is formalised as a protocol." The sender of an email also adds a random number to this metadata called a "nonce". The metadata and nonce then are hashed to produce a seemingly random-looking number. The "trick" of "hashcash" was that not every hash is considered "valid". "Instead, the binary version of the hash must start with a predetermined number of zeroes", for example 20 zeroes. The only way for the sender to produce a hash starting with exactly 20 zeroes is to use a "nonce" that randomly adds up correctly. The sender has one option: trial and error until the intended result is achieved. Unless the sender finds the valid combination, the recipient will reject the email. Back explained on the Cypherpunks mailing list, "this would put spammers out of business overnight, as 1,000,000 × 20 = 100 MIP years", exceeding their computing power.

Back did not create a digital cash system as the name of his product implies. However, subsequent work on decentralised electronic cash systems incorporated the concept of hashing. For example, Bitcoin uses hashing—proof of work—to incentivise miners to produce a valid proof of work, decide which transactions are approved, and receive a reward.

Nick Szabo

Nick Szabo combined programming and cryptographic skills with philosophy and economic history. His vision, inspired by Ayn Rand's "Galt's Gulch", was to create a digital domain where individuals could trade freely, in a totally anonymous manner. Having read Friedrich Hayek, Szabo attempted to transfer the infrastructure of a free market to an online stateless domain. By the mid-1990s, Szabo proposed "smart contracts". Believing that trusted third parties are holes, Szabo used computer protocols to facilitate, verify, and enforce the negotiation of contracts, without third-party intermediation.

However, to achieve his objective, Szabo understood that "smart contracts" were a solution only to part of the problem. He needed: money. Having worked with Chaum and the company "DigiCash", Szabo realised the weaknesses of a centralised database; it was too vulnerable to attack. "Szabo knew that he wanted to create a new form of money that did not depend on trust in any third party". His "money required three characteristics: (1) secure from accidental loss or theft, (2) its value had to be "unforgeably" costly and considered valuable, and (3) its value determined by simple methodology. Szabo wanted to create something that was both digital and scarce, and independent of any third party. In his essay "Shelling Out: The Origins of Money", Szabo described the unforgeable scarcity of precious metals and searched for a cyberspace equivalent. He came up with Bit Gold—a "protocol whereby unforgeably costly bits could be created online with minimal dependence on trusted third parties, and then securely stored, transferred and assayed with similar minimal trust." Van Wirdum states that, "with Bit Gold, Szabo was inches away from inventing Bitcoin" (van Wirdum 2018).

The central property of Bit Gold was scarcity based on Back's proof-of-work requirement for Hashcash. The expenditure of real-world resources represented the "unforgeable costliness of Szabo's money. Bit Gold posted a "first candidate string", or a random number. A person wanting to generate Bit Gold would be required to add another random number to the "candidate string" to produce a hash. Like Back, Szabo used a binary system where a valid hash had to start with a predetermined number of zeroes. The solution to the "first candidate string" was Bit Gold, in effect another candidate string to be subject to another proof of work. The monetary system consisted of chains of proof of work hashes. The person solving the "hash" problem was the owner of the string or Bit Gold. Szabo introduced a digital ownership registry where hashes were linked to the public keys of their owners. Owners spent their money by initiating a transaction with a cryptographic signature. In his decentralised network, "property club" members kept ledgers of Bit Gold ownership. Szabo proposed a security system based on the "Byzantine Quorum System" whereby agreement by the majority of servers established the valid registry of Bit Gold. In a Sybil attack, the honest minority could break off and create a new chain. Users then would choose which chain to follow, presumably the honest chain.

Bit Gold also dealt with the phenomenon of inflation. Szabo realised that increasing computing power would make it easier to generate hashes, thereby reducing scarcity and introducing dilution by abundance. His solution was to timestamp each valid hash with an earlier-in-time hash worth more than a later-in-time hash. Markets then determined the relative value of hashes. Solving for fungibility, that is, each currency unit equal to another currency unit, Bit Gold would be bundled into baskets of combined equal value regardless of year stamped. While the work of Szabo was not cited in the 2018 *Bitcoin Magazine* paper, it is "not difficult to see Bit Gold as an early draft of Bitcoin" (van Wirdum).

Wei Dai's B-Money

While Chaum, Back, and Szabo were fierce advocates of online privacy, Wei Dai took the concept to its logical conclusion. He stated: "(I)n crypto-anarchy the government is not temporarily destroyed but permanently forbidden and permanently unnecessary. It's a community where the threat of violence is impotent because violence is impossible, and violence is impossible because its participants cannot be linked to their true names or physical locations" (van Wirdum). Dai was a prolific contributor to the Cypherpunks mailing list, writing on a broad swath of topics, including digital cash deemed essential for efficient cooperation. He called his proposal b-money. Since there are two versions, only Version 2 is discussed.

In Version 2, not everyone maintains a version of the ledger of transactions involving b-money. There are two types of users: regular users and servers. Only the "servers" linked through a network like Usenet maintain the b-money ledgers. The modification is required to solve the double spending problem. Assume Alice wants to buy a product from Bob, and both are b-money users, with public/private keys and adequate b-money units. Alice creates a transaction in the form of a message: "2 b-money from A to B". Alice signs this message with her private key corresponding to A. The signed message is broadcast to the servers. Alice and Bob must verify, independently from the servers, the transaction. Each server had to put up something of value to participate in the network, foreshadowing proof-of-stake consensus. Dai, borrowing from Szabo, also introduced smart contracts on his network.

Where b-money differs significantly from Bitcoin is in Dai's monetary policy. The value of b-money was linked to a basket of goods. For example, 100 b-money units would be worth one basket of goods. The same 100 b-money units would buy the same basket of goods in the past, in the present, and in the future. Issuing new coins required servers to determine the value of a basket of goods relative to the difficulty of the computational problem: the proof of work. Assume a basket of goods should cost $80 at a specific point in time, then the server performing the proof of work had to show that the value of the proof of work on average would cost $80. The first server to produce a valid proof of work would be credited with 100 b-money units by all servers and users of the system. "No one would be incentivised to produce proofs of work unless they intended to use b-money, limiting inflation to the growth of the b-money" market (van Wirdum 2018). B-money was never implemented, but b-money is the first citation in the Bitcoin white paper.

Conclusion

The history of the Genesis Files demonstrates unequivocally the cypherpunks' commitment to online privacy in general, not limited to cashless payment systems. This unrelenting commitment to privacy conflicts with contemporary general practice on Internet transactions, where users provide identification for free, for example on Facebook. Transactions in cryptocurrencies are pseudonymous, not anonymous. All users can see the public list of cryptocurrency addresses. These addresses are privately created by user's wallets. Obtaining a wallet often requires name and identification. Therefore, transactions are vulnerable to tracing, by connecting an address to a wallet. In effect, the dream of the founders already has been destroyed.

Questions

1. Who are "cypherpunks" and what did they mean by "online privacy"?
2. Explain Chaum's creation of "blind signatures". Why did Chaum find "blinding" necessary for his implementation of a cashless payment system?
3. From the point of view of cypherpunks, like Szabo and Dai, what was wrong with Chaum's eCash, according to the vision of secure anarchic electronic space?
4. Back's hashcash is a misnomer, because it is not a payment system. What is "hashcash" and why is it important for electronic cashless payment systems in general?
5. Szabo introduced the first "smart contract". What is a "smart contract"? What objectives was Szabo trying to achieve with the introduction of "smart contracts"?
6. Explain the origin and value of Bit Gold. What was the source of the scarcity of Bit Gold?
7. How did Szabo try to manage inflation of Bit Gold?
8. Van Wirdum says Dai's B-Money was the first draft of Bitcoin. What features of Dai's B-Money are virtually identical to Bitcoin (hint: ledger technology and consensus system)?

Bibliography

David Chaum, Achieving Electronic Privacy, 96 Scientific American (1992)

Timothy C. May, The Crypto Anarchist Manifesto, 1988 at https://www.activism.net/cypherpunk/crypto-anarchy.html

Aaron van Wirdum, The Genesis Files: How David Chaum's eCash Spawned a Cypherpunk Dream, https://BitcoinMagazine.net 12 July 2018, at https://bitcoinmagazine.com/articles/genesis-files-how-david-chaums-ecash-spawned-cypherpunk-dream

Aaron van Wirdum, The Genesis Files: Hashcash Or How Adam Back Designed Bitcoin's Motor Block, 4 June 2018, at https://bitcoinmagazine.com/articles/genesis-files-hashcash-or-how-adam-back-designed-bitcoins-motor-block

Aaron van Wirdum, The Genesis Files: With Bit Gold, Szabo Was Inches Away From Inventing Bitcoin, 12 July 2018 at https://bitcoinmagazine.com/articles/genesis-files-bit-gold-szabo-was-inches-away-inventing-bitcoin

Aaron van Wirdum, The Genesis Files: If Bitcoin Had A First Draft, Wei Dai's B-Money Was It, 14 June 2018 at https://bitcoinmagazine.com/articles/genesis-files-if-bitcoin-had-first-draft-wei-dais-b-money-was-it

9 Cryptography

Introduction

"Cryptography is the science of secret writing with the goal of hiding the meaning of a message," from third-party eavesdropping. It is an ancient science going back to the emergence of writing *itself*. By contrast, "Cryptanalysis is the science and sometimes art of breaking cryptosystems."[1] Singh argues correctly that cryptography and cryptanalysis evolve in a Darwinian competition for survival (Singh). Cryptography is split into three main branches: (1) symmetric, (2) asymmetric, and (3) cryptographic protocols. In symmetric algorithms, two parties share the same key to encrypt and decrypt messages. In cryptography, a "key" is a piece of data that, working in conjunction with an algorithm, a term derived from the Islamic mathematician al-Khwarizmi, encrypts or decrypts plaintext messages. "Symmetric cryptographic schemes are also referred to as symmetric-key, secret-key, and single-key schemes or algorithms" (Paar and Pelzl).[2] In asymmetric algorithms, parties share key pairs, usually a public and private key pair. Cryptographic protocols involve numerous instruments. However, for purposes of this text, we discuss only cryptographic hash algorithms. Although cryptology is shrouded in arcane vocabulary, the underlying objectives are simple: keep communication confidential between sender and receiver, prevent interception, and verify authenticity.

Historical Symmetric Ciphers

Pre-mathematical symmetric ciphers comprise "ad hoc" efforts to encrypt and decrypt messages. They generally transform plaintext into code by using small, fixed-length language elements divorced from the meaning of the word or phrase in the message. The term "plaintext" refers to unencrypted text, such as the word "paradise", and the term "code" operates on semantics, usually mapped to a codebook. Pre-mathematical ciphers come in two general categories: "substitution ciphers"

J. JA Burke, *Financial Services in the Twenty-First Century*, https://doi.org/10.1007/978-3-030-63967-9_9

and "transposition ciphers". The term "cipher" refers to an algorithm for performing encryption or decryption—a series of well-defined steps that may be followed as a procedure. Ciphers operate on syntax (symbols). Ciphers can be simple such as substitution or transposition ciphers. In codes, the codebook is shared; in ciphers, a key is shared. Substitution ciphers replace each letter in a message with a different letter or symbol using a mapping called a "cipher alphabet". Transposition ciphers rearrange letters of a message but do not substitute new letters for existing letters in the message.[3] "Codes" use plaintext language, like syllables, words, or phrases, to replace the plaintext word or phrase. For example, codes may use a codeword like "paradise" to refer to the plaintext "stop". Symmetric ciphers transform each individual letter of plaintext to produce a cryptogram, the encrypted text. History is replete with examples of symmetric ciphers and codes.[4]

The Caesar Cipher

The Caesar cipher is the most famous example of a symmetric algorithm.[5] The Caesar cipher is a substitution cipher using a shifted alphabet. "The idea is very simple: We substitute each letter of the alphabet with another one."[6] Julius Caesar spoke classical Latin or Greek and likely determined the number of "shifts" using one of these languages. However, for purposes of illustration, we take the English language, as a *monoalphabetic substitution cipher*, and use a three-shift key (including the starting point), to illustrate the Caesar cipher. Shift ciphers work by using the "modulo operator" to encrypt and decrypt messages. The shift cipher has a "*K*", which is an integer from 0 to 25, assuming we use the English alphabet. First, each letter of the plaintext alphabet is assigned a number beginning with "0" to produce the following table (Fig. 9.1):

Modular Arithmetic: An Essential Detour

Let's encrypt the plaintext phrase "veni vidi vici" using the Caesar cipher. We get the ciphertext "sbkf sfgf sfzf". To decrypt, we just shift each letter to the left by a factor of three. But where is the mathematics? We use modular math and the shift cipher. Modular arithmetic or clock arithmetic sits at the heart of cryptography both ancient and modern. "In modular arithmetic, mathematicians consider a finite group of numbers arranged in a loop, rather like the numbers on a clock" (Singh). It is rich in one-way functions: easy to do, and hard to undo. Modular arithmetic thus must

A	B	C	D	E	F	G	H	I	J	K	L	M	N	O	P	Q	R	S	T	U	V	W	X	Y	Z
0	1	2	3	4	5	6	7	8	9	10	11	12	13	14	15	16	17	18	19	20	21	22	23	24	25

Fig. 9.1 Caesar cipher. (Source: Paar and Pelzl)

be comprehended, without mastering the field. Imagine a clockface with six numbers from 0 to 6 as depicted called (mod 7) since it is composed of seven digits (Fig. 9.2):

In traditional arithmetic 2 + 3 = 5 and 2 + 6 = 8. These results do not necessarily hold true in modular arithmetic. For example, 2 + 3 (mod 7) = 5, but 2 + 6 (mod 7) = 1, because we move around the clock of numbers. So, six moves from 2 leads to 1 on the clock or in modular arithmetic. Instead of visualising clocks, mathematicians perform calculations using normal arithmetic. Then, if the mathematician wants to know the result in (mod x), he/she divides the normal result by x. For example, finding 11 × 9 (mod 13) requires us to multiply 11 × 9 to get 99. We then divide 99 by 13, the modulus. The result is 7 with a remainder of 8, so 11 × 9 = 8 (mod 13). The erratic behaviour of modular arithmetic often requires building of tables that may take hours to assemble. This unusual property of modular arithmetic combined with prime numbers underpins innovations in cryptography. A simple demonstration is found in the Caesar cipher.

The message is denoted by "M". Convert every letter in the alphabet into its corresponding number. Calculate: Y = (X + K) mod 26. Convert the number Y into a letter that matches its order in the alphabet starting from "0". For example, we agree that Y = 19 corresponding to the letter "S". Take the message "kill". K = 10; i = 8; and l = 11, and use mod 26 to get the following table (Fig. 9.3).

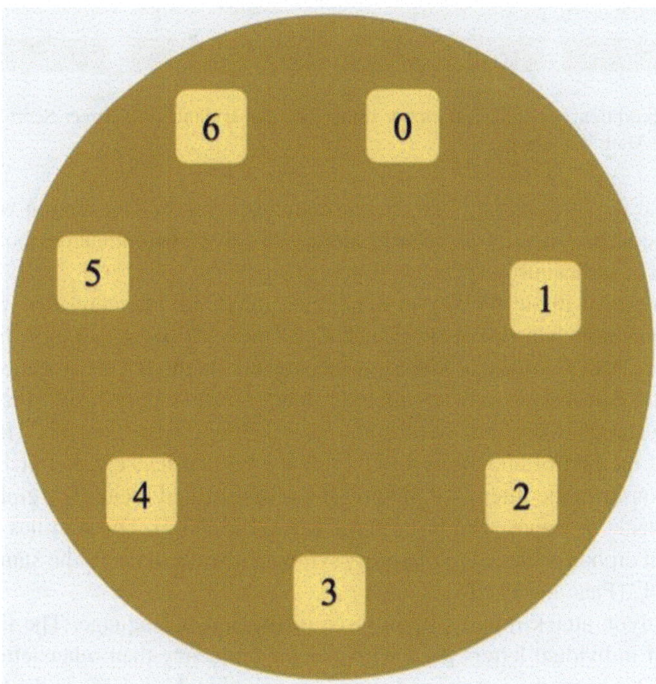

Fig. 9.2 Modular arithmetic. (Source: Author)

K	I	L	L
10	8	11	11
+19	+19	+19	+19
29	27	30	30
3	1	4	4
D	B	E	E

Fig. 9.3 The modular arithmetic of the Caesar cipher. (Source: Scott Sutherland 2005, MSTP Math Workshop)

D	B	E	E
3	1	4	4
- 19	-19	-19	-19
-16	-18	-15	-15
10	8	11	11
K	I	L	L

Fig. 9.4 Decryption of the Caesar cipher using modular arithmetic. (Source: Scott Sutherland 2005, MSTP Math Workshop)

Note that the differential is 26, because we use mod 26. Decryption works in a reverse operation using mod 26 arithmetic. We give our colleague the message "DBEE". The colleague decrypts as follows (Fig. 9.4):

Conceivably, without the key to the cipher, messages intercepted by an enemy would be incomprehensible. However, if Eve intercepts the ciphertext, she can try all possible 26 keys of the alphabet to recover the method. This is called a brute force attack. But there is a better method: letter frequency analysis, since ciphers leave fingerprints when one writes messages. "Frequency analysis" is a well-established method of attack used by cryptanalysts and hackers. Letter frequency analysis examines the internal structure of the cipher, and breaks the cipher by an analytic attack, as opposed to brute force (Paar and Pelzl). The Achilles heel of a substitution cipher is that each plaintext symbol "always maps to the same cipher-text symbol" (Paar and Pelzl).

The analytic attack reposes upon three properties of language. The first is the property of individual letters used with greater frequency than other letters in the language. This property permits code breakers to build tables showing the frequency of every letter in the language. Since plaintext letters map to ciphertext symbols, the frequency distribution of ciphertext symbols follows closely the frequency distribution of plaintext symbols. The second property of languages is the phenomenon of pairs, triples, or quadruples where discrete letters often follow one another. In the English and French languages, the letter "q" invariably is followed by the letter "u". In the English language, triples are found in words such as "The", "And" or "But". If a pair, triple, or quadruple is found in the ciphertext symbols, then this property of the underlying language may be used to identify which ciphertext symbol maps to "q" and "u". The third property is word separators, that is blank spaces between words. If ciphertext symbols follow this pattern, then it may be possible to map words such as "the" or "and" to ciphertext symbols. These techniques often are combined to break substitution ciphers (Paar and Pelzl).[7]

The following figure shows relative letter frequencies of the English language (Fig. 9.5).

In English, the most frequently occurring letters are usually given in the order of ETAOINSHRDLU. "The technique of frequency analysis is to do the same count of letters for the ciphertext, and then use those counts to guess at the letters of the

Letter	Frequency	Letter	Frequency
A	0.0817	N	0.0675
B	0.0150	O	0.0751
C	0.0278	P	0.0193
D	0.0425	Q	0.0010
E	0.1270	R	0.0599
F	0.0223	S	0.0633
G	0.0202	T	0.0906
H	0.0609	U	0.0276
I	0.0697	V	0.0098
J	0.0015	W	0.0236
K	0.0077	X	0.0015
L	0.0403	Y	0.0197
M	0.0241	Z	0.0007

Fig. 9.5 Letter frequencies of the English language. (Source: John Dooley, History of cryptography and cryptanalysis)

ciphertext. Thus, in English, the most frequently occurring letter in the ciphertext should represent 'e'. The next most frequently occurring should represent 't', then 'a', etc." (Dooley). An Islamic scholar "al-Kindi"[8] exposed this weakness "in a few short paragraphs and [with this insight] revolutionized cryptanalysis".[9] Assume a sender and receiver select the permutation: K, D, G … 0. The plaintext "point" is encrypted to "MJBXZ". Here is a jumbled ciphertext alphabet where the order of the ciphertext letters is a key (Fig. 9.6).

The receiver, who knows the randomly chosen permutation, replaces each ciphertext letter on the bottom row with the corresponding plaintext letter in the top row. The ciphertext "MJBXZ" is decrypted to "point".

Nevertheless, in spite of these weaknesses, there is one perfect method of encryption called the "one-time pad", based on randomness (or Vernam encryption). Shifts are random and equal to the length of the message. Assume Alice rolls a die with 26 sides, and copies the results. Alice shares the results with Bob. Since the shifts do not repeat, there is no fingerprint left behind. For example, each letter in the name "Alice" is represented by 26 possible combinations, that is, 26*26*26*26*26 = approximately 12 million combination possibilities. The "one-time pad" is impossible to break in a practical sense, since it would take too much time.

The basic concepts of encryption are (Fig. 9.7):

Encryption is mapping from some message using an encryption key to produce a ciphertext message.

But our purpose in providing a foundation to understand cryptography does not require an exhaustive history of cryptology but a focus on twentieth-century developments when number theory replaced language and when computer technology strengthened and standardised ciphers and introduced multiple algorithms in the pursuit of confidential communication. The story is not devoid of political statecraft and conflicting philosophies. Hence, we turn to computer-based symmetric algorithms, asymmetric cryptography, digital signatures, and hashes.

A	B	C	D	E	F	G	H	I	J	K	L	M	N	O	P	Q	R	S	T	U	V	W	X	Y	Z
K	D	G	F	N	S	L	V	B	W	A	H	E	X	J	M	Q	C	P	Z	R	T	Y	I	U	O

Fig. 9.6 Jumbled ciphertext alphabet. (Source: John Dooley, History of cryptography and cryptanalysis)

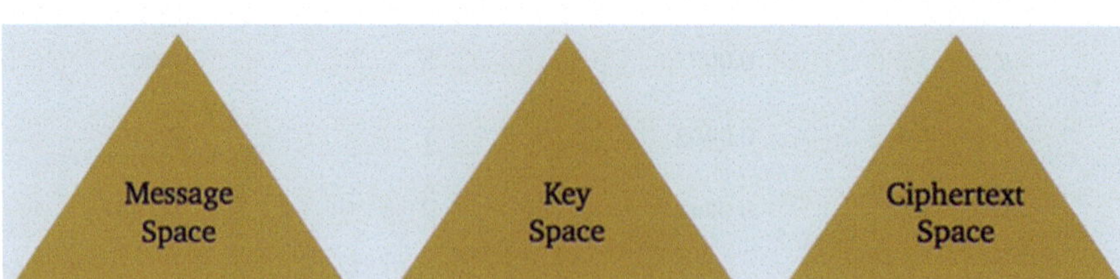

Fig. 9.7 The basic concepts of encryption. (Source: Author)

Modern Cryptography

The Twentieth Century moved cryptology from an esoteric "ad hoc" field to the discipline of statistics and mathematics. Modern cryptography operates on binary bit sequences and generally relies upon shared keys in symmetric cryptography and key pairs in asymmetric cryptography. It offers a suite of security services: (1) confidentiality, (2) data integrity, (3) authentication, and (4) non-repudiation. Confidentiality keeps data from interception by an unauthorised person; it is equivalent to privacy and secrecy. Data integrity assures the receiver that the information transmitted by the sender has not been altered or modified. Authentication assures the identity of the origination of the data; it assures the receiver that the sender is the verified sender. Non-repudiation is a service ensuring that the sender of the data cannot deny the transmission of the data. The term "cryptography primitives" refers simply to the tools and techniques in cryptography: (1) encryption, (2) hash functions, (3) message authentication codes (MACs), and (4) digital signatures. The following figure shows primitives and the particular security service they can achieve alone (Fig. 9.8):

Cryptographic primitives often are combined to achieve the desired suite of security services. However, we start with the elements of digital key encryption.

Symmetric Key Encryption

Modern cryptographic primitives take digital data and convert the text into binary digits (bits) and process these bits using a specific encryption system. Symmetric encryption systems can be classified into two primary schemes: block ciphers and stream ciphers. In a block cipher, plaintext "bits" are processed in blocks. The size and number of blocks differ depending upon the type of encryption scheme. The Data Encryption Standard (DES) has a 64-bit block size; the Advanced Encryption Standard (AES) has a 128-bit block size. Stream ciphers process plaintext one bit at a time and produce one bit of ciphertext. Encryption

Primitive Service	Encryption	Hash Function	MAC	Digital Signature
Confidentiality	Yes	No	No	No
Integrity	No	Sometimes	Yes	Yes
Authentication	No	No	Yes	Yes
Non-Repudiation	No	No	Sometimes	Yes

Fig. 9.8 Cryptography primitives. (Source: Tutorialspoint.com)

standards process the binary digits by sequential rounds of permutation until the algorithm completes the encryption process.

Three scientists, William Friedman, Lester Hill, and Claude Shannon, were the vanguard of this revolution and established the framework for use of number theory and later computers to dominate the science of cryptology. Friedman established his mark by helping to resolve the German Enigma machine. Hill and Shannon built upon his work by changing the firmament of cryptology from language to number theory thereby altering the methodology concealing and then revealing messages. While each scientist made his personal contribution to the field, the United States government standardised mathematically based cryptology by adopting in 1977 the Data Encryption Standard (DES), at that time a widely used encryption algorithm (Paar and Pelzl). "In 2001 a much stronger algorithm, the Advanced Encryption Standard (AES) that was vetted by a new burgeoning public cryptologic community, replaced it. It must be remembered that both DES and AES" are symmetric ciphers relying upon a single shared key.[10] This section introduces Hill and Shannon and explores the details of the DES (including its embellished version "3D") and the AES.

Lester Hill

In 1929, Hill published a paper entitled "Cryptography in an Algebraic Alphabet" applying abstract algebra to cryptology. The substance of his paper was a new system of polygraphic encryption and decryption that used "invertible square matrices", a concept taken from linear algebra, as the key elements and did all the arithmetic modulo 26 (Dooley). This is now known generally as matrix encryption, or the Hill cipher. Polygraphic encryption takes place when more than two letters (algebraic alphabet) are substituted for one letter. Since Hill used "modulo 26", letters of the text are converted into numbers ranging from 0 to 25, then applied to an invertible "N × N" square matrix to produce the cipher. Decryption requires finding an inverse matrix modulo 26. Hill was instrumental in placing cryptography squarely within statistics and mathematics.

Claude E. Shannon

Claude E. Shannon contributed both to cryptology and to data science. By education, he was a mathematician and an electrical engineer. "His master's thesis was the first published work that linked Boolean algebra with electronic circuits – the basis of all modern computer arithmetic."[11] In 1948 he published his work on communications systems as "A Mathematical Theory of Communication", the foundational paper in information theory (Dooley). In 1949 he followed with another seminal paper, "Communication Theory of Secrecy Systems" (Dooley). In his 1948 paper, Shannon "defined in mathematical terms what information is and how it can be transmitted in the face of noise."[12] He took various forms of communication—telephone, telegraph, radio, and television—and unified them into a single theory. Combined with his discovery of a link between Boolean logic and electrical circuits, he demonstrated how language may be reproduced in binary units used in computers: "true" or "false" and "0" and "1". He defined the quantity of information in a text by a formula similar to that used in thermodynamic entropy. He also analysed the ability to send information through a channel (today, for example, Wi-Fi LAN) and how to reduce "noise" in the system, that is, reduction of errors. Finally, he proved that unbreakable cryptography was possible by showing that the Vernam cipher, or the one-time pad explained above, was impossible to break. Quantum cryptography vindicated Shannon's claim by means of quantum key distribution. Quantum mechanics generates a random key identical at both ends of the quantum communication channel so that no person may eavesdrop and "lift" the key.

Horst Feistel

While working at IBM, Horst Feistel conducted research on cryptology and developed a program called *Lucifer* (Dooley). IBM marketed and sold the program in the United States and a "light version" outside the United States. "Then, in 1973, the National Bureau of Standards put out a call for cryptographic algorithms that would be a federal standard and would be used to encrypt unclassified government data."[13] IBM submitted *Lucifer* as a candidate, knowing that if the program was approved, it would become a commercial success. "It turned out that *Lucifer* was the only acceptable algorithm and a modified version of it was adopted as Federal Information Processing Standard 46 (FIPS-46) on 15 July 1977 and renamed the federal Data Encryption Standard or DES" (Dooley). "DES" is a symmetric block cipher algorithm using a 64-bit key: the standard operates on data in 64-bit blocks (eight characters at a time), using a 56-bit key. "It passes each block through the heart of the algorithm – a round – 16 times before outputting the result as ciphertext. Each round breaks the 64-bit block into two 32-bit halves and then implements a Shannon-style substitution-permutation network using part of the key, called a sub-key, to produce an intermediate ciphertext that is then passed back again for the next round."[14]

In spite of the recombination of rounds, DES is insecure because the key is too short, the length having been mandated by NSA. A 56-bit key yields a key space of 2^{56} possible keys. The number equates to 10^{18} or about a quintillion keys. While this number appears large, it is modest compared to the computing power needed to break the encryption by brute force. "In 1997 a network of thousands of computers on the Internet broke a DES key in a little over a month's time. And a year later, a special-purpose computer built by the Electronic Frontier Foundation for less than $250,000 broke a DES key in less than 3 days."[15] It is a simple function of Moore's Law: "Moore's Law refers to Moore's perception that the number of transistors on a microchip doubles every two years, though the cost of computers is halved. Moore's Law states that we can expect the speed and capability of our computers to increase every couple of years, and we will pay less for them. Another tenet of Moore's Law asserts that this growth is exponential."[16] Correcting for this weakness, the National Institute of Science (NIS) released a new version of DES called 3DES. Because of the greater length of time to encrypt a message using 3DES, the NIS, in 1997, sent out a call for potential successors for the DES. A Belgian team submitted *Rijndael*. In August 2000, *Rijndael* was selected as the next standard and the new advanced encryption standard abbreviated "AES" (Dooley). The latter uses three different key lengths: 128,192,256. "There is currently no analytical attack against AES known which has a complexity less than a brute-force attack. An elegant algebraic description was found, which in turn triggered speculations that this could lead to attacks. Subsequent research showed that an attack is, in fact, not feasible. By now, the common assumption is that the brute force approach will not threaten AES."[17]

Architecture of Modern Cryptography

Symmetric Cryptography

In symmetric cryptography, persons are paired and use identical keys for encryption and decryption. Thus, there is one key per pair of persons. The keys are generated by a mathematical process using the product of large prime numbers belonging to a single set and are accessed by users through a key management system. The keys may be transmitted over an insecure channel by using AES to encrypt the key. Symmetric cryptography is widely used because it is fast and easy to scale. In addition, the new protocols: 3DES and AES have strengthened the security services it provides. However, it has flaws. First, a single organisation, the entity most likely to adopt symmetric cryptography, must generate enough keys to allow pairs to communicate (Paar and Pelzl). For example, assume an organisation of 2000 persons that adopts a symmetric cryptographic system, the number of keys that the organisation needs is calculated using the following formula: $n \times (n - 1)/2$, or more than 4 million keys (Paar and Pelzl). Second, symmetric cryptography cannot provide non-repudiation. The following illustrates how symmetric cryptography operates (Fig. 9.9):

Problem: Lack of Secure Key Exchange

Symmetric cryptography presents substantial security problems. First, there is the issue of sharing the same key. A courier may be hired to physically transfer the key from Alice to Bob, Alice and Bob may meet physically and exchange the key, or the key may be encrypted using DES, for example. However, even if the bank uses DES, then the client, the receiver of the key, not only needs to have a copy of DES on its computer but also must know which key was used to encrypt the message. The bank is back to square one. The problem of solving the key delivery plagued cryptographers for centuries. Singh observes, "Key distribution might seem a mundane issue, but it became the overriding problem for post-war cryptographers" (Simon Singh 2018).

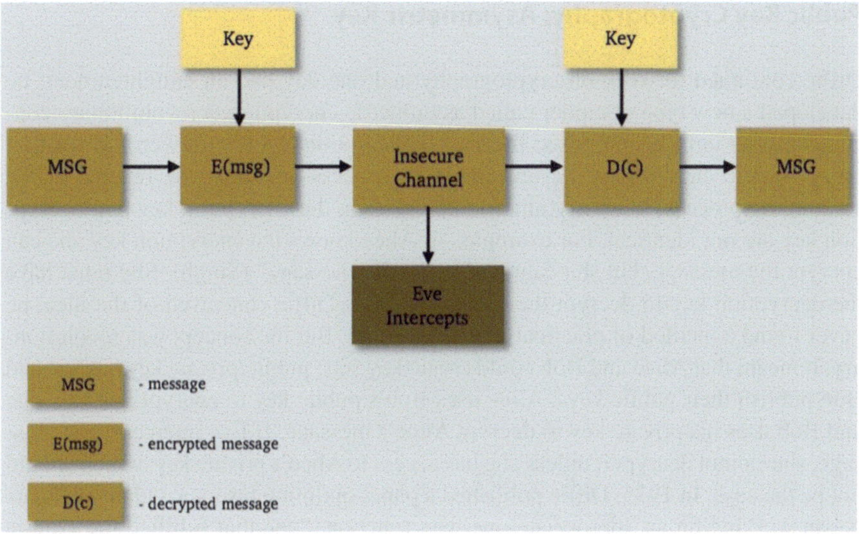

Fig. 9.9 Symmetric key Cipher system model (a shared key system). (Source: John Dooley, History of cryptography and cryptanalysis)

The Diffie-Hellman-Merkle Key Exchange Scheme

In 1974, Whitfield Diffie, a distinguished engineer at Sun Microsystems, met Martin Hellman, a then professor at Stanford University. Each shared a common vision to solve the issue of key distribution. Ralph Merkle joined them later. They used mathematical functions. A mathematical function is any mathematical operation that turns one number into another number. Computer encryption acts as a mathematical function by turning plaintext into ciphertext. The scientists searched for what is called a one-way function—an operation easy to do in one direction, but hard to undo in the opposite direction. They also relied upon modular arithmetic and prime numbers: numbers divisible only by one or the number itself. The idea rested upon a one-way function using primes and modular arithmetic in the form Y^x (mod P). Alice and Bob agree on values for Y and P. These numbers are public, since it does not matter that Eve or anyone else knows them. Alice and Bob then each select a secret number, say 3 for Alice labelled "A" and 6 for Bob labelled "B". Alice then puts her secret number 3 into the one-way function, that is, Y^3 (Mod 11) = 343 (mod 11) = 2, and calls it *alpha*. Bob then puts his secret number 6 into the one-way function, that is, Y^6 (mod 11) = 117,649 (mod 11) = 4 and calls it *beta*. They swap their results: the 4 and the 6, since even if intercepted, these numbers are not the keys. Alice takes Bob's beta 4 and raises it by her secret number 3, such that 4^3 (mod 11) = 64 (mod 11) = 9. Bob takes Alice's alpha 2 and raises it by his secret number 6 such that 2^6 (mod 11) = 64 (mod 11) = 9. The number 9 is the key and it is practically infeasible for Eve to reproduce that number without knowing either Bob's or Alice's secret number. Singh states, the Diffie-Hellman-Merkle key exchange system "is one of the most counterintuitive discoveries in the history of science, and it forced the cryptographic establishment to rewrite the rules of encryption" (Singh).

Public Key Cryptography: Asymmetric Key

Diffie continued to work on cryptography and one day had an enlightenment: he developed a new type of cipher called asymmetric encryption, a revolutionary concept since up until his proposed theory, all encryption techniques were symmetric. In symmetric encryptions the unscrambling process is simply the reverse of the scrambling process. In an asymmetric key system, the encryption key and decryption key are not identical. For example, "if Alice knows the encryption key she can encrypt the message, but she cannot decrypt the message" (Singh). She must have the decryption key to decrypt the message. While Diffie conceived of the idea, he never found a method of practical implementation. But the concept was revolutionary. It meant that Alice and Bob could create key sets: public/private keys. Alice and Bob publish their public keys. Alice uses Bob's public key to encrypt her message and Bob uses his private key to decrypt Alice's message. If Eve intercepts the message, she cannot decrypt it unless she has access to Alice's private key, which should not be the case. In 1975, Diffie published a paper outlining his idea. Other scientists began working on an appropriate one-way function, "one that fulfilled the criteria for an asymmetric cipher" (Singh).

In 1977, Rivest, Shamir, and Adleman solved the puzzle. The solution reposed upon a component known as "N" of the one-way function. Each person can choose a different "N". In order to choose her "N", Alice picks two prime numbers, say p and q, and multiples them together. Borrowing from Singh, Alice chooses her prime numbers to be $p = 17$ and $q = 11$. This choice is used for purposes of illustration, since the prime numbers must be large. Multiplying these numbers gives her 187. Alice then selects another number, say $e = 7$. "N" plus e is Alice's public key. Assume Bob wants to send a message to Alice. The plaintext message first must be converted into a number denoted "M". Singh says Bob simply wants to say "kiss" by using the symbol "X". Bob converts X into a number by using ASCII binary digits. In ASCII, the letter X is represented as 1011000, equivalent to 88 in decimal, so M is 88. Bob encrypts the message by using Alice's N and her second published number such that $C = 88^7 \pmod{187}$. This calculation is not a straightforward task but when completed it produces the ciphertext C = 11 that Bob sends to Alice. Alice then decrypts the message first by calculating a special number "d" her private key as follows:

$$e \times d = 1 \pmod{(p-1) \times (q-1)}$$
$$7 \times d = 1 \pmod{16 \times 10}$$
$$7 \times d = 1 \pmod{160}$$
$$d = 23$$

Decryption proceeds such that:

$$M = C^d \pmod{187}$$
$$M = 11^{23} \pmod{187}$$
$$M = 11^1 \pmod{187} \times 11^2 \pmod{187} \times 11^4 \pmod{187} \times 11^6 \pmod{187} \pmod{187}$$
$$M = 11 \times 121 \times 55 \times 154 \pmod{187}$$
$$M = 88 = \text{X in ASCII}$$

Digital Signatures

A digital signature is the equivalent of a signature written in ink on a physical piece of paper. Because neither Alice nor Bob can, or want to, sign physical pieces of paper, cryptography provides a method for validating a signature proving that Alicc or Bob signed message, and that the signature cannot be repudiated. Digital signatures are one of the most important cryptographic tools, and they are widely used today (Paar and Pelzl), because "they provide a method to assure that a message is authentic to one user, i.e., it in fact originates from the person who claims to have generated the message" (Paar and Pelzl). A digital signature scheme is based upon public key cryptography.

In this model, Alice and Bob have key pairs: one private and one public. To illustrate, Bob creates a message and signs the message with his private key, intending to send the signed message to Alice. "The signature algorithm is a function of Bob's private key, k_{pr}" (Paar and Pelzl).[18] Upon receipt of the message, Alice uses Bob's public key to decrypt the message. The public key verifies that Bob created and signed the message, as both the message (x) and the signature (s) are inputs to the signature algorithm. A generic digital signature protocol is illustrated as follows (Fig. 9.10):

Each person adopting this model has a public-private key pair. In general, the key pairs for encryption/decryption and signing/verifying are different. The person sending and signing the data first produces a hash of the data. While hashes are explained below, the "primitive" reduces data, no matter the size, to a distinct serial identifier. The hash and the signature key are passed through the signature algorithm that produces the digital signature on the hash. The receiver/verifier uses the signer's public key applying it to the signed hash. The application of the public key to the data received produces another hash value. If the hash values are identical, then the receiver/verifier is certain of the origin of the message. The signer cannot repudiate the signature.

Alice Bob generate kpr,B, kpub,B kpub,B ← ———————————— publish public key sign message: s = sigkpr (x) (x,s) ← ———————————— send message + signature verify signature: verkpub,B (x,s) = true/false From this set-up, the core

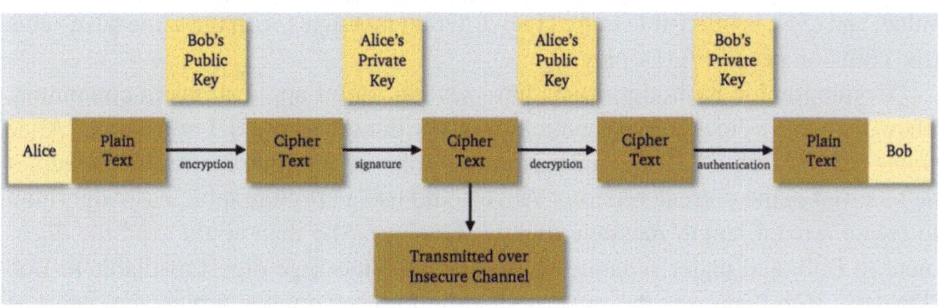

Fig. 9.10 Digital signature model (simple two key encryption). (Source: John Dooley, History of cryptography and cryptanalysis)

property of digital signatures follows: a signed message can unambiguously be traced back to its originator since a valid signature can only be computed with the unique signer's private key (Paar and Pelzl). "Only the signer has the ability to generate a signature on his behalf. Hence, we can prove that the signing party has actually generated the message" (Paar and Pelzl). This proof has legal significance since it can be used to enforce contractual obligations, for instance, within the meaning of the Electronic Signatures in Global and National Commerce Act (ESIGN). The basic protocol of digital signature cryptography fails to provide confidentiality of the message, since the message x is being sent over a channel where it may be intercepted. "The message can be kept confidential by also encrypting it, for example, with AES or 3DES. Each of the three popular public-key algorithm families, namely integer factorization, discrete logarithms and elliptic curves, allows us to construct digital signatures" (Paar and Pelzl).

Hashes

Chapter 8 discussed hashes in the context of Adam Back's work. Here, a general overview is provided. A hash function, say H, takes an input of a variable-length message, say M, and produces an output of a fixed-length hash value h (also called a message digest). So we have h = H(M). "A hash function is not a cipher system because the hash function is not invertible; the amount of effort required to recover the original block of data M is infeasible" (Dooley). "A crucial idea in implementing a cryptographic hash function is that if one applies the hash function to a block of data (a book, a program, a music file, etc.) one will get a unique fixed-length hash" (Dooley). If the bits of that block of data change, applying the hash function yields a different hash. In this way, one can tell if a file has been tampered with or if errors have been introduced during transmission by comparing the before and after hashes. The main function of cryptographic hash functions is to guarantee data integrity. An excellent hash function has five properties: (1) the same message always results in the same hash value, (2) the hash function is fast, (3) it is infeasible to generate a particular message from its hash value, except by trying all possible messages in the message space, (4) a small change to a message changes the hash value so extensively that the new hash value appears uncorrelated with the old hash value, and (5) it is infeasible to find two different messages with the same hash value (the collision property) (Dooley).

"Cryptographic hash algorithms have several useful applications in computing. They can serve as message authentication algorithms" (Dooley). For example, Alice wants to send Bob a confidential report and Bob wants to make sure that the report he received is the correct version. "Alice could use a cryptographic hash algorithm to create a fixed length message digest" (Dooley). She then could send the document to Bob, and under separate cover, make the message digest available to Bob (Dooley). Bob then uses the same hash algorithm to compute a message digest of the document he received and compares the two hash values (Dooley). "If the hash values are identical, then Bob is confident that he has received an uncorrupted document" (Dooley). "A second application for cryptographic hash functions is password protection" (Dooley). The user's password is converted into a cryptographic hash algorithm. In a multi-user network, passwords *per se* cannot travel over the network since they could easily be intercepted. Hashing the password and storing the hash preserve the integrity of the password. "When a user logs into the system they provide their password to the login program, the login program executes the hash function to produce a new message digest. The new message digest is then compared to the stored message digest for that user. If they match, then the user can be admitted to the system" (Dooley). Even though hash functions have many applications in modern cryptography, they are perhaps best known for the important role they play in the practical use of digital signatures, as indicated earlier.

Global System for Mobile

The mobile telephone plays an important role in FinTech financial services. Therefore, a diversion to introduce the basics of its technology is warranted, especially given the new 5G technology. A cellular phone is a telecommunications device using radio waves over a networked area (cell) to make wireless calls over a wide range. The cellular phone comprises a mobile system consisting of equipment and a Subscriber Identity Module (SIM) card capable of transmitting voice, messages, and video files by connecting to the Internet or a fixed landline. The Global System for Mobile Communications "standard is the most widely used digital mobile telephone protocol in the world" governed by the European Telecommunications Standards Institute (ETSI) (Dooley). The protocol is a set of rules enabling the connection of the cellular phone to a network, as the following figure illustrates (Fig. 9.11).

The mobile connection proceeds in stages similar to operating systems making a connection over the Internet. First, the mobile phone queries the network and asks

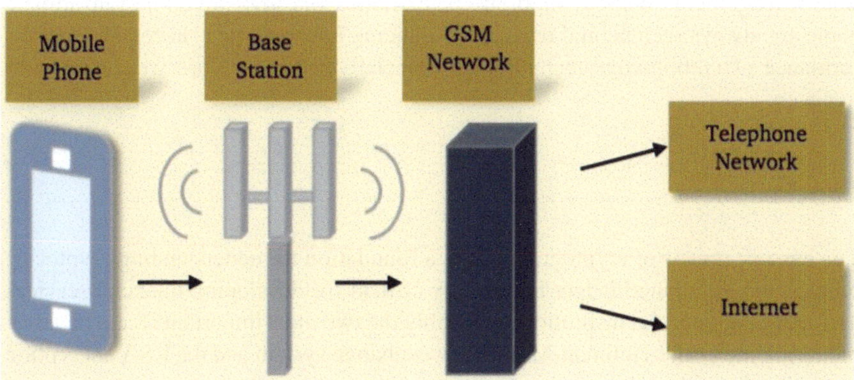

Fig. 9.11 GSM cellular telephone network. (Source: John Dooley, History of cryptography and cryptanalysis)

to join. The request consists of the phones unique ID number (the IMEI or International Mobile Equipment Identity number) to the server. Second, the network server produces a random number and sends it to the phone as a "challenge." Third, "the phone uses the random number, the mobile keyword, and the A3 algorithm and generates an encrypted 'response' that it sends to the server" (Dooley). Fourth, the server uses the A3 algorithm, the phone's keyword (retrieved from the phone company where the user has a subscription service, using the IMEI), "and the random number to generate an encrypted message" (Dooley). Fifth, "the server then compares the two encrypted messages and if they match, it establishes the connection with the mobile phone" (Dooley). The data is secured by three algorithms performing three functions: authentication, key generation and data encryption. The first two algorithms are stored in the SIM card. The algorithm called A3 authenticates the phone and user to the network.

5G is the fifth generation of wireless networking technology (Wired Magazine 2019). According to *Wired* magazine, "5G isn't a single technology or standard, but rather a constellation of different technologies, and deploying them could require a radically different approach than building 4G networks" (Wired Magazine). The novelty of 5G is the use of millimetre-wave technology, a largely unused range of bandwidth, that comprises the range of the wireless spectrum above 24 GHz or 30 GHz. This bandwidth is fast, providing speeds of up to 10 gigabits per second, that is, 600 times faster than typical 4G speeds. In addition, 5G technology has the capacity to connect multiple devices to wireless networks, such as artificial intelligence, self-driving cars, and telemedicine. The limitation of the 5G bandwidth spectrum is its disruption by obstacles, like trees, rain, and people, thereby preventing transmission over long distances. The underlying infrastructure therefore is extremely important and, since it does not yet exist, the system must be built.

Equally important as speed to 5G is its ultra-low latency. The term "latency" is "the gap time, or transmission time for a packet of data" (Qualcomm 2019). Single-direction latency is the time between when a packet is sent and when it is received by the recipient. Roundtrip latency is the time between transmission and receipt of acknowledgement. Without high speed, activities like live streaming an athletic game are always seen behind real time. Reducing latency time is necessary for performance of cutting-edge technologies especially when they are woven together in a web.

Conclusion

The cursory review of cryptography lays a foundation for understanding cryptocurrencies and distributed ledger technology critical for developing financial services and changing financial institutions. Arguably the two most important recent achievements are the Diffie-Hellman-Merkle key exchange system and the RSA encryption algorithm. This chapter provides a segue to understanding the first attempts to create an electronic cashless payment system without using the intermediation of a trusted third party. The overview of GSM standards potentially foreshadows improved delivery of financial services as they are presently built around smartphones. A Qualcomm report estimates the "total contribution of 5G to Real Global GDP growth" is expected to be $2.1 trillion by 2035, establishing further support that innovation, not finance *per se*, drives real economic growth.[19] Quantum computing may pose a threat to contemporary encryption systems.

Questions

1. What is cryptography and why is it important for financial services?
2. What is the difference between symmetric and asymmetric cryptography?
3. Explain public/private key technology and digital signatures.
4. Conduct research and provide a current report of 5G rollouts.

Notes

1. Christof Paar and Jan Pelzl, "*Understanding Cryptography*" A Textbook for Students and Practitioners (Springer International Publishing 2009) p. 3. (Kindle edition).
2. *Ibid.* at 4.
3. Block ciphers and stream ciphers are defined later.
4. For example, "in 1467, architect Leon Battista Alberti described a curious device. It was a disk made up of two concentric rings: the outer ring engraved with a standard alphabet, and the inner ring, engraved with the same alphabet but written out of order. By rotating the inner ring and matching letters across the disk, a message could be enciphered, one letter at a time, in a fiendishly complex way". Kevin Sands, Top 10 Codes, Keys and Ciphers, The Guardian 10 Sep 2015 at https://www.theguardian.com/childrens-books-site/2015/sep/10/top-10-codes-keys-and-ciphers
5. "A cipher is a set of steps (an algorithm) for performing both an encryption, and the corresponding decryption." https://www.tutorialspoint.com/cryptography/traditional_ciphers.htm
6. Paar and Pelzl, *ibid*, n.1.
7. Without explaining the details, Paar and Pelzl provide an example of how letter frequency analysis breaks two lines of ciphertext symbols using blank spaces and the English language as plaintext symbols into a comprehensible message (Paar and Pelzl at 8.).
8. "The period around the ninth century C.E. is considered to be the beginning of the Islamic Golden Age, when philosophy, science, literature, mathematics, and religious studies all flourished in what was then the peace and prosperity of the Abbasid Caliphate. Into this period was born Abu Yūsuf Ya-qūb ibn Isāq as-Sabbāh al-Kindi (801–873 C.E.), a polymath who was the philosopher of the age. Al-Kindi wrote books in many disciplines including astronomy, optics, philosophy, mathematics, medicine, and linguistics, but his book on secret messages for court secretaries, A Manuscript on Deciphering Cryptographic Messages, is the most important to the history of cryptology. It is in this book that the technique of frequency analysis is first described." John F. Dooley, *History of Cryptography and Cryptanalysis: Codes, Ciphers, and their Algorithms* Springer International Publishing, 659 (Kindle edition).
9. *Ibid.* at 783–786.
10. *Ibid.* at 5292.
11. *Ibid* at 5324–26.
12. Graham P. Collins, Claude E. Shannon : Founder of Information Theory, Scientific American 14 October 2002.
13. *Ibid.*, Dooley at 5356–5359.
14. *Ibid.* at 5363–5366.

15. *Ibid.* at 5415.
16. Investopedia.
17. Paar and Pelzl, *ibid*, n.1, at 116.
18. *Ibid.* at 262, Kindle location 4264.
19. The 5G Economy at https://www.qualcomm.com/invention/5g/economy

Bibliography

John F. Dooley, *History of Cryptography and Cryptanalysis: Codes, Ciphers, and their Algorithms* (Springer International Publishing 2018)

Christof Paar and Jan Pelzl, "*Understanding Cryptography*" A Textbook for Students and Practitioners (Springer 2009)

Simon Singh, The Code Book: The Science of Secrecy from Ancient Egypt to Quantum Cryptography Anchor Books (1999)

Kevin Sounds, *Top Ten Codes, keys and ciphers*, The Guardian, 10 Sep. 2015

Klint Finley, *The WIRED Guide to 5G*, Wired Magazine, 12 December 2019 at https://www.wired.com/story/wired-guide-5g/

How 5G low latency improves your mobile experiences (Qualcomm 2019) at https://www.qualcomm.com/news/onq/2019/05/13/how-5g-low-latency-improves-your-mobile-experiences

FinTech

10

Introduction

Every innovation solves a problem. In this respect, FinTech is no different. The question arises what problems did FinTech solve in the financial services industry. The answer requires a reconstruction of the pre-FinTech world of financial services. This reconstruction of context is limited to five areas: stability, democracy, payments, lending, and smartphones.

Financial Instability: The Norm

Reinhart and Rogoff have demonstrated that financial crises of various kinds permeate centuries of history involving globe-spanning advanced and emerging countries with no end in sight. The financial folly reposes upon on a mentality that "this time is different" (Reinhart and Rogoff 2009). In the United States, during the run up to the "Second Great Contraction", the mindset of "this time is different" was expressed as: "Everything is fine because of globalization, the technological boom, our superior financial system, our better understanding of monetary policy, and the phenomenon of securitized debt" (Reinhart). Contrary to this optimism, housing prices doubled, equity prices soared, and external borrowings reached unsustainable levels. During the period 1970–2017, Laeven and Valencia have identified 151 banking crises, 236 currency crises, and 74 sovereign crises (IMF Working Paper 2018). Financial instability is a permanent feature of the financial ecosystem (Fig. 10.1).

Financial Services: An Elitist Club

The non-democratic nature of the global financial system is revealed by those whom the system serves and those whom it excludes. "In 2005, out of a total world

J. JA Burke, *Financial Services in the Twenty-First Century*,
https://doi.org/10.1007/978-3-030-63967-9_10

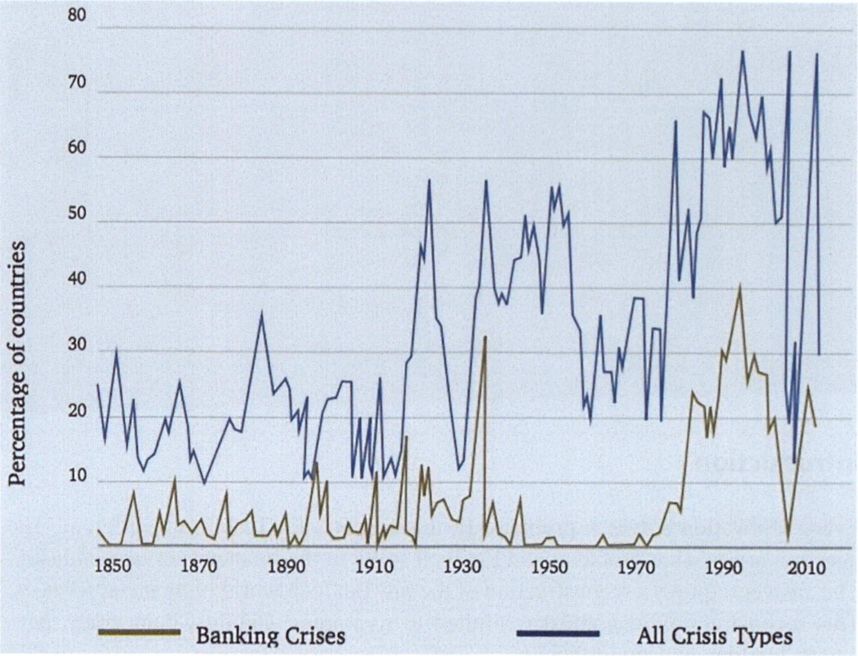

Fig. 10.1 Incidence of banking crises. (Source: Bank of England 2016)

population of 6.4 billion people, 4.7 billion were adults" (Chaia et al. 2009). Research concluded that 2.5 billion adults, or just over half the world's adult population, did not use formal financial services to save or borrow. Approximately 2.2 billion of the unbanked lived in Africa, Asia, Latin America, and the Middle East (Chaia) (Fig. 10.2).

Of the 1.2 billion adults using formal financial services in Africa, Asia, and the Middle East, slightly more than 800 million lived on less than $5 per day (Fig. 10.3).

Differences between the poorest and richest regions of the world are telling. "In Sub-Saharan Africa, 80% of the adult population, 325 million were unserved, as compared to only 8% in high income OECD countries" (Chaia). Financial inclusion, a stated goal of most governments, had not happened. Unbanked does not include the "underbanked". According to the Federal Reserve, in 2010, "underbanked consumers have either a checking or savings account, but also rely on alternative financial services. The Federal Deposit Insurance Corporation (FDIC) estimates that the underbanked population includes about 43 million adults and 21 million households in the United States. These households use non-bank money orders or non-bank cheque-cashing services, payday loan institutions, rent-to-own agreements or pawn shops on a regular basis. Blacks, Hispanics and Native Americans are the most likely Americans to be underbanked" (Martha Perine Beard 2010).

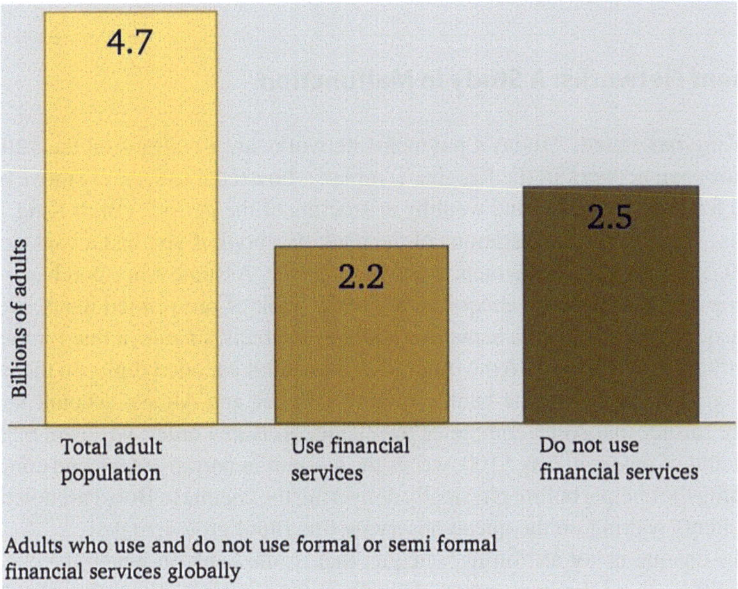

Fig. 10.2 2.5 billion adults globally do not use formal or semi-formal financial services. (Source: Honohan, 2008: Human Development Index: Work Bank)

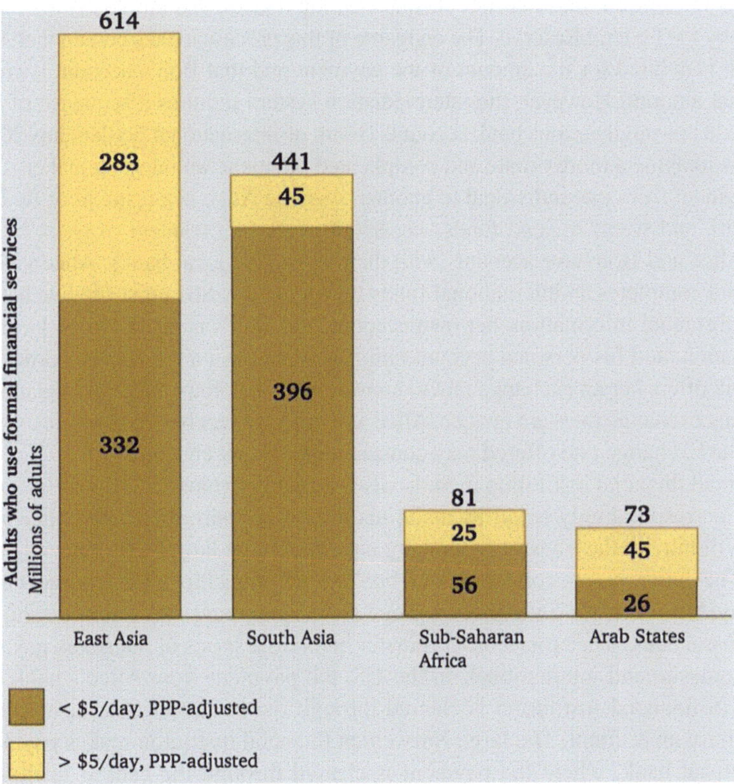

Fig. 10.3 Hundreds of millions of adults who use financial services live on less than $5/day, PPP-adjusted. (Source: Honohan, 2008: Human Development Index: Work Bank)

Payment Networks: A Study in Malfunction

Brett King has stated, "Today's payments networks are iterations on the 12th century European network of the Knights Templar, who used it to securely move money around for banks, royalty, and wealthy aristocrats of the period" (Brett King 2018). Likewise, debit cards are iterations of the bank passbook if you had a bank account in 1850. Take a domestic payment made by a cheque. Assume Alice purchases items at a shop and pays Bob by cheque. Alice has a book of pre-printed blank cheques. The cheques contain Alice's name and address, the bank's name, a line for the date, a line after the words "pay to the order of" and several encoded digits on the bottom of the cheque, generally the bank's routing number and Alice's account number. Assume further that Alice completes the cheque to Bob's order, writes in numerals the amount of payment, say $100, writes the amount in narrative text, and concludes by signing the cheque before physically delivering the cheque to Bob. Parenthetically, those clients waiting on the queue observing this ritual grow irritated.

If the cheque is not an "on-us" cheque, that is, the bank on which the cheque is drawn differs from the bank where deposited, the clearing and settlement process takes place through interbank mechanisms.

While cheques are truncated into electronic items, nevertheless the clearing and settlement process is ornate, passing through correspondent banks using the Federal Reserve's Fedwire Funds Service, cheque clearing houses, and ultimately to be finally posted by the Federal Reserve. The endgame of this process makes certain that Alice's account is debited for the amount of the payment and that Bob's account is credited with that amount. However, the intermediation system requires a sequence of debits and credits through various bank accounts (Bank of International Settlements 2012).

Now imagine a more ornate and complicated payment: an international cross-border payment from one individual to another. Assume Alice is a resident of St. Louis, Missouri, and wants to send funds, say $5000 to Bob, a resident of Oslo, Norway. Both Alice and Bob have accounts with their respective local banks. Alice visits her bank and completes an international funds transfer order. She must provide her bank with substantial information: her own account, and Bob's name, address, local bank information, and his personal account number. Alice pays a fee for the "order", and her bank offers her an exchange rate to convert her US dollars into Norwegian krone. Currency exchange rates are opaque. Alice will unlikely receive a wholesale exchange rate. The Exchange rate offered may conceal hidden bank charges.

A small financial institution in St. Louis is unlikely to have a commercial account with a correspondingly small financial institution in Oslo; therefore, Alice's local bank will initiate the transfer by making a payment to a larger US financial institution. The latter has a correspondant banking relationship with a large bank in Norway. We further assume that the large Norwegian bank has a relationship with Bob's local bank. The cross-border transfer involves a series of interbank payments, both domestic and international. In the US, the payment from Alice's bank to the large US financial institution is cleared through the Federal Reserve, where both banks have an account. The large Norwegian financial instituton makes payment to Bob's local bank, where the payment is cleared through the central instituton in Norway to clear and settle interbank payments. In our simplified example, the payment is cleared and settled upon two separate domestic rails. In addition, one or several intermediary banks may be used to complete the transaction. The Society for Worldwide Interbank Financial Telecommunication (SWIFT) transmits messages to banks involved in the international funds transfer. SWIFT does not transfer any money. The funds transfer is a sequence of debits and credits through the intermediation system necessary to debit the account of Alice in US dollars and ultimately to credit the account of Bob in Norwegian krone. The transaction may take days, and neither Alice nor Bob has any idea of the progress of the transfer at any point in time, as they might with sending a package by FedEx. International funds transfers are expensive, opaque, and inefficient.

Lending: The Universe of Multiple Monopolies

Lending to households traditionally is the province of financial institutions. Secured debt generally is used to provide loans for purchases of homes and automobiles. Unsecured debt generally is used to provide consumers with lines of credit on a credit card or similar instrument. Levels of secured lending follows the business cycle. In a boom period, financial institutions loosen their credit criteria and provide lending to households often leading to asset inflation and eventual reduction of value of the purchased asset. In a bust period, financial institutions tighten credit criteria making it difficult to qualify for a loan or increasing the required loan-to-value ratio (Figs. 10.4 and 10.5).

In the EU, cross-border mortgages virtually do not exist comprising only 1% of all EU mortgages. "According to Matthias Tiemer, head of legal affairs at the European Mortgage Federation (EIF), lenders are ready to offer their services across borders, but are put off by issues such as the length and complexity of some procedures". In spite of the EU banking passport, mortgage lending consists of country-specific bank monopolies.

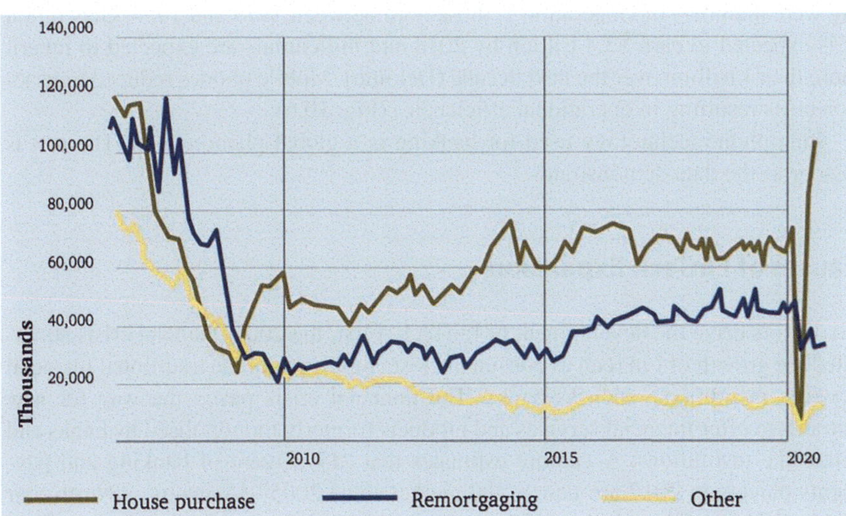

Fig. 10.4 Total number of sterling approvals secured on dwellings. (Source: Bank of England 2020)

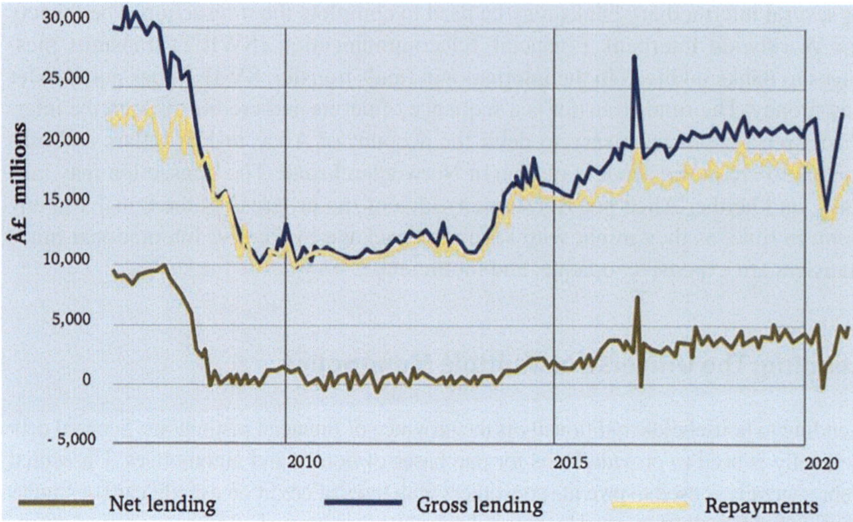

Fig. 10.5 Total value of sterling lending secured on dwellings. (Source: Bank of England 2020)

Mobile Phone Technology

Prior to the "Second Great Contraction", bank customers began to conduct banking operations with their mobile phones. "From 2005–2010, mobile banking usage [in the United States] increased at nearly 100% compounded annual growth rate, with most of that growth occurring after 2007, the year that Apple Inc. introduced its revolutionary iPhone and App Store" (Deloitte "Mobile Banking" 2010). The 2007 Apple iPhone was not the first smartphone, but it was the first to get the user interface right (Justin Meyers 2011). Chief among those to use mobile phones for banking were members of Generation Y, those born between 1979 and 1994. Generation Y is expected to earn $3.4 trillion by 2018 and millennials are expected to inherit more than 1 trillion over the next decade (Deloitte). Mobile phones reduced transaction costs resulting in operational efficiencies (Fig. 10.6).

Smartphone technology used for banking is a global phenomenon. The rest is history as the data demonstrates.

Causes of FinTech Expansion

Six factors drive the development of FinTech. First, the 2008 financial crisis stimulated the growth of FinTech as consumers lost confidence in the traditional financial services institutions, such as banks. The financial crisis paved the way for new entrants to offer financial services and products formerly monopolised by banks and other like institutions. Accenture estimates that "17 percent of banking and payments players in 2017 are new to the market since 2005" (Accenture "North Star Gazing" 2018). Second, the 2007 release of the iPhone, and subsequently smartphones, opened the door to mobile payment systems, especially in developing

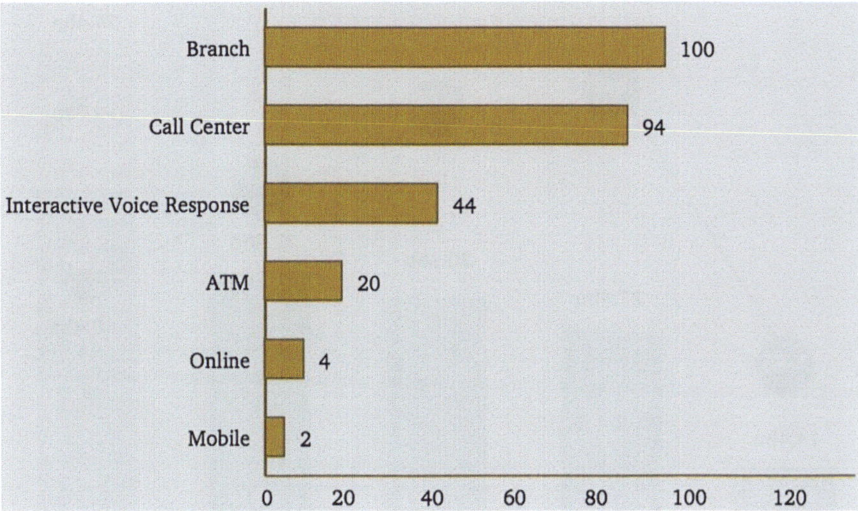

Fig. 10.6 Relative transaction cost per channel usage. (Source: Tower Group)

countries where average persons could not open bank accounts but possessed smartphones. Third, accumulated advancements in technology offered FinTech the opportunity to build infrastructure required to meet the changing demand for financial products and compete against incumbent banks.[1] Fourth, consumer preferences for digital financial services allowed FinTech companies to outmanoeuvre legacy financial system entrenched in obsolete programming languages and corporate organisations blocking quick change in banking models. Fifth, FinTech firms have a "mindset" ready to question the "raison d'être" of financial institutions, products, and processes. Sixth, regulatory reform pushing "open banking" such as PSD2 in the European Union has paved the highway of FinTech innovation. There are six developing FinTech models: payment, crowdfunding, wealth management, peer-to-peer lending, capital markets, and insurance services (Suryono et al. 2019).

Definition

FinTech is a contraction of the term "financial technology" and means technology-enabled financial solutions.[2] Arner et al. note that there is nothing new about the application of technology to advance the delivery of financial services. First, in 1866, the Atlantic Telegraph Company laid the first transatlantic cable and provided the infrastructure for the first period of financial globalisation. Second, the introduction of the automated teller machine (ATM) in 1967 by Barclays Bank marks the modern evolution of FinTech. Third, since the late 1980s, the financial services industry has been one of the foremost investors in information technology (IT), spending more than $197 billion in 2014, and that trend is accelerating. Based on recent reports, over $157 billion has been invested into FinTech in the United States during the period 2014–2018 (Fig. 10.7).

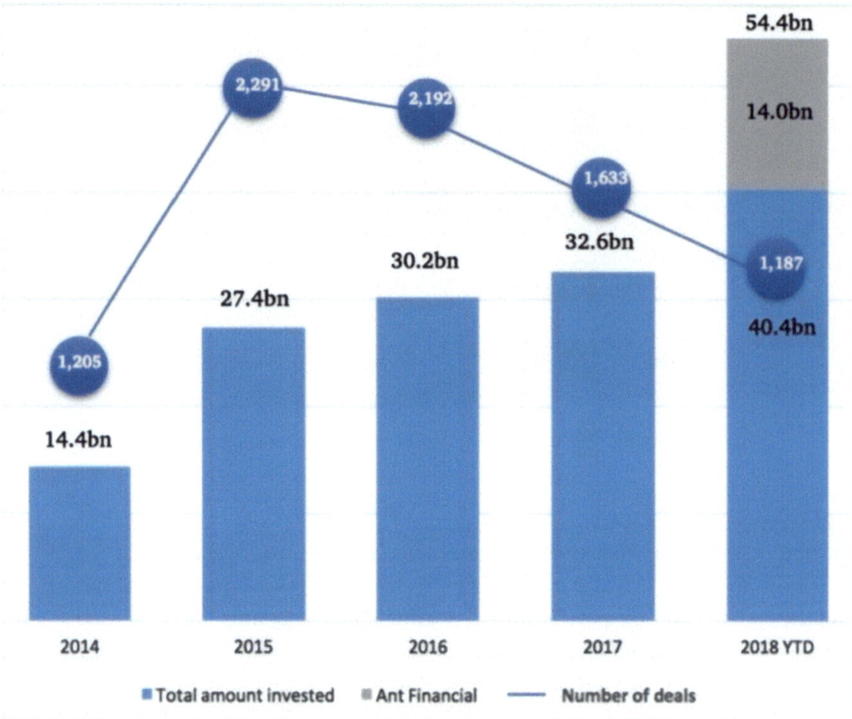

Fig. 10.7 Global FinTech investment, 2014—Q3 2018 (USD, number of deals). (Source: FinTech Global)

FinTech investment is not limited to the United States. While the United States leads in number of deals and amount, FinTech investment is global (Fig. 10.8).

In contrast to "evolving financial innovation", FinTech is distinguished from "evolving financial innovation" by its pace of innovation and its objective of disruption. FinTech seeks to identify weaknesses in legacy financial systems and then exploit those weaknesses to destabilise the *status quo*. It is financial guerrilla warfare. Particularly well-positioned to co-opt FinTech strategies are telecommunication companies and technology companies like Google that can leverage user accounts to offer financial services.[3] These combined factors have the potential to benefit consumers using financial services: lower costs, increased competition, and easier access to financial products and markets. Goodspeed aptly notes that "Financial technology is an umbrella term that incorporates a wide range of new business models and technical innovations that have the potential to transform the financial sector". Breakthroughs in technology have produced new ways to raise funds, for example, "crowdfunding, peer-to-peer lending, robo-advisers, high frequency trading, and distributed autonomous organisations". In addition, FinTech has increased "financial inclusion" to the underbanked or non-banked populations, principally found in Asia, Africa, and South America. Further, and most

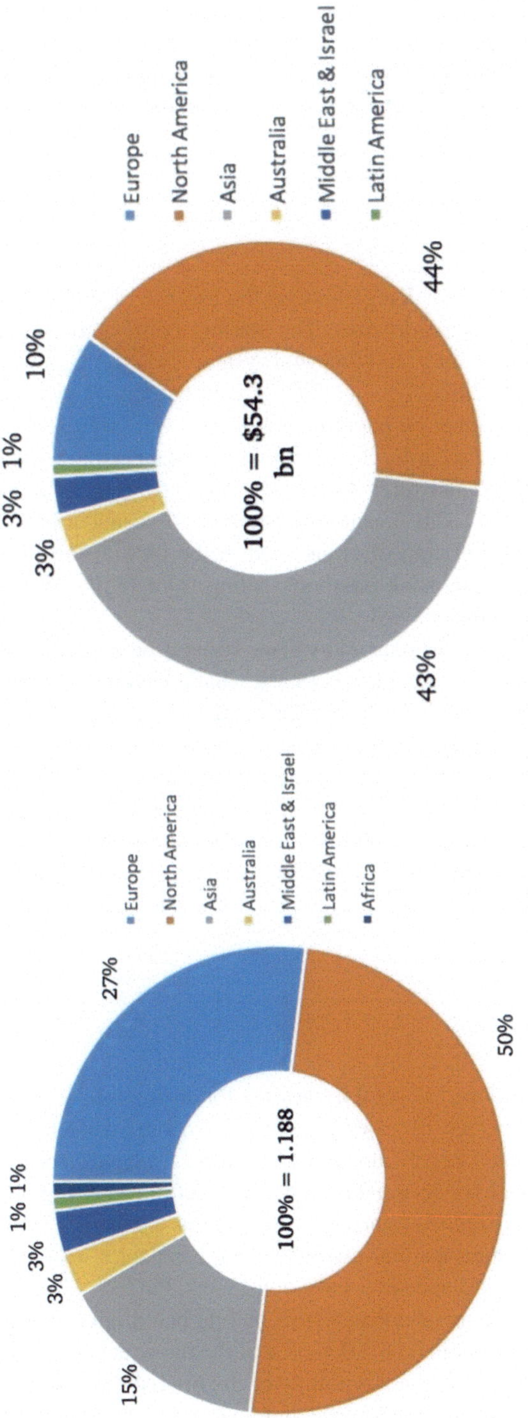

Fig. 10.8 Global FinTech investment by region, Q1—Q3 2018 (number of deals). (Source: FinTech Global)

importantly, FinTech takes advantage of changing consumer behaviour and customer evolution. For example, "66 percent [of customers] execute half their banking transactions online and 71 percent are open to automated support" (Accenture Report). Incumbent, or legacy, banks are far behind the curve of meeting consumer preferences in a digital age.

First Principles

In his book *Bank 4.0*, Brett King captures the essence of FinTech innovation and disruption: design on a *tabula rasa*. The starting point is to ask, if you were to design a "banking, monetary, and financial system" from scratch, would it look like the existing financial edifice. I quote, "Would you start with physical bank branches, insist on physical currency on paper or polymers, "wet" signatures on application forms, passbooks, plastic cards, cheque books, and the need to rock up with 17 different pieces of paper and three forms of ID for a mortgage application?" The answer clearly is "no". Today's banking system is a descendent of the Middle Ages. Paper currency is an iteration of coins used in the first century. Debit and credit cards are iterations of the bank passbook dating from 1850. "Wet" signatures are insecure and easily compromised.

The key to designing a financial system, without being distracted by existing, obsolete, and baroque architecture, is to ask what a bank does that other organisations do not do. Stripped down to first principles, King says banks provide three utilities: (1) a value store; (2) money movement; and (3) access to credit (Brett King 2018). These activities describe utility and functionality, not financial products, nor the byzantine structure built around the business of banking. King posits, "Technology now affords us the ability to radically eliminate that friction and create banking *embedded* in the world around us, delivering banking where and when we need it" (King). Going back to first principles and reinventing utility defines FinTech.

Framework

Arner et al. have developed a useful framework for distinguishing periods of developments of FinTech. FinTech 1.0 extends from 1866 to 1967 whereby the financial services industry remained largely analogue. FinTech 2.0 extends from 1967 until 2008 whereby the financial services industry became not only more globalised but also deeply digitalised. FinTech 3.0 starting in 2008 marks a paradigm shift whereby non-banks, mainly new start-ups and established IT companies, entered the market to deliver financial products and services to consumers. FinTech 3.5 is characterised by developments in emerging markets where mobile-based payments are synthesised with developments from FinTech 3.0, to sketch the future development of FinTech.

Arner et al. have developed a typology of the FinTech industry. "FinTech today comprises five major areas: (1) finance and investment, (2) internal operations and risk management, (3) payments and infrastructure, (4) data security and monetization, and (5) customer interface". Traditional financial institutions have the capital to dominate the FinTech industry; however, at least until the present time, these institutions are hampered by: (1) rigorous regulation that has not yet been applied to their counterparts in the IT industry, thereby giving the latter an edge until governments expand the scope of regulations; and (2) infrastructure based on outdated programming languages such as COBOL.

FinTech drives innovation in financial services by applying relatively recent technology to solve customer disillusionment with legacy banking. These technologies are: (1) smartphones, (2) distributed or decentralised ledger technology (blockchain), (3) big data, (4) artificial intelligence, and (5) machine learning. In addition, FinTech start-ups use state-of-the-art hardware and programming language thereby avoiding the barnacle-encrusted infrastructure of legacy banks often the result of myriad mergers and acquisitions and reliance upon obsolete programming languages like COBOL. Legacy banks are stuck with expensive branch networks for which the digital generation expresses dis-preference and the underbanked and underserved customer never used.

FinTech intersects financial services and technology sectors (PwC Global FinTech Report 2016).[4] Technology companies or start-ups reinvent financial products and services, formerly provided by traditional financial institutions, and offer them to customers, on novel infrastructures and platforms. FinTech is a movement of disruptive innovation precisely because FinTech firms build correct systems from the start, take risks, and have a culture of efficient operational design (Philippon 2016). Critical to this mission is the reconstruction of broken systems and dismissal of obsolete ideas. FinTech requires not only "thinking outside the box" but also "thinking as if there is no box".

Changing Financial Systems Architecture

Accenture "conducted a wide-ranging quantitative study to determine structural change and revenue migration in the banking and payment industry" during the period 2005–2017. Accenture analysed more than 20,000 institutions across seven geographies: "Australia, Brazil, Canada, China, the European Union, the United Kingdom, and the United States" (Accenture 2018). The study found that the "combination of the aftershocks of the global financial crisis, more active regulatory intervention, and the emergence of digital-native customers are … reshaping the global banking industry". New entrants in the banking and payment industry fell into four broad categories: (1) challenger banks, (2) non-bank payment institutions, (3) credit intermediation platforms, and (4) "BigTech" (Accenture 2018).

Challenger banks "seek to replace a traditional banking relationship with something better." Examples are: N26, Atom, Monzo, Starling, and Ally. Challenger banks stress "customer experience enabled by technology innovation (AI, Big Data, Analytics Cloud, APIs and so forth)". Some like BMW Bank are subsidiaries of non-financial corporates trying to cash in on their brand name. Some like Tyme in South Africa are subsidiaries (here the Commonwealth Bank of Australia) of existing banks entering a new market or trying out a new model. A review of the websites of these challenger banks demonstrates that the devil is in the detail. For example, many challenger banks lack a convenient way to deposit cash and, after several interbank transfers, start to charge transfer fees. In addition, no bank can get around the problem of mandatory physical residence. The latter restriction imposes friction upon expats trying to open or maintain accounts in their country of origin.

Non-bank payment institutions are category-killer businesses, specialising mainly in payment services, a domain where incumbent banks have failed to deliver quality services at cost-based rates. Regulatory changes such as the PSD2 have encouraged competition in payment services by mandating European banks to give third-party access to customer-permitted accounts and transaction data through application programming interfaces (APIs) "and allowing those third parties to initiate payment transactions on behalf of their customers". Regulatory innovation is not limited to the EU; Australia, Canada, and Hong Kong are following suit.

Credit intermediation platforms match borrowers with savers. These players span a range from B2C (SoFi, LendingClub) to B2B (Kabbage, OnDeck) generally using peer-to-peer funding technologies. LendingClub is a US peer-to-peer lending company headquartered in San Francisco, California, having started in 2006. LendingClub offerings are registered with the U.S. Securities and Exchange Commission (SEC) and its shares trade on the secondary market under the symbol "LC". Both individuals and institutions may purchase positions in a portfolio of LendingClub loans. By contrast, Kabbage provides small business funding: inventory purchases, line of credit, and cash flow.

"*BigTech*" refers to large technology firms, like Google, Amazon, Baidu, Alibaba, and Tencent, that encroach upon the banking and payment services industry, pivoting off their large customer base. To place in perspective the success of "BigTech", Alipay in 2015 delivered 87,000 transactions per second while, during that same period, Visa processed 9,000 transactions per second across its network. In addition, Ant Financial (Alipay) "is on track to become the largest single financial institution in the world" (King).

Case Study in International Payments: TransferWise

Note: this explanatory text was written prior to TransferWise's decision to re-brand itself as "Wise" in 2021. Post-rebranding, the procedure to initiate a funds transfer differs from the original system. Now, a client using Wise must first order its bank to make a domestic wire transfer to Wise's designated financial institution in the jurisdiction of the bank holding the originating funds. The two-step procedure is predicated upon arguments of consumer protection. However, the "new" procedure imposes additional costs upon the user of Wise's service since the user must pay the cost of the domestic wire transfer, plus the fees charged by Wise for the international funds transfer.

Assume Alice, a resident of the United States, wants to pay Bob, a resident of France €10,000. Alice opens an account with TransferWise (TW) online. To make a transfer, she will provide TW details about the bank account from which the funds are to be withdrawn. She also must provide to TW details about Bob's account where the funds are to be deposited. Because the USD/EUR exchange rate constantly changes, Alice will probably be unable to deliver exactly the €10,000 amount to Bob, but she will get very close.

Alice then instructs TW to transfer $11,000 from her account to Bob's. TW immediately provides the actual amount to be delivered, including the fee and the exchange rate, say €9,850. If Alice agrees with the terms, Alice instructs TW to withdraw the money from her account. Those funds are sent to a US financial institution where TW has an account. TW will notify Alice by email when TW has received the funds. TW also provides an estimated date of deposit into Bob's account. When the funds are deposited into Bob's account in France, TW notifies Alice that the transfer has been completed.

However, TW does not transfer money from one country to another but from person to person thereby avoiding using the international intermediary banking system. Rather, TW uses a program to find matches between Alice who has sent TW $11,000 and a person expected to receive that amount in the United States. TW replicates this matching search in Europe seeking a person that has transferred to TW Europe the sum of €9,850. That amount is paid to Bob in France. Funds never leave the country or region where TW has its bank accounts. TW makes series of domestic payments (Fig. 10.9).

Illustrative of FinTech disruption is "TransferWise" (TW), a UK company that executes cross-border payments, relying on an easy-to-use interface, speed, low cost, and advantageous exchange rates. TW is a P2P transferring service linking sending and receiving locations. "It was founded in 2011 by two Estonians, Taavet Hinrikus and Kristo Käärmann, to solve a problem of sending money from the UK to Estonia without being ripped off by hidden transfer fees from their bank" (Austin Grey Maxwell 2018). Founded in a small apartment in Tallinn, TW now is worth more than

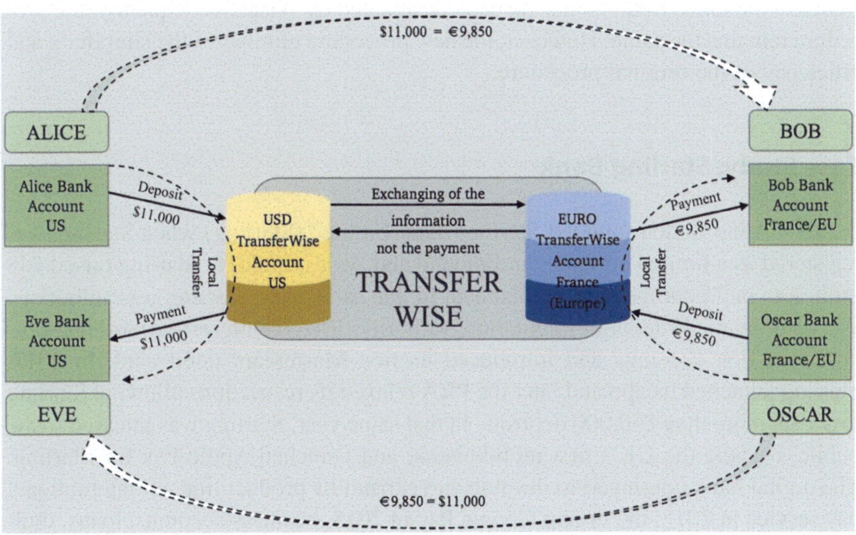

Fig. 10.9 How TransferWise works. (Source: Author)

$1 billion. I have a TransferWise account and I explain upon personal experience. It works as follows. You open an account subject to KYC/AML rules of the FCA, the UK regulator that regulates TW. Second, you tie your TW account to a funding account, usually a bank account. Third, when you request a transfer, TW sends a notice of confirmation of request to your email account and provides data on cost and currency conversion. If you agree to the terms, TW notifies the time when the funds were withdrawn from the originating institution and estimates time of delivery to destination institution and beneficiary account. The website interface allows users to track the progress of the transfer similar to tracking delivery of a package through FedEx, unlike a funds transfer originating from a bank instruction. The currency conversion rate is transparent as are the fees deducted to conduct the transfer. When the funds arrive, TW sends an additional notification. Duration of time from login to withdrawal of funds takes less than one minute. By contrast, many incumbent banks require presence at a branch to complete an Electronic Funds Transfer form, with a wet signature. The bank cannot track the movement of the funds. It is as if the funds have entered "void" and the originator must hope the funds arrive at the beneficiary institution. Incumbent bank cross-border transfers are more expensive and less transparent than the service provide by TW.[5]

As stated in the "Note", the foregoing explanation is no longer accurate. As of 2021, a "Wise" client first executes a funds transfer from his/her bank to a domestic bank designated by Wise. This step requires a physical visit to the bank holding the funds to be transferred or an elaborate pre-authorised procedure. For example, contrary to the pre-branding process, now I must do the following. First, based upon a written and signed authorisation executed in person at my bank in the US, I must write, sign, and scan a second letter of authorisation to transfer funds. Receipt by my bank of the letter alone is insufficient. I must call the bank and verify all details of the transfer. If the bank is satisfied that my authorisation is genuine, the bank transfers the funds to the domestic bank designated by Wise. Subsequently, the procedure remains the same. However, the new procedure eliminates the simplicity and efficiency of the original procedure.

Case Study: Starling Bank

In 2014, Anne Boden founded Starling Bank Limited (Starling) when Starling was registered as a limited company in England and Wales. In 2016, Starling raised £48 million to build out the bank as planned. In that same year, Starling was authorised as a bank by the Prudential Regulation Authority (PRA), with restrictions, and produced its first accounts and introduced its first Mastercard debit card. In 2017, Starling launched its app and later the PRA relaxed its restrictions allowing Starling to accept more than £50,000 deposits. In that same year, Starling was released to the public, became the UK's first mobile bank, and launched Apple Pay for Starling. The digital bank continued to develop and expand its product line: an international pay service in 2018, the in-app Google Pay in 2018, business accounts, loans, multiple currency accounts, additional software apps such as Sparqa Legal and

QuickBooks. In 2019, Starling opened its one millionth account and in 2020 broke even for the first time in its history.

Starling offers multiple accounts but this discussion focuses on the personal current account. Starling's website states that the current account does not charge monthly fees for: making electronic payments, receiving payments, domestic transfers, cash deposits, or ATM withdrawals. The current account pays interest of 0.05% on balances up to £85,000; Starling does not pay interest on balances exceeding that amount. Cheques up to £500 may be deposited from the customer's mobile phone by photograph. Instant messages notify client of banking activity, and personalised data shows your spending habits and suggests how to improve budgeting. Starling states, "Bank wherever, whenever" and "Think of us as your app-based bank with real-world benefits".

Starling has solved many of the problems of legacy banking noted by King. There are no branches, so opening an account takes place entirely online without reliance upon paper documents and signatures. Payments are simplified and additional apps provide improved customer service. Critical is the total digital experience of banking. Notwithstanding these successes, Starling limits its customer base to UK residents, though no fault of its own but a result of PRA regulation. The menu of services also is limited. Starling does not provide secured lending for real property and the amount of its loans to personal customers is limited: £500 to £5000. The APR (annual percentage rate) offered depends on individual circumstances.

Having reviewed the broad outlines of the personal account, I began to wonder how Starling makes money, since a wide swath of services are free. Hence, I downloaded the "Current Account Terms and Conditions" dated 4 November 2020, the "Rates, Fees and Charges Sheet" of the same date, and the "2019 Annual Report". The audited income statements indicate that Starling derives substantial income in fees and commissions totalling £11,095,000 and secondarily from interest income totalling £6,895,000. More than 61% of income is generated in fees. A review of the "Personal Account Contract" and "Rates, Fees and Charges Sheet" show the provenance of fees. The overdraft facility, if approved, imposes a specific rate of interest viewable on the app and interest accrues every day. Subscription services such as "Starling Kite", a debit card for a non-adult, costs £24 annually or "Connected" cards cost £24 annually per card. If a customer uses CHAPS (Clearing House Automated Payment System) to send money, then the payment is not free. Rather Starling charges a fee of £20 per CHAPS payment. Starling also imposes fees for sending money outside the UK. When an international payment instruction is received, Starling posts an exchange rate and fee viewable on the app before payment is made. The "Rates, Fees and Charges Sheet" does not provide specific amounts. While not received by Starling, other banks in the international payment process may deduct fees during the transfer. Transfers of funds among Starling accounts if not made in BPS are subject to exchange rates and fees.

In terms of its competitors, based on 2019 data, Starling appears well-managed and able to control costs best (Fig. 10.10):

	Starling	Monzo	Revolut
Reporting date end	Nov' 19	Feb' 20	Dec' 19
Revenue	£17m	£67.2m	£162.7m
Revenue growth from 2018 (%)	455%	241% +	180% +
Losses (post-tax)	£52m	£113.8m	£107.4m
Customers	1.08m	3.9m	10m
Deposits	£1.07bn	£1.39bn	£2.36bn
Card as % total revenue	45%	55%	63%

Fig. 10.10 Comparison chart of interchange fees. (Source: Starling Bank Annual Report, 2020)

It has the highest revenue growth rate and the lowest post-tax loss rate compared to 2018, while having a substantial level of deposits given its smaller customer base compared to Monzo and Revolut. Recall that Starling broke even in 2020, so the data is inaccurate as to Starling. Nevertheless, the data shows that digital banks rely heavily on "interchange fees" to produce revenue. Starling has prepared for Brexit by intending to establish a presence in Ireland thereby securing the bank passport to the EU.

In sum, Starling has accomplished a remarkable series of achievements in its short history. The question: has Starling changed banking? In a way, yes. Starling has shown that the digital banking experience is preferred by consumers, that banking is technology, and as devices get smarter, digital banks may offer a wider range of services, potentially superior and cheaper than their legacy counterparts, to customers and attract customers away from legacy institutions. However, the goal of toppling "big banks" remains a distant and uncertain goal.

Case Study: P2P Lending

"Peer-to-Peer lending platforms, which emerged around the 2008 financial crisis, allow individuals and small business to borrow without the presence of traditional financial institutions" (Huang Tang 2018). Technology-based lenders accounted for about 30% of unsecured instalment loans in 2016. LendingClub (LC) is the largest online P2P lending platform in the United States. LC may be viewed from three perspectives: the platform, individual lenders, and individual borrowers. The platform is a marketplace for non-bank loans. LC earns income from origination fees.

The applicant completes an online application, reporting name, address, purpose of loan, and amount to be borrowed. The platform uses the applicant's identity to construct a credit report. The platform deems ineligible any applicant whose FICO score is below 630 or whose debt-to-income (DTI) ratio is below 0.35. In the event the applicant is qualified, the platform presents the applicant with a menu of loans of different amounts, maturities (either 30 or 60 months) and interest rates. When the applicant selects a loan, the request for the loan is listed on LC's website and becomes accessible to investors (Tang).

Lenders then may search the loan request list to determine which loans to fund. Alternatively, LC classifies loans based on the credit quality of the borrower from low to high risk: A, B, and C, with the A-loans being the most secure, that is, the most likely to repay. The C-loans pay higher interest rates but potentially pose greater risk of default. The platform then allows the lender to select the category and percentage of lending made into each slice, and allow the platform to make investments automatically. Interest payments also may be reinvested automatically or swept into a connected bank account. Loans are not funded by single individuals or entities. Rather, investment funds are broken down into small notes so that an aggregation of small notes provisions each loan to mitigate risk for lenders.

Prices of loans depend upon "35 credit grades – A1 to G5 – based on the borrower's credit score, DTI ratio, credit history, requested loan amount, and loan maturity" (Tang). The price of loans is nation-wide and not dependent upon specific regions. Interest rates for loans are established by assigning a loan grade, "calculating the interest rate as the platform's base rate for that grade plus an upward adjustment reflecting the quoted factors" (Tang). Based on Tang's study of loans from 2009–2012, the average interest rate was 13.3%, "ranging from 5.4% to 24.9%" (Tang). Parenthetically, in the author's personal experience as an investor, during the period November 2019 to December 2020, investments in A and B grade loans have resulted in zero defaults and an annual return of 16.75%.

Case Study: Ripple[6]

Ripple is a San Francisco-based company in the United States, which has developed an international payment system using distributed ledger technology. Originally named OpenCoin and founded in 2012, the company was renamed Ripple Labs Inc. in 2015. Ripple has developed a protocol that runs on a distributed network to provide a de-localised payment system that settles transactions in seconds and in real time. Ripple arguably has solved problems with cross-border payments.

The international payment system is broken (Rosner and Kang 2016). Even the Federal Reserve System acknowledges the need to overhaul both domestic and international payment systems (FRB Strategy Report 2015). Cross-border payments are complex, because of Nation State boundaries and different domestic payment systems, and present heightened risk. "[T]here is no global central settlement system institution that holds the accounts of banks across national borders" (Rosner and Kang, 656). Many cross-border payments also require settlement in multiple currencies and "thus depend on a foreign-exchange (FX) transaction".

Definitions of "payments" and "clearing and settlement" are set forth to lay a basis for understanding Ripple's solution. A payment system is a set of instructions and rules governing the transfer of funds from one bank to another bank and providing a method for banks to settle their obligations. A payment system dictates the movement of money. However, "money" is not currency; rather, it is a bank obligation. These obligations also do not "move"; rather, these obligations are created and extinguished by a series of credits and debits. Clearing and settlement of payments takes place when "banks update their ledgers to adjust deposit balances" (Rosner and Kang). When one bank pays another bank, clearing and settlement requires the two banks to adjust balances through a "central" institution, where both banks have accounts and hold balances. "By adjusting the deposit balances of the payer's and payee's respective banks, the settlement institution provides the key mechanism to facilitate a funds transfer" (Ibid). In the United States, the Federal Reserve is the central clearing and settlement institution. The US operates two systems to facilitate settlement: Fedwire for wholesale, large value payments and the Automated Clearing House (ACH) for retail payments. While Fedwire is time sensitive, the ACH is not. Therefore, retail payments may take days to settle, introducing uncertainty and friction into the system.

"Ripple is an open-source Internet software that enables users to conduct payments across national boundaries in multiple currencies as seamlessly as sending an email" (Rosner and Kang 650). Ripple moves money through distributed ledger technology, a subject elaborated in the next chapter. In effect, Ripple applies blockchain technology to international funds transfers. Ripple links together computers participating in its distributed ledger network. In distributed settlement, Ripple's protocol operates on a single ledger held by all nodes. There is no central "party". The ledger, combined with the protocol, is the payment system. Since the network transcends physical borders, Ripple is a completely de-localised payment and clearing and settlement system. Users of Ripple initiate payments by instruction. Payments are executed when a super-majority of nodes (80%) approve a change to the single ledger by a process of consensus. The consensus mechanism solves the "double spending" problem.

In addition, Ripple solves the problem of Denial-of-Service (DoS) attacks. A DoS attack occurs when a malicious actor creates many identities in a P2P network to exert a disproportionate influence and paralyse the network. Ripple's solution is a digital currency called XRP, a math-based currency like Bitcoin. "The Ripple protocol requires each account to hold a small reserve of XRP in order to create ledger entries" (Rosner and Kang 660). XRP is Ripple's native currency, although Ripple is currency agnostic. The modest reserve requirement is "a significant cost for attackers who wish to flood the network with many false transactions" (Ibid). This makes DoS attacks extremely costly for attackers thereby functioning as a deterrence mechanism.

Unlike legacy systems, Ripple offers real-time settlement for cross-border payments. Ripple achieves this objective by deploying market-makers to create liquidity. Market-makers are entities that match buyers and sellers and profit off a spread between the bid and ask price. The Ripple protocol routes a transaction not only to the cheapest market-maker but also to the cheapest path, causing market-makers to compete for spreads. If a market-maker cannot handle the transaction, the Ripple protocol searches for an alternative. If none can be found, the transaction is dead. This is called the "atomic" or all or nothing settlement for cross-border payments. There is no possibility of a payment being stuck in the system. Because transactions happen in real time, parties know their positions immediately.

Structural Changes in the Financial Services Industry

The magnitude of structural changes in the industry varies by country as shown in the following figure (Fig. 10.11).

Country	2005	2017	Percent of new players
Global Change	~ 24,000	~ 19,300	17 %
EU	~ 8,400	~ 6,800	20 %
USA	~ 8,000	~ 6,150	19 %
China	~ 5,300	~ 4,300	7 %
Brazil	~ 1,800	~ 1,400	7 %
UK	~ 350	~ 760	63 %
Australia	~ 230	~ 234	38 %
Canada	~ 60	~ 140	47 %

Fig. 10.11 The magnitude of industry structure change varies by country. (Source: Accenture Research Analysis)

Revenue Migration

The percentage of revenue migration to new entrants is lower than their share of the market (Accenture 11). For example, in the UK, the most dynamic market in the world for FinTech companies, 63% of institutions are new, but their share of revenue is only 14%. However, incumbent banks must focus not only on the supply of new entrants but also upon the direction of the flow of revenue. Accenture estimates that "new entrants have captured six to seven percent of revenues in Europe", "three to four percent in the U.S.", and "one-third of new revenue creation in Europe".

The numbers are more striking in Asia. Alipay and WeChat have a combined more than 1.3 billion mobile users and "account for 94 percent of that market". "In Japan, Rakuten, the e-commerce giant, is now the largest online bank, with some six million customer accounts". In China and Japan, incumbent banks, though possessing larger balance sheets than their online rivals, will have a difficult, if not impossible, task, to gain any meaningful penetration of these markets, no matter what new model they adopt for the future. Existing banks rationalise wrongly that these new entrants are simply banks wearing digital clothing.

Structural Changes in the Financial Services Industry

The term "financial inclusion" refers to an underbanked or unbanked population. Africa is probably the pre-eminent example of a territory and population where incumbent banks failed to offer adequate financial services. The consequence is fertile ground for FinTech start-ups, and FinTech companies have taken advantage of this lacuna. M-Pesa ("M" for mobile and "Pesa"—Swahili for money) arguably is the most successful non-bank company to provide financial services to the financially excluded. M-Pesa was launched in 2007 by Safaricom and Vodacom, the largest mobile networks in Kenya and Tanzania, respectively. The company offers mobile-based money transfers and microfinancing. M-Pesa is a branchless banking service. Customers deposit and withdraw money at designated "banking agents" and their funds are stored on their mobile device. Customers may make mobile payments using their devices. In Kenya, approximately 25% of GDP moves through the M-Pesa system and the client base comprises more than 17 million persons.

The underbanked or unbanked populations are not limited to third-world countries. In the United States, based upon a 2017 study by the FDIC, 25% of households are either underbanked or unbanked. The latter of those "are people who either don't have a bank account, or have an account, but still use financial services outside the banking system like payday loans to make ends meet" (CNBC). The reasons cited: (1) more than 50% of those surveyed stated that they lacked sufficient funds to open a bank account, (2) 30% stated that they did not trust banks, and (3) 9% stated that bank locations were inconvenient. At present, community development financial institutions (CDFIs) are attempting to remedy the lack of access to affordable financial services.

Conclusion

FinTech firms have impacted the delivery of financial services and have used accumulated advances in technology to challenge legacy banks and attract disgruntled customers. To what extent FinTech firms can continue to take market share from incumbent institutions remains unclear, since the latter have monopolised the market for decades and have enormous financial resources. Because of existing anachronisms and regulations, many FinTech firms "piggy-back" off existing bank infrastructure thereby preventing the reinvention of the banking and financial services sectors. FinTech has a substantial "Achilles heel". FinTech is premised upon thinking outside the box. However, FinTech operates inside multiple boxes: the legal regulations of jurisdictions in which they are incorporated and the legal regulations of jurisdictions where they operate.

FinTech also poses several questions. Customers "bank" by using smartphones, but that use comes at a cost. Payments that were previously made in cash and, in principle, free of charge and anonymous, now cost money to make and leave an audit trail. Interchange fees account for the greatest percentage of neo-bank income. Loans when available are limited in amount and the interest rate is substantial as shown by a Starling demonstration of a £5,000 loan extended at more than 11% APR. Financial inclusion raises two questions: "what constitutes meaningful inclusion?" and "what does it mean to be 'banked'?". For example, M-Pesa offers payment by telephone to the formerly unbanked who now take cash to an exchange office to fund their phone. Is that what it means to be "banked"? TW has implemented a clever scheme to solve the problems and costs of cross-border funds transfers by making them domestic payments. Hence, the international payments system remains fragmented, expensive, slow, and opaque. Finally, while no fault of FinTech, the gap between income and capital inequality incessantly widens. The simple fact remains: smart bank or not, without sufficient funds, customers are paying a premium to use mobile technology. Wealth creation, never mind management, is independent of the technology deployed to simplify financial transactions.

Questions

1. In 150 words or less, explain the distinction between "financial innovation" and FinTech.
2. This question requires comparative analysis and independent research. Take FinTech firms operating in the same economic space. Identify their "disruptive" character. Compare the services offered by the FinTech firms and explain whether, or if, they provide advantages over incumbent banking services.
3. Explain why many FinTech firms are stuck "piggy-backing" upon extant incumbent banking infrastructure. For example, the difference between pre- and post-FinTech payment systems is the use of non-banks, such as Google, Apple, or Facebook, to initiate, monitor, and provide verification of payment. The common denominator, and ostensible limitation, of these novel payment systems is that

they are "piggy-backed" on legacy banking systems. All apps require connection to bank accounts or to cards issued by banks thereby effacing some of the gloss of mobile payment.
4. Regulatory reform is said to smooth the way to "open banking". Explain why. Every Nation State has its own rules and regulations governing financial services and banking. Explain why this lack of unification creates "speedbumps" in the delivery of financial services and provide your opinion upon whether lack of uniform law impedes progress in development of new financial entities.
5. Visit the Ripple web page https://ripple.com/ripplenet/. Understand the existing system and why Ripple decided to construct a novel solution to global payments for banks and payment providers, based upon blockchain. Read the articles on the web page https://ripple.com/insights to gain a better understanding of Ripple. In addition, IBM and Stellar are launching a global payments system based on blockchain. Compare and contrast the two systems.

Use Case

Payment Systems

PayPal may be considered the original FinTech model of payment, and it has continued to evolve to provide enhanced services, such as Xoom. New smartphone payment systems include: Venmo (acquired by PayPal), Square Cash, Zelle (legacy bank consortium), Apple Pay, Google Wallet, and Facebook Messenger. Each mobile payment system works by creating a wallet on the mobile device that is tied to a bank account or bank card(s). The novelty consists in cashless payments by using the phone (mobile device) at the point of sale, using the phone to send or receive money using email addresses, telephone numbers, or instant messaging, and the provision of electronic financial recordkeeping. For example, "Zelle" allows payment to friends or family directly from the user's bank account provided the receiver has an account at a participating bank. (Note that Zelle is a US-based consortium of more than 100 banks.) Since many large banks are participating members, the customer base is large, and the payment is made the same day in real time.

The Venmo network reported payment volumes of approximately $77.8 billion since Q1 of 2017 to Q3 2018. The popularity of P2P apps captured the attention of financial institutions that launched "Zelle" in 2017. Transfers are made directly between user accounts within the Zelle system. Zelle outperformed Venmo during the seven-quarter period 2017–2018 by reporting payment volumes of $160 billion in the aggregate. Legacy banks adopting FinTech payment concepts are well-positioned to enter the market given their large customer base.

Notes

1. S&P Global, Market Intelligence, An Introduction to fintech: Key sectors and trends, October 16, 2016.
2. Douglas W. Arner, Jànos Barberis, and Ross P. Buckley, *The Evolution of FINTECH: A New Post-Crisis Paradigm*, 47 Georgetown J. Int'l L. 1271 (2016). The authors argue correctly that financial technology and finance have a long history. See also, Ingrid Goodspeed, *Financial technology – an introduction*, SA Financial Markets Journal (25th ed. May 2017). The authors note an acceleration of the marriage of finance and technology since the 2008 financial crisis, and advocate regulation of innovative financial products.
3. Ingrid Goodspeed, at 1.
4. PwC, *Blurred Lines: How FinTech is Shaping Financial Services*, p. 4 Global FinTech Report March 2016, Retrieved from URL https://www.pwc.com/gx/en/inductries.financial-services/fintech-survey/blurred-lines.html
5. By contrast, Xoom, a PayPal service, allows users to send funds cross-border by using an app installed on a smartphone. The user initiates the transfer by entering the amount, and the location where the beneficiary can pick up the funds, if in Russia, in cash up to €20,000. Unlike TW that allows transfers up to an equivalent of £1,000,000, Xoom transfers currency only in USD or EUR and imposes a maximum limit of €20,000.
6. On 22 December 2020, the Securities and Exchange Commission filed an action against Ripple Labs Inc. and two of its executives, alleging that they raised more than $1.3 billion through an unregistered offering. The complaint stated Ripple, beginning in 2013, sold digital assets known as XRP in an unregistered offering to investors in the United States and worldwide. The complaint further alleged that the two executives – Larsen and Garlinghouse – sold personal unregistered XRP assets totalling approximately 600 million. The SEC seeks injunctive relief, disgorgement with pre-judgement interest, and civil penalties. The litigation is pending. SEC Press Release, *SEC Charges Ripple and Two Executives with Conducting $1.3 Billion Unregistered Securities Offering*, Press Release 2020–338.

Bibliography

Accenture, *Beyond North Star Gazing: How are four winning bank models map to actual market evolution*, 2018, at https://www.accenture.com/_acnmedia/PDF-85/Accenture-Banking-Beyond-North-Star-Gazing.pdf

Accenture, Star Shifting: Rapid Evolution Required – Banks can grow by accelerating their move to digital, 2018 at https://www.accenture.com/_acnmedia/PDF-87/Accenture-Banking-Rapid-Evolution-Required.pdf

Albero Chaia, Aparna Dalal, Tony Goland, Maria Jose Gonzalez, Jonathan Morduch, and Robert Schiff, Half the World is Unbanked, Financial Access Initiative Framing Note October 2009.

Douglas W. Arner, Jànos Barberis, and Ross P. Buckley, *The Evolution of FINTECH: A New Post-Crisis Paradigm*, 47 Georgetown J. Int'l L. 1271 (2016). The authors argue correctly that financial technology and finance have a long history

Business Wire, Banks' Revenue Growth at Risk Due to Unprecedented Competitive Pressure Resulting from Digital Disruption, Accenture Study Finds, retrieved https://www.businesswire.com/news/home/20181017005055/en/Banks'-Revenue-Growth-Risk-Due-Unprecedented-Competitive

Carmen M Reinhart and Kenneth S. Rogoff, This Time is Different: Eight Centuries of Financial Folly (Princeton University Press 2009).

Earthport Payment Network, Shapeshifting: a look at the evolving landscape of cross-border payments, retrieved https://www.bankingtech.com/files/2019/05/2019_Earthport_Shapeshiftingpaymentslandscape_whitepaper.pdf

Niall Ferguson, *The Ascent of Money: A Financial History of the World* 70 (Penguin Books 2008)

Finleap Insights, Fintech Trends: The Underbanked, retrieved https://www.finleap.com/insights/fintech-trends-the-underbanked/

FinTech Australia, "Digital challenger banks off and away in Australia", 25 May 2018; retrieved https://fintechaustralia.org.au/digital-challenger-banks-off-and-away-in-australia/

Ingrid Goodspeed, *Financial technology – an introduction*, SA Financial Markets Journal (25th ed. May 2017)

Brett King, *Digital Bank 4.0*, Marshall Cavendish International (Asia) Pte. Ltd. under license by John Wiley & Sons. (2018)

Y. Nichkasova and S. Bila, The Ontology of Financial Markets, Functions and Structural Evolution: Theoretical and Methodological Aspect, V.1 Bulletin of National Academy of Sciences of the Republic of Kazakhstan, Nr. 377 (2019), 236–248

PwC, *Blurred Lines: How FinTech is Shaping Financial Services*, p. 4 Global FinTech Report March 2016, at https://www.pwc.com/gx/en/inductries.financial-services/fintech-survey/blurred-lines.html

PwC, Redrawing the Lines: FinTech's growing influence on Financial Services (Global FinTech Report 2017) at https://www.pwc.com/jg/en/publications/pwc-global-fintech-report-17.3.17-final.pdf

S&P Global, Market Intelligence, An introduction to fintech: Key sectors and trends, October 16, 2016

TransferWise. https://transferwise.com

Lukas Wellen and Meine Pieter van Dijk, New Financial Technologies and the 4th Industrial Revolution in the Third World (The Example of Customer Care of M-Pesa, Kenya), The "EUrASEANs: journal on global socio-economic dynamics", V.2 (9); March-April, Year 2018, retrieved https://www.euraseans.com/2(9)

Yapstone, *12 Top Fintech Companies to Watch*, 28 February 2018 retrieved at: https://www.yapstone.com/press/12-top-fintech-companies-to-watch/

Ryan Randy Suryono, Betty Purwandari, Indra Budi, Peer to Peer (P2P) Lending Problems and Potential Solutions: A Systematic Literature Review, Science Direct 2019 at www.sciencedirect.com

Huan Tang, Peer-to-Peer Lenders Versus Banks: Substitutes or Complements?, The Review of Financial Studies, v. 32. Issue 5, May 2019, pp. 1900–38 at https://academic.oup.com/rfs/article/32/5/1900/5427773

Martha Perine Beard, 2010, Reaching the unbanked and underbanked, Central Banker, Federal Reserve Bank of St. Louis, Issue Win.

Deloitte, Mobile banking: A catalyst for improving bank performance (2010 Deloitte Development LLC).

Marcel T. Rosner and Andrew Kang, Understanding and Regulating Twenty-First Century Payment Systems: The Ripple Case Study, 114 Mich. L. Rev. 649 (2016)

Starling Bank, Current Account Terms and Conditions, General Part 4 November 2020

Starling Bank, Rates, Fees and Charges Sheet, 4 November 2020

Starling Bank, Annual Report 2018–29 at https://www.starlingbank.com/docs/annual-reports/Starling-Bank-Annual-Report-2018-19.pdf

Gunnar Camner, Caroline Pulver, Emil Sjöblom, GSMA Mobile Money for the Unbanked, What Makes a Successful Mobile Money Implementation? Learning from M-PESA in Kenya and Tanzania 2009

Distributed Ledger Technology 11

Introduction

The building blocks of "distributed ledger technology" preceded Bitcoin and blockchain technology. "The Genesis Files" laid out the precursors of the Bitcoin Network allowing Satoshi Nakamoto to assemble the parts in the right order and to construct a peer-to-peer e-payment system in the absence of financial institutions. However, other concepts critical to the development of DLT go further back. In 1982, Lamport et al. solved the Byzantine Generals Problem in the context of computer systems sharing information operating in an adversarial environment (Lamport et al. 1982). In 1992, Haber and Stornetta introduced cryptographically linked data blocks secured with digital timestamps in distributed systems using hashing functions and Merkle trees (Haber and Stornetta 1991). In 1999, Castro and Liskov created an algorithm to tolerate Byzantine faults (Castro and Liskov 1999). None of these developments attracted significant attention in contrast to the overwhelming interest in cryptographically secured digital assets and digital tokens transferred on DLT systems. The rising use of DLT systems therefore makes it imperative to establish a consensus definition.

The concept of a distributed ledger per se is not new. Its use can be traced to 500 CE on the Micronesian island of Yap. The Yapese used large Rai stones as currency; these stones often weighed 200 kilograms or more and were located in different parts of the Micronesian island, making them difficult to move (Neel Mehta, Adi Agashe, and Parth Detroja 2020). Because the stones were immovable, "the Yapese collectively remember(ed) who own(ed) each stone and kept a mental log of past transactions" (Ibid). For example, if a person wanted to buy a boat from the carpenter, the owner of the stone, say the one on the beach, announced to the village that the rai stone she controlled now belonged to the carpenter. The villagers broadcast this announcement to all villagers to inform them that the rai stone on the beach now belonged to the carpenter. Likewise, the carpenter had the capacity to transfer

J. JA Burke, *Financial Services in the Twenty-First Century*,
https://doi.org/10.1007/978-3-030-63967-9_11

control of the stone to someone else, and everyone's mental records were adjusted accordingly (Ibid.).

The rai stone system is a form of intangible money without the operation of a middleman. Legend has it that a ship carrying a rai stone sank but was never recovered (Mehta). The villagers reasoned that the stone still must exist and continued to use this stone as a mechanism of payment. The physical location of the stone was irrelevant thereby giving the stone the character of intangible money. In addition, the decision as to who owned a stone, or a fractionalised part, was not made by a single administrator in charge of maintaining a ledger of accounts. The decision of ownership was taken by consensus agreement of the villagers.

The collective memory ledger was fairly fault-tolerant and difficult to corrupt, though lacking a central administrator. The analogy between the Yapese distributed ledger using Rai stones and the Bitcoin Network using digital records and cryptography demonstrates the core concept of distributed ledger technology. However, the analogy is too primitive to understand contemporary DLT models.

The Cambridge Report

The Cambridge Report first notes the broad swath of DLT definitions, from the extremely narrow, which exclude DLT systems, to the overly broad, which incorporate alternative systems. The report then focuses on identifying "the essential minimum requirements of a DLT system", that is, "the necessary and sufficient conditions, as opposed to articulating the full set of properties that a DLT system might ideally possess" (Rauchs et al. 2018). The critical characteristics separating DLT systems from traditional databases are: (1) consensus about shared data and its validity reached within a multi-party system, (2) operating in an adversarial environment, (3) without a central coordinator, and (4) delegating trust to endpoint users. In short, a "DLT system is a system of electronic records that enables independent entities to establish a consensus around a shared ledger – without relying on a central coordinator to provide the authoritative version of the records" (Ibid). The fundamental distinction between a DLT system and other databases is control over "how data is stored, processed, and executed" (Ibid). The following illustration shows the "control differences" among three systems: (1) a centralised database, (2) a traditional distributed database, and (3) distributed ledger technology (Fig. 11.1).

The Cambridge Report then provides its formal definition of a DLT. Paraphrasing the report, a DLT is a system of (1) electronic records enabling a network of independent participants to establish a consensus about, (2) the authoritative ordering of cryptographically signed transactions, (3) made persistent by replicating the data across nodes, (4) secured against alteration by linking them to cryptographic hashes, (5) ultimately leading to a definitive ledger of records.

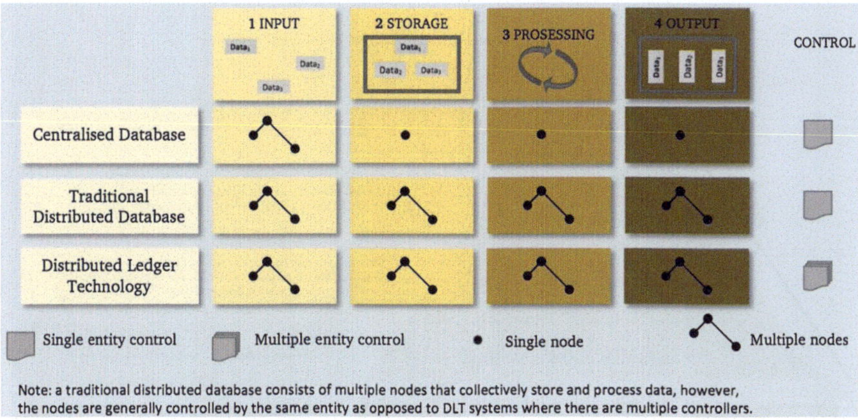

Fig. 11.1 From centralised database to distributed ledgers. Note: A traditional distribution database consists of multiple nodes that collectively store and process data, however, the nodes are generally controlled by the same entity as opposed to DLT systems where there are multiple controllers. (Source: Cambridge report 2018)

Essential Terminology

Before examining how DLT systems work, terminology must be clarified. The following terms are set forth in reverse hierarchical order. A "transaction" is a request to change the state of the ledger. A transaction need not have an economic value such as making an electronic payment. Transactions often are denoted "TX". A transaction is an authorised attempt to change the state of the ledger, since it is cryptographically signed by the user's private key. A "log" is a set of diverse transactions held by a node, not yet incorporated into a record "subject to network consensus rules" (Rauchs et al. 2018). It is an unconfirmed transaction. A "record" comprises a group of transactions that have been subject to network consensus rules. If a record has not been broadcast to the network, it is called a "candidate record". A "journal" is a set of records held by a node. Nodes may hold inconsistent records since "journals are partial, provisional and heterogenous" (Ibid). The "ledger" is the "authoritative set of records collectively held by a significant portion of network participants unlikely to be erased or amended" (Ibid). The flow from transaction to ledger is depicted in the following illustration (Fig. 11.2):

The Cambridge Framework

DLT systems consist of three layers: (1) protocol, (2) network, and (3) application depicted in this table (Fig. 11.3).

The protocol layer is the base layer upon which the other layers repose. The protocol layer contains the software instructions that determine how the system operates and codifies its architectural design. It is equivalent to a constitutional document

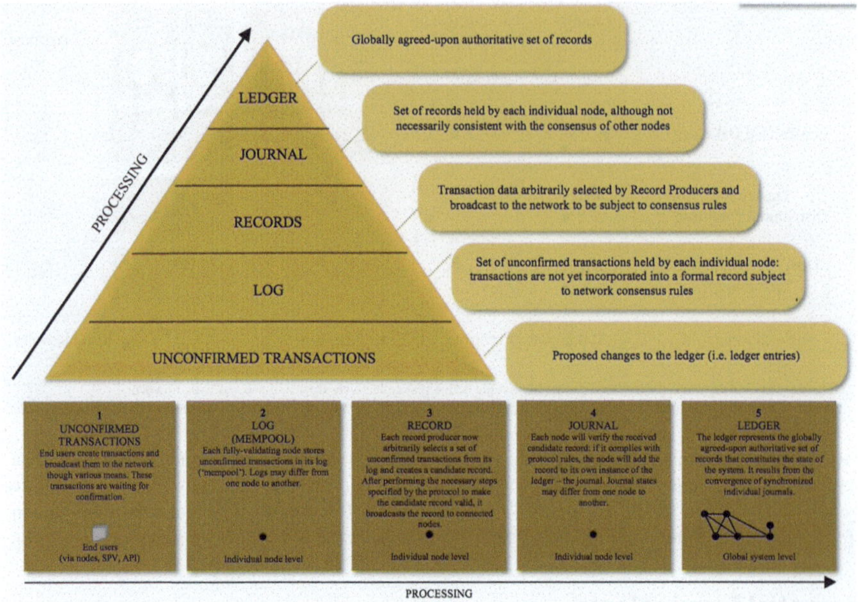

Fig. 11.2 From transaction to records. (Cambridge report 2018)

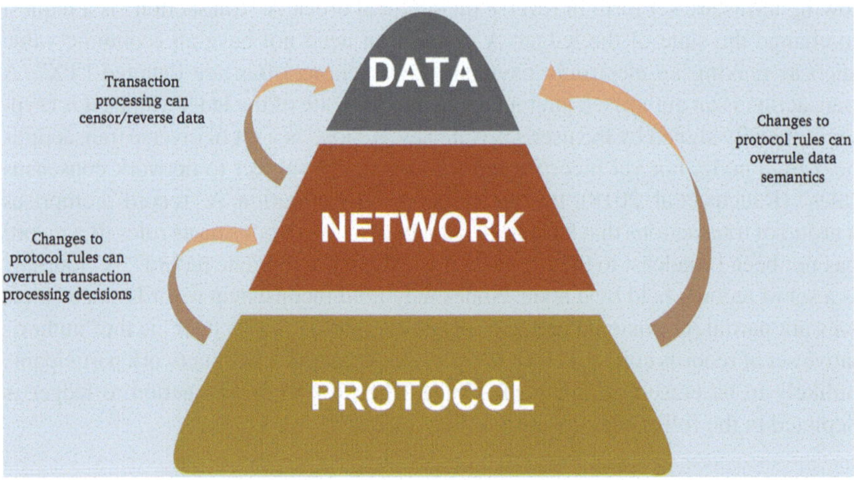

Fig. 11.3 Layer impact hierarchy. (Cambridge report 2018)

governing the behaviour of an organisation. The protocol layer has two components: the genesis component and the alteration component. The genesis component specifies the protocols governing the DLT system at launch, while the alteration component specifies how the original set of protocols may be amended. In other words, the alteration component defines how the original protocols evolve and are implemented over time.

The network layer (NL) is the practical implementation of the protocol layer and consists of the interconnected actors: storing, sharing, and processing data. The NL controls access to the network, specifies how data is handled, and provides rules as to how the data is shared, updated, and ultimately verified. The NL has three core components: (1) communications, (2) processing of transactions, and (3) validation. The NL communications component specifies which actors can become members of the network (open vs. closed) and who may initiate authorised transactions (unrestricted vs. restricted). The transactions processing component identifies how the "ledger" is updated, which participants have the authority to update the ledger (permission-less vs. permissioned), and specifies the rules of consensus. The validation component sets out the actions by which "auditors" verify the compliance of transactions with protocol rules, whether they are valid or invalid. The data layer refers to the information "processed and stored by the DLT system in the form of records" (Rauchs et al. 2018). The data layer delivers the objectives of the DLT system: a shared data structure—the authoritative ledger (set of authenticated records).

The data layer has two components: operations and journal. The operations component specifies the operations to be performed on data to produce a ledger, and the journal contains the content of the confirmed records. The ledger possesses critical features usually expressed as transparency, persistence, standardisation, and censorship resistance or transparency, immutability, and decentralisation.

Actors Within the DLT System

There are many actors within a DLT system. An actor is an entity or individual interacting with the DLT system. One person or entity may play a single role or multiple roles. Actors fall within one of four groups: (1) developers, (2) gateways, (3) administrators, and (4) participants. Developers function at many layers. First, they write the foundational software instructions at the protocol layer. Second, they build DLT clients so that users may access the system. Third, they design applications that run on the application layer. Fourth, they construct protocols allowing the DLT to function with third-party systems. Administrators control access to the codebase and "can decide to add, remove and amend code to change the system rule" (Rauchs et al. 2018). Administrators play an important role in the governance system of a DLT. The administrator's role varies upon the implemented system. In a closed and permissioned system, the administrator may exercise the authority of a central coordinator. By contrast, in an open and permission-less environment, administration is likely to devolve upon a group of volunteers. These volunteers do not impose changes, rather they propose changes to be accepted by independent users of the system. Gateways perform the role of linking distinct DLT systems to the external world to receive data exogenous to the system, such as custodians, exchanges, and issuers. Finally, participants refer to a diverse group of entities or individuals that interact with the DLT system. Auditors check the validity of records or submitted transactions; they audit the system state, and sometimes are referred to

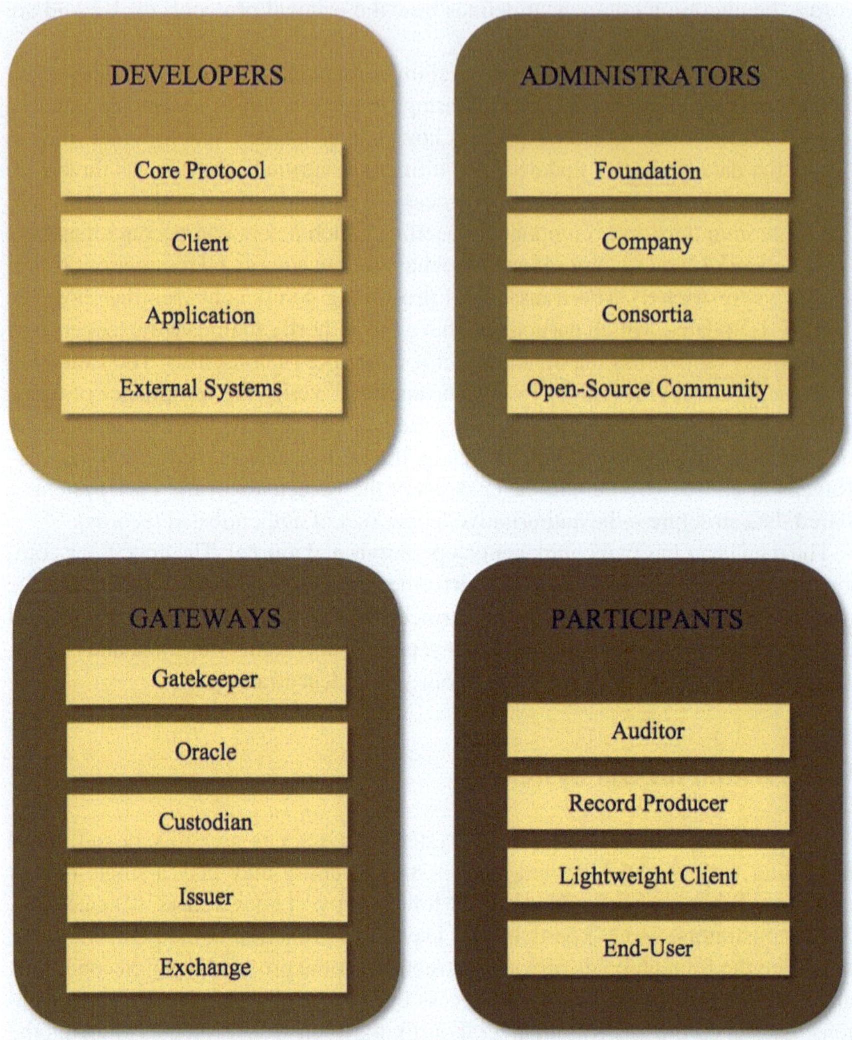

Fig. 11.4 Actor types found in DLT systems. (Cambridge report 2018)

as fully participating nodes. Record producers, or miners, propose candidate records for inclusion in the ledger. End users are those who require access to the system (Fig. 11.4).

Layer Interdependence

Layers do not operate independently of one another. It is important to understand the relationship between and among the layers and how they impact one another.

The protocol layer is king since it has the capacity to influence directly the network and application layers. For example, changes to protocol rules can override transactions processing information at the network layer and can overrule data semantics at the application layer. It follows that a system attempting to achieve independent layers requires decentralisation at the protocol and network layers. Design considerations in the construction of a DLT system therefore must decide on the relative independence of each layer in the network. "Each design decision involves a complex set of trade-offs", and ultimately determines the degree of decentralisation of a DLT (Rauchs et al. 2018).

What Is Decentralisation?

In the literature, the term "decentralisation" is as poorly defined as the term "distributed ledger technology", noted by Vitalik Buterin in 2017 (Vitalik Buterin 2017). According to Buterin, there are three types of (de)centralisation: (1) architectural (de)centralisation—how many computers compose the network, and how many computers may fail before the system does not function?; (2) political (de)centralisation—how many individuals or groups control the computers within the network?; and (3) logical (de)centralisation—do the interface and data structures resemble a single monolithic block or an amorphous swarm? (Buterin). The Cambridge Report takes the concept of "control" to its logical conclusion and offers a precisely focused definition. DLT systems have multiple layers, and multiple processes involving multiple decisions made by multiple actors. Decentralisation hence is not a "binary property" but rather a fluid concept dependent upon examining the factors contributing both to centralisation and decentralisation respecting functions taking place within a DLT. To assess whether a DLT system is centralised or decentralised requires identifying the "power dynamics" acting out at each layer of the system, and how power has "spill over" effects between and among layers. In this regard, a distributed system must be distinguished from a decentralised system. In a distributed system, data storage and operations upon data are "divided into parts" and spread across multiple nodes. A distributed process may be centralised by relying upon central coordination of the nodes' activities. By contrast, a decentralised system lacks central coordination; each node in the system has exactly the same data and conducts operations upon that data independently and redundantly. Consequently, the degree of decentralisation in a DLT results from design choices at each layer (Fig. 11.5).

Use Case: Bitcoin

Satoshi Nakamoto's Problem and Solution

In his 2008 seminal paper, Nakamoto observed that commerce on the Internet had "come to rely almost exclusively upon financial institutions serving as trusted third

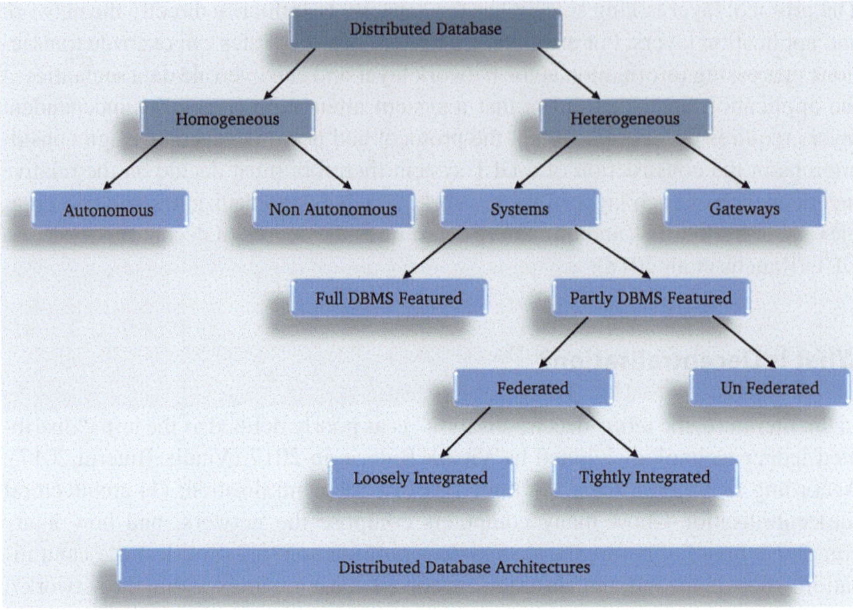

Fig. 11.5 Different design of DLT. (Source: PACKT)

parties to process electronic payments" (Satoshi Nakamoto 2008). The "trust-based model" suffered from the inability to conduct "completely non-reversible transactions" because financial institutions, committed to resolving disputes, had the authority to reverse transactions leading to increased transaction costs and making impractical small/micro-payments. The threat of reversal also spread the need for trust and required users of the payment system to provide unnecessary and invasive personal information to mitigate distrust. Consequently, Nakamoto sought to establish "an electronic payment system based on cryptographic proof instead of trust" (Nakamoto). Under his scheme, two parties transact directly with one another without a third-party financial institution, and transactions are computationally infeasible to reverse. He proposed "a peer-to-peer distributed timestamp server to generate computational proof of the chronological order of transactions to eliminate trusted third parties and solve the "double spend" problem" (Nakamoto).

A Bitcoin blockchain is open, transparent, and permission-less. Any person may join the network and have a copy of the ledger allowing that participant to see individual transactions and blocks. All copies of the ledger are synchronised across all nodes to guarantee the existence of a valid and single ledger. A special type of node called a "miner" makes certain that changes to the ledger are authentic. Bitcoin uses a consensus algorithm called "proof of work" to maintain the ledger. When a new block is broadcast to the network, miners compete, using computational power and electricity, to solve a mathematical puzzle. The first miner to solve the problem broadcasts the result to the entire network. When consensus is reached among nodes, the new block is added to the chain and the miner is rewarded with a certain number of Bitcoins, plus transaction fees. In the context of distributed ledger technology, consensus is a process of reaching agreement among disparate actors on the network as to a "common truth". The "common truth" is reached by adherence to protocols and mathematics. In other words, we do not trust individual actors on the distributed network to reach agreement outside of the required protocols and mathematics. This methodology allows consensus or agreement upon a "common truth" without having to trust participants on the distributed network. "We trust the general protocol and the math behind it". This leads to a system of "trust – without trust".

Application of Cambridge Report DLT Framework to Bitcoin

The question is whether the Bitcoin Network constitutes a DLT within the meaning of the Cambridge Report. Applying the Cambridge definition of DLT to the Bitcoin Network reveals that the Bitcoin Network is the DLT *par excellence* remaining true to May's, Dai's, and Szabo's anarchist dream. We begin by examining the Bitcoin architecture.

The Protocol Layer

"Bitcoin was released as open-source software in the form of a reference client (now Bitcoin Core)" and constitutes a self-sufficient system (Rauchs et al. 2018). Bitcoin does not have a formal protocol specification; "the reference client specifies the rules [that have] tended to be followed by alternative client implementations (e.g., bitcoind, libbitcoin, Bcoin)" (Ibid). The governance is anarchic since Bitcoin lacks formal procedures to adopt changes to the protocol. Participants run the reference client that implements the sets of rules they deem valid. Proposed changes to the protocol require "global coordination to convince nodes to upgrade to the new client version" (Ibid). Nodes refusing to upgrade cause a split in the network leading to a new DLT system where both systems share the same history up until the point of the fork. Competing sub-networks fragment the value of the network to participants. Users are incentivised to upgrade to the new protocol. The reference client "Bitcoin Core" has a standardised process to discuss protocol changes, but the proposals are not mandatory. Changes are effective only if the majority of nodes agree to upgrade the client software.

The Network Layer

Communications: Bitcoin is completely open with unrestricted access. Anyone can join, leave and re-join by downloading and running the client software. All data is broadcast to anyone on the network. Full nodes have identical copies of unconfirmed transactions in their memory pool and confirmed transactions in the form of the blockchain. Anyone can initiate a transaction. End users external to the network use "wallets" to make transactions; these transactions are sent to nodes that then broadcast the transaction to the entire network.

Processing of Transactions: Miners or "record producers" (Cambridge Report) assemble and order individual transactions into candidate "blocks" and attach a valid proof of work. The valid solution to the specified hash output requires the miner to expend substantial computational power or hash power. Miners are incentivised to build blocks by the prospect of economic reward in transaction fees and new units of Bitcoin.

Validation: Full nodes verify the validity of unconfirmed transactions twice. First, transactions are scrutinised before being broadcast to the network, since non-scrutinised transactions, if broadcast, would squander network resources. Second, full nodes verify blocks that now include the confirmed transactions by checking the hash. If the block passes the test, "the node updates its journal and broadcasts the block to connected peers" (Rauchs). Because settlement in Bitcoin is probabilistic, in practice merchants wait for six confirmations to consider a transaction finalised. Six confirmations mean waiting for six blocks to be built on top of the block containing the transaction in question.

The Application Layer

Data: The main purpose of Bitcoin is the secure transfer of the native asset – Bitcoin. It also can be used to timestamp data and to run simple smart contracts.

Journal: "Bitcoins exist exclusively within the boundaries of the Bitcoin system as entries in the Bitcoin ledger." The records are entirely internal values and are unrelated to any external system. Every transaction occurs on chain.

Recall that the Cambridge definition of DLT systems set forth five criteria: (1) the system provides a means for independent participants to establish a consensus around, (2) authoritative ordering of signed transactions whereby (3) these records are persistent and replicated across multiple nodes, and (4) linked together by cryptographic hashes to make them tamper-evident for purposes of establishing, (5) an authoritative version of the records. Bitcoin satisfies all five criteria. The system consists of shared recordkeeping, multi-party consensus, and independent validation. In addition, the system can detect alterations and is tamper-resistant.

Mechanics of the Bitcoin Network

The Coin

The existential properties of Nakamoto's electronic coin, Bitcoin (BTC), are first addressed. Nakamoto defined "an electronic coin as a chain of digital signatures", reminiscent of Szabo's candidate strings though Szabo is not referenced in the paper. This definition of a coin differs substantially from a physical coin since the electronic coin contains a record of its history. The first observation is Nakamoto's complete reliance upon public/private key cryptography and hashing, clearly drawing upon Adam Back's "hashcash", to construct a method of transferring a coin from one owner to the next. The genesis coin owned by "Owner 0" has a previous hash, inferring the coin came into existence by computational proof. One Bitcoin owner transfers a coin to someone else by signing a hash of the previous transaction and the public key of the next owner (Coinbase). In this example, the owner of the genesis coin transferred ownership to "Owner 1" by using his/her private key to sign the hash of the prior transaction and the public key of the next owner, here Owner 1, and appending this data to the end of the coin. "A payee can verify the signatures to verify the chain of ownership" (Nakamoto). The electronic coin is totally unlike a physical coin because the electronic coin contains a record of its entire transfer and ownership history. In effect, the electronic coin has memory. Nakamoto's illustration is reproduced to demonstrate transfer of coin ownership (Fig. 11.6).

Nakamoto realised that his transfer system did not solve the double spend problem. A payee could not be certain that prior transferors of the coin did not transfer or attempt to transfer the coin to another party. The solution is the public ledger comprising "a single history of the (chronological) order" in which transactions were received and verified by participants maintaining the ledger. In this system, all transactions are broadcast to the network. When a majority of nodes agree to a single history of the order in which the transactions were received, the transactions are confirmed and made practically impossible to reverse. Nakamoto states, "the earliest transaction is the one that counts, so we don't care about later transactions to double-spend" (Nakamoto). Borrowing from Haber and Stornetta, referenced in the paper, Nakamoto acknowledged that his solution required a timestamp server. A timestamp server takes a hash of "a block of items" to be timestamped and then the hash is broadcast to the network. The timestamp proves that all data in the hash could not have been created *after* the hash was published. Each timestamp also

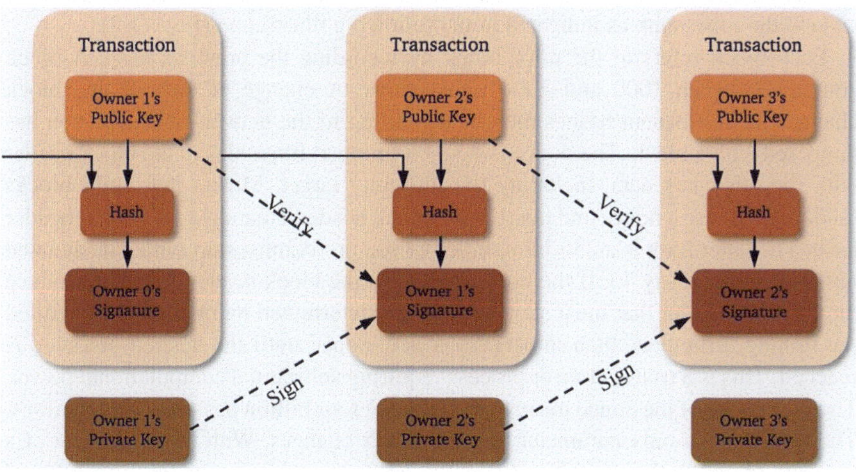

Fig. 11.6 Coin transactions. (Source: Satoshi Nakamoto)

includes previous timestamps in its hash. This forms a chain of records of the order in which transactions took place. Transactions timestamped on the blockchain and mathematically related to previous ones are practically irreversible and tamper-resistant. Thus blockchains are born.

Architecture of the Bitcoin Blockchain

A blockchain starts with a genesis block. Subsequent blocks are linked to one another through cryptographic hashes to prevent alteration and fraud and to establish a ledger containing a history of legitimate transactions. This architecture relies upon several concepts some already touched upon: digital timestamps, hashes, digital signatures, and consensus algorithms. A "digital timestamp" provides strong legal evidence "that the contents of work existed at a point-in-time and has not changed since that time". (Digistamp.com)[1] A "digital timestamp" creates "a unique identifier, or fingerprint, for the file" called a SHA hash. (Ibid.) A hash is a mathematically calculated number that is virtually impossible to recreate. Even if one character in the message is altered, a different hash output is produced. The hash ordinarily consists of 256 characters. This is a large number 2^{256} making an inverse infeasible. The probability is $1/2^{30}$ or 1/1,000,000,000. The term "digital signature" comprises a pair of keys: a private key (sk) and a public key (pk). A digital signature cannot be forged unless the owner loses his/her private key. The private key encrypts the message. The signature is a function of the message and sk, producing a signature consisting of digits. When the intended receiver of the message obtains the message, the receiver uses the public key to decrypt the message. The verification process comprises the function (message, signature, pk) and the output is T/F. If true, then the receiver is certain that the message was sent by the person who signed it with the private key.

A block consists of: (1) block #, (2) transaction root, (3) previous hash, (4) nonce, and (5) the timestamp as indicated in the following illustration (Fig. 11.7):

Each block refers to the prior block by recording the previous hash. A block contains between 1000 and 3000 transactions. A change of data in one block changes all subsequent hashes thereby signalling to the network that a person has tampered with a block. The nonce is a 32-bit number. It remains in the block header with the other key data, including the difficulty target. Miners that build blocks randomly choose a nonce and put it in the block header, creating a new block header hash. The latter hash is a 256-bit number whose prefix must start with a designated number of zeros, say 40. If the nonce posted in the block header does not produce the 256-bit number that must start with the predetermined number of zeros (called the mining difficulty), then miners try a new nonce until the desired outcome is reached. This is a trial-and-error process requiring substantial computational power. The 32-bit size of the nonce means that there are four billion possible combinations. The nonce is the only parameter that the miner changes. With the consensus of a majority of nodes, the miner that finds the "golden nonce" announces the result and adds that block to the blockchain.

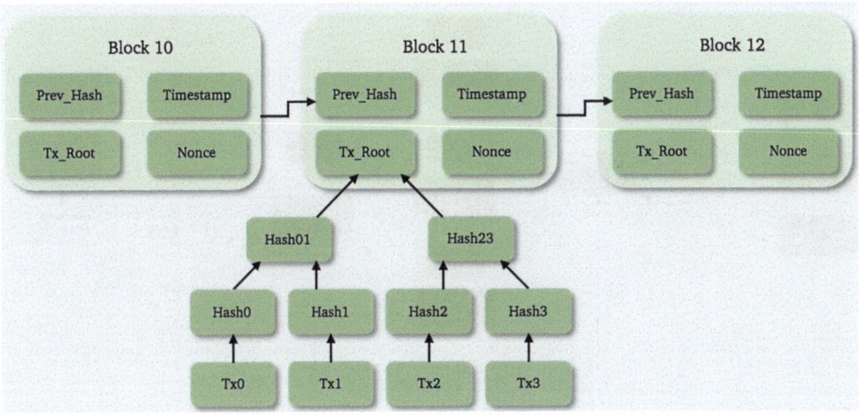

Fig. 11.7 Building blocks with nonces. (Source: Ben Whittle, coincentral.com, 2018)

Mining Difficulty

The Bitcoin protocol sets the difficulty of "mining". The difficulty consists in finding the hash starting with the fixed number of zeros. Increasing the level of difficulty requires increasing the number of starting zeros, say from 40 to 41. Decreasing the level of difficulty requires the opposite operation. Computational difficulty adjusts every 2016 blocks, about every two weeks. The Bitcoin protocol also assumes blocks are added at a rate of every ten minutes. Adjustments to "difficulty" aim to make certain that blocks are produced at the rate of one per ten minutes; currently about 120 blocks per day. Bitcoin currently uses the SHA-2 algorithm to produce hashes, as SHA-2 is the strongest existing algorithm. Nakamoto capped the total amount of Bitcoin at 21 million coins, expected to be mined by 2140. The amount Bitcoin miners receive to validate blocks is cut in half every 210,000 blocks. As of 2020, a miner receives a reward of 6.25 BTC.

Having reviewed the architecture and mining process of Bitcoin, it is timely to depict the mechanics of a Bitcoin transaction between two parties. Assume Alice wants to transfer 50 BTC to Bob. Both Alice and Bob have public and private keys. The term "VKa" is Alice's public or verification key; "VKb" is Bob's public key. The term "SKa" is Alice's private or signature key; "SKb" is Bob's private key. Assume further that Alice has 65 BTC in her wallet derived from three prior transactions: 25 BTC from Bill, 20 BTC from Carol, and 20 BTC from Nancy. Alice applies a series of cryptographic hash functions to each previous transaction and then cryptographically hashes the group of hashes with her Ska. Anyone on the network can verify the chain of ownership of the coins. Alice starts a transaction to transfer 50 BTC to Bob, with 14 BTC back to her. Alice takes all data and digitally signs it using her private key Ska, and appends the contents to the transaction record. One coin is reserved to pay a miner a transaction fee. The following illustration reproduces the transaction (Fig. 11.8):

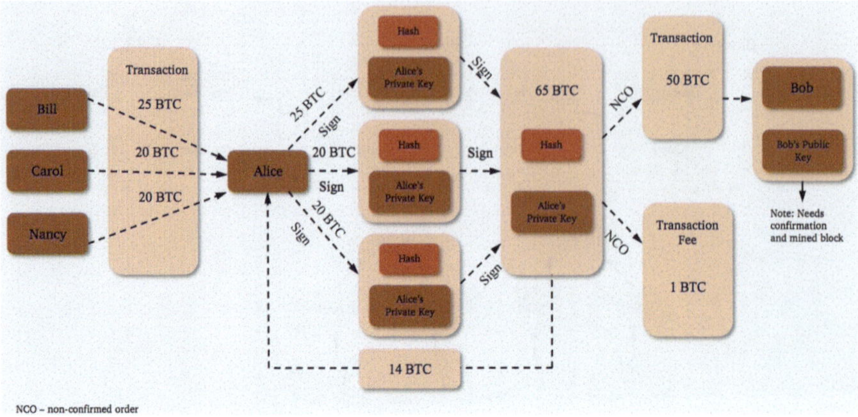

Fig. 11.8 Illustrative coin transactions. (Source: Author)

Bitcoin Network: Vulnerability

In a "51%" attack a person or group attempts to control 51% of the computational or hashing power of the network attempting to change the hashes in all previous blocks to make the link look valid. The resources required to re-engineer the ledger outweigh the economic expenditure required to accomplish the fraud. Therefore, economic incentives deter malicious nodes. In the event of a "fork", the general rule in Bitcoin is that the longest blockchain is the valid ledger. Longest refers not to number of blocks but the chain that has expended the most power or proof of work.

Ethereum

Ethereum is "an open-source, globally decentralised computing infrastructure that executes programs called *smart contracts*" (Andreas M. Antonopoulos 2015). In 1996, Nick Szabo defined a smart contract as: "a set of promises, specified in digital form, including protocols within which the parties perform on these promises" (Nick Szabo 1996). Like Bitcoin, Ethereum organises transactions in blocks, and "nodes", called validators, ensure that the blockchain synchronises and stores the system's state changes. Ethereum has a native cryptocurrency called "*ether* to meter and constrain execution resource costs" (Antonopoulos). Unlike Bitcoin, Ethereum's purpose exceeds a currency payment network. It is "designed to be a general-purpose programmable blockchain that runs a virtual machine capable of executing code of arbitrary and unbounded complexity" (Antonopoulos). Early attempts to achieve this objective tried to build on top of Bitcoin. However, Bitcoin-imposed constraints prevented broader applications from running on this hybrid model forcing developers to produce workarounds, go off-chain or start to build a new blockchain. In 2013, Vitaly Buterin published a "white paper" proposing Ethereum.[2] In 2015, Buterin and Gavin Wood co-founded Ethereum, a next-generation blockchain after Bitcoin. Ethereum is the great innovation to solve the problem of going beyond the constraints of Bitcoin.

The core invention is the Ethereum Virtual Machine (EVM). The EVM is a Turing-complete 256-bit virtual machine. The question arises what does "Turing-complete" mean? Alan Turing was an English mathematician who in 1936 created a "mathematical model of a computer consisting of a state machine that manipulates symbols by reading and writing them on sequential memory" (Antonopoulos). A Turing machine is a hypothetical machine that can simulate any computer algorithm, no matter its complication. Hence, a Turing-complete machine is simply one that simulates any Turing machine. A Turing-complete system has a significant limitation: there are classes of problems that are unsolvable. For example, Turing proved the "halting problem": it is not possible to determine whether any given program will stop running.

The EVM has the "ability to execute a stored program while reading and writing data to memory" thereby making it a Turing-complete system (Antonopoulos). Ethereum's ground-breaking innovation is combining "the general-purpose computing architecture of a stored-program computer with a decentralized blockchain, thereby creating a single state world computer" (Antonopoulos). Contrary to the implication of the term "Turing-complete" as a machine with a special feature, Turing-completeness poses risks in open access systems because of the "halting problem". For example, if a printer, a Turing-complete machine, freezes, it can be turned off and then on again, but that is not possible in a public blockchain. Ethereum answered this challenge by introducing a mechanism called "gas". When the EVM runs a smart contract, it gauges every instruction or execution deployed by the smart contract. Each activity is assigned a cost in terms of "gas". When a "smart contract" is executed on the EVM, it is introduced with proof of purchasing sufficient "gas" to complete its purpose. The EVM terminates the program if the "gas" consumed exceeds the "gas" available in the transaction. "Gas" is purchased with Ethereum's native asset called "ether". The price of "gas" is not fixed, but must be purchased for each transaction. Any unused "gas" is refunded to the sender.

Started as a way to make a general-purpose blockchain, Ethereum quickly expanded to become a platform for programming DApps. The latter represent a broader concept than smart contracts. In the Ethereum system, a smart contract refers to immutable computer programs that run deterministically on the EVM. By contrast, a DApp is a smart contract wrapped with a web user interface. "More broadly, a DApp is a web application that is built on top of open, decentralized, peer-to-peer infrastructure services" (Antonopoulos). DApps are meant to take the World Wide Web to its next evolutionary level called *web3*. There are many types of "DApps". I discuss DeFi DApps that allow anyone to create stablecoins (coins whose value is tied to the US dollar), take out a loan, lend out money, and "implement automated, advanced investment strategies" (Sid Coelho-Prabhu 2020). Since smart contracts are the root of DeFi DApps, once deployed to the blockchain, DeFi DApps run themselves with minimal human intervention limited to upgrade or fix bugs but unmanaged by any financial institution. DeFi DApps are global from time of creation making them available to anyone on the world. There are no gatekeepers.

"Users interact directly with the smart contracts from their crypto wallets" (Coelho-Prabhu). Ethereum's DeFi DApp holds promise to take financial services away from banks and put it squarely in the hands of the public.

Ethereum encompasses other features to expand its use and functionality. Ethereum uses "oracles" to load information extrinsic to the network onto the network. "In the context of blockchains, an oracle is a system that can answer questions that are external to Ethereum, such as the price of gold or capital markets data, in a trustless way" and place them on the platform to be executed by a smart contract (Antonopoulos). Oracles can be thought of "as a mechanism for bridging the gap between the off-chain world and smart contracts, allowing smart contracts to enforce contractual relationships based on real world events and data" (Antonopoulos). Some oracles provide information through an external "trusted source" such as governments or universities. This data cannot be provided without trust, as its truth depends on appeal to the authority of the source.

Further versatility is found in Ethereum's use of tokens. The word "token", derived from Old English, means a symbol or sign. In the context of blockchains, "tokens" often represent assets, currency, or access rights. Issuers often provide tokens to raise funds in what is called a "crowdfunding campaign", usually funds needed to start a new business. The initial coin offering (ICO) is a poignant example. An ICO is a derivative of initial public offering (IPO), a highly regulated activity. The promoter offers to exchange tokens for ether. Ether has a value determined by the open market; by contrast, the token may have no established market value. The underlying representations of the issuer usually in a white paper are key. Setting aside the economic and legal effects, tokens may be exchanged for ether on Ethereum.

Ethereum's Proof of Work

Ethash is Ethereum's proof-of-work (PoW) algorithm. It is an evolution and fusion of algorithms developed by Buterin called "Dagger" and Thaddeus Dryja's called Hashimoto. Ethash depends upon analysis of a large dataset known as a directed acyclic graph or "DAG". The "DAG" had an initial size of 1 GB but it will increase slowly and linearly being updated approximately every 125 hours. The purpose of "DAG" is to make PoW dependent upon "maintaining a large frequently accessed data structure" (Antonopoulos). The objective was to reduce the concentration of "mining power" held by industrial mining operations by reducing the speed needed to resolve a PoW to a magnitude no greater than an average GPU (graphics processing unit). Reduction of speed decentralised mining power since any person with a GPU could participate in the mining process. Exercising a monopoly of mining power undermines the security of the consensus algorithm. In any event, Ethereum plans to transition to proof of stake.

Ethereum 2.0 (Serenity)

Since its inception in 2015, Ethereum has undergone numerous upgrades. The latest version, Ethereum 2.0, called Serenity is expected to launch on 1 December 2020 in three phases. The main differences are switching from PoW to proof of stake (PoS) and improving scalability, the ability of a system to react to different quantities of demand without losing any capacity. Serenity also upgrades the virtual machine using "ewasm", Ethereum WebAssembly, where ewasm aims to run code in the browser resulting in execution at native speed (Bashir 2020). We look at select features of Ethereum 2.0. Presently, Ethereum can process 13–15 transactions per second compared to Visa at 20,000 transactions per second. If Ethereum wants to replace Visa payments with digital currency, it must increase its capacity. "Plasma" is one of Ethereum's scalability solutions. Plasma conducts off-chain transactions while relying on the Ethereum blockchain. In effect, Plasma creates "child blockchains" called blockchain trees; there is no limit to the number that may be created, and they are all tied in hierarchical form to the Ethereum blockchain.[3]

Serenity also introduces "Casper" replacing proof of work with proof of stake. The concept is that proof of work wastes energy and computing power. There are two implementations of Casper: friendly finality gadget (FFG) and correct by construction (CBC). FFG combines proof of work with proof of stake serving as an "off-ramp" to get people to change to pure proof of stake. CBC is solely proof of stake. The consensus system of proof of stake requires miners to put up a deposit in ether to obtain the right to validate blocks. If the validation is fraudulent, the miner loses its deposit thereby taking away incentives to cheat. In addition, two-thirds of the validators must reach consensus on the transaction. In proof of work, the validators must always be online.

Another innovation is called the "beacon chain". The beacon chain is a proof-of-stake chain running parallel to Ethereum's proof-of-work chain. The beacon chain sits between the Ethereum blockchain and the shards, explained below. "It is like a connective tissue providing a heartbeat. A smart-contract on the current Ethereum blockchain will allow validators to participate in the proof-of-stake protocol by taking deposits of 32 Ether" (Nirolution 2018). Nodes that made deposits are put into the pending validator set on the beacon chain; participating nodes may become validators. The beacon chain then "generates a random number for a random sample of validators for block proposal and voting duties" (Ibid). Random sampling prevents validators from colluding to influence the system. In effect, the beacon chain manages the validators conduct. "Sharding" is similar to adding new chains to process more transactions and therefore solve the scalability problem. In the Ethereum environment, transactions must be processed in distinct order; different transactions cannot be processed at the same time. Each shard is a "separate blockchain with its own state and transaction history" (Ibid). Instead of putting the burden of validating transactions on a single blockchain, sharding splits the chain into smaller networks, each containing specific accounts and designated validators, to speed up the process of block validation. When Serenity is implemented, Ethereum has the capacity to compete with Visa, Mastercard, and American Express and revolutionise payment by digital currency without a trusted third-party intermediary. Ethereum 2.0 "pledges to be capable of handling up to 100,000 transactions per second" (Bybit Learn 2020).

Hyperledger

In 2015, the Linux Foundation, in conjunction with multi-national companies, established the launch of Hyperledger. Multi-national companies—for example, IBM, J.P. Morgan, Microsoft, Intel, and Huawei—expressed an interest in understanding and exploring the potential of blockchain space and approached the Linux Foundation to coordinate efforts. Hyperledger now has more than 230 organisations as members covering well-known industry leaders from Airbus to VMware, 15 projects, and 28,000 participants. According to the Linux Foundation, "Hyperledger is an open source collaborative effort created to advance cross-industry blockchain technologies" (The Hyperledger White Paper Working Group 2018). The Linux Foundation sees the future of enterprise-level blockchains as modular, open source platforms that are easy to use. The collaborative effort has several advantages over siloed efforts: reduction of costs, elimination of duplication, and increased quality of code.

Hyperledger has adopted "open governance", meaning that technical decisions are taken by a "group of community-elected developers drawn from a pool of active participants" (Linux White Paper). The "Technical Steering Committee" (TSC) decides which projects to sponsor and develop. The TSC is supported by legal and marketing teams. While Hyperledger relies upon volunteer software developers, the projects are driven by large industries in technology, finance, banking, and manufacturing. As of October 2020, Hyperledger consisted of more than 15 projects, many of which were distributed ledger frameworks. The "Hyperledger Modular Approach" looks as follows (Fig. 11.9):

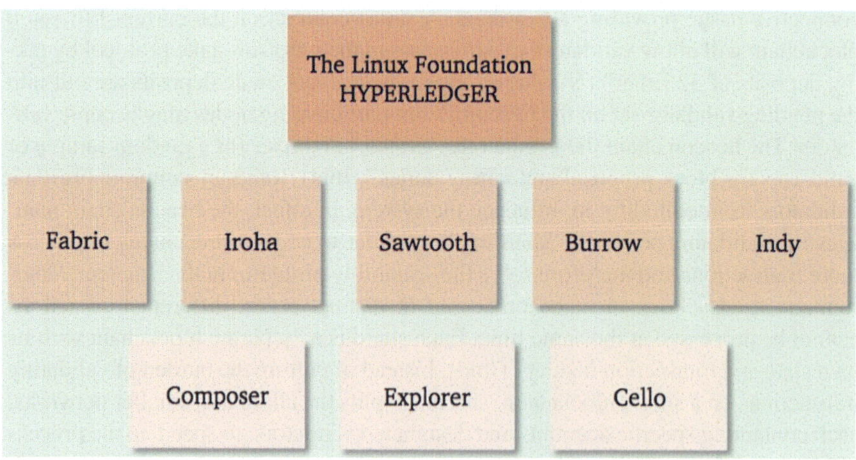

Fig. 11.9 Hyperledger Modular Approach. (Source: Linux foundation)

Hyperledger "is a unique platform that is developing permissioned distributed ledger framework specifically designed for enterprises, including those in industries with strong compliance requirements" (Kris Bennet et al., n.d.). Hyperledger projects must be: modular, highly secure, interoperable, cryptocurrency-agnostic, and complete with APIs. Modular means that common building blocks can be used across multiple projects to avoid the waste of "reinventing the wheel". Security follows from the nature of enterprise-level blockchains likely to involve high-value transactions or sensitive data. Interoperability is key since Hyperledger is designed to connect distinct blockchains. "Most smart contracts and applications should be portable across many different blockchain networks" (Linux White Paper). Hyperledger will never issue a cryptocurrency since Hyperledger exists to create blockchain software for enterprises. However, the design philosophy does not prohibit creation or management of coins. APIs enable "external clients and applications to interface quickly and easily with Hyperledger's core distributed ledger infrastructure" (Linux White Paper).

Use Case: Bank Loan

Assume an individual wants to borrow money from a bank to purchase real property. The problem: banks seek to lend but must distinguish between good and bad borrowers. This vetting of applications requires banks to collect personally identifiable information (PII) from anyone seeking to obtain a loan. The documents cover a broad range: passports, tax returns, income information, employment verification, and credit score, to name a few items. From the customer perspective the process is agonising and must be repeated with each potential lender. Using a combination of modular Hyperledger projects can facilitate the process.

Hyperledger Indy solves the identity problem. Hyperledger Indy "is a distributed ledger purpose-built for doing distributed identity" (Bennett). Identity is a critical issue not only for distributed ledger technology but also for data shared on the Internet. Hyperledger Indy is designed to transfer control of your personal identity from third parties, like financial entities, back to you. "If you have an identity, it belongs to you, and only you, and no one can pull the plug on you" (Bennett). One of the main use cases of Hyperledger Indy "is to create a global public utility for identity that's being created by the Sovrin Foundation" (Bennet). The consequence is a paradigmatic shift in control over personal identity. When implemented, you "own" your identity and decide how to share that identity, composed of silos of data, with third parties on an as-needed basis. "Applicants can share only the information the banks need to make a decision" (Linux White Paper). "Anyone seeking a loan can apply to 100 different lenders in milliseconds, without placing any sensitive personal data into a hackable database" (Linux White Paper). Rather than disclosing PII, applicants use "zero-knowledge proofs" to verify their PII. Banks can lend with confidence of repayment while applicants can safeguard their identity.

A "zero-knowledge proof" is a method to present the "correctness of an assertion without revealing the actual proof" (Saarland University 2014). Following protocol, we start with an example taken from Wikipedia. Assume that Peggy knows the secret word to open a magic door in a cave that is circular in shape. There is an entrance and in the middle of the cave tunnel there is the "magic door" splitting the paths of the cave into two parts labelled "A" and "B". Victor wants to know if Peggy really knows the secret word, but Peggy does not want to tell him. So, Peggy enters the cave and begins to walk along one side of the circular cave, say the "A" side, and then is blocked by the door. If Peggy has the key, she can open the door and walk out the cave using the path labelled "B". Victor stands at the entrance to the Cave and yells out, in random order, which path—"A" or "B"—he wants Peggy to use to enter the cave and to exit the cave. If Peggy knows the secret word, she can always return along the desired path. Peggy has proved that she knows the magic word without revealing the word to Victor. Zero-knowledge proofs have varied practical applications in the verification data without revealing the data.

Other Hyperledger projects can improve on the use case. Hyperledger Burrow, originally contributed by Monax and co-sponsored by Intel, is a modular blockchain with a permissioned "smart contract interpreter partially developed to the specification of the Ethereum Virtual Machine (EVM)" (hyperledger.org). Hyperledger Burrow fills a distinct role within the Hyperledger ecosystem. It is explicitly designed to one thing well: "run EVM style smart contracts in a permissioned environment. The codebase is fast, easy to use and simple" (Hyperledger Burrow).[4] Hence, Hyperledger Burrow can turn the loan contract into a smart contract. Hyperledger Fabric offers a modular architecture, allowing components such as consensus and membership services to be plug and play. Entities conduct confidential transactions without channelling information through a central authority. Hyperledger Fabric supports permissioned deployments, and leverages container technology to host smart contracts. Consequently, Hyperledger Fabric "can drive a membership system by linking to the pre-existing, self-sovereign identity on the loan application" (Linux White Paper).

Use Case: Supply Chain Management

Hyperledger Sawtooth Lake "is a modular enterprise blockchain platform for building, deploying, and running distributed ledgers" (Kelly Olson, Mic Bowman, James Mitchell, Shawn Amundson, Dan Middleton, Cian Montgomery).[5] Sawtooth Lake assures the distribution of ledgers and the security of smart contracts. It uses yet another consensus algorithm called "proof of elapsed time" (PoET). Proof of elapsed time follows the following strategy: (1) each participant in the blockchain waits a random amount of time, and (2) the first participant to finish waiting is appointed leader of the new block. Two conditions must be met: the lottery winner must demonstrate the time chosen was randomly selected, and second, the lottery winner must actually finish the waiting time before starting to validate the block. Hyperledger Sawtooth Lake may be used to demonstrate the provenance of "goods and assets" from fish to diamonds so that the end user is assured of origin, quality, transport; in other words, a record of the entire supply chain.

Take a seafood supply chain for example. Sensors are attached as soon as fish are caught to record data such as physical location, temperature, and humidity. The data is recorded in a ledger along with information obtained later down the supply chain line: "ownership, storage temperature, and transport company" (Linux White Paper). The traceability prototype captures the entire history of the fish from the time it is caught until the time it is purchased by the consumer (Fig. 11.10).

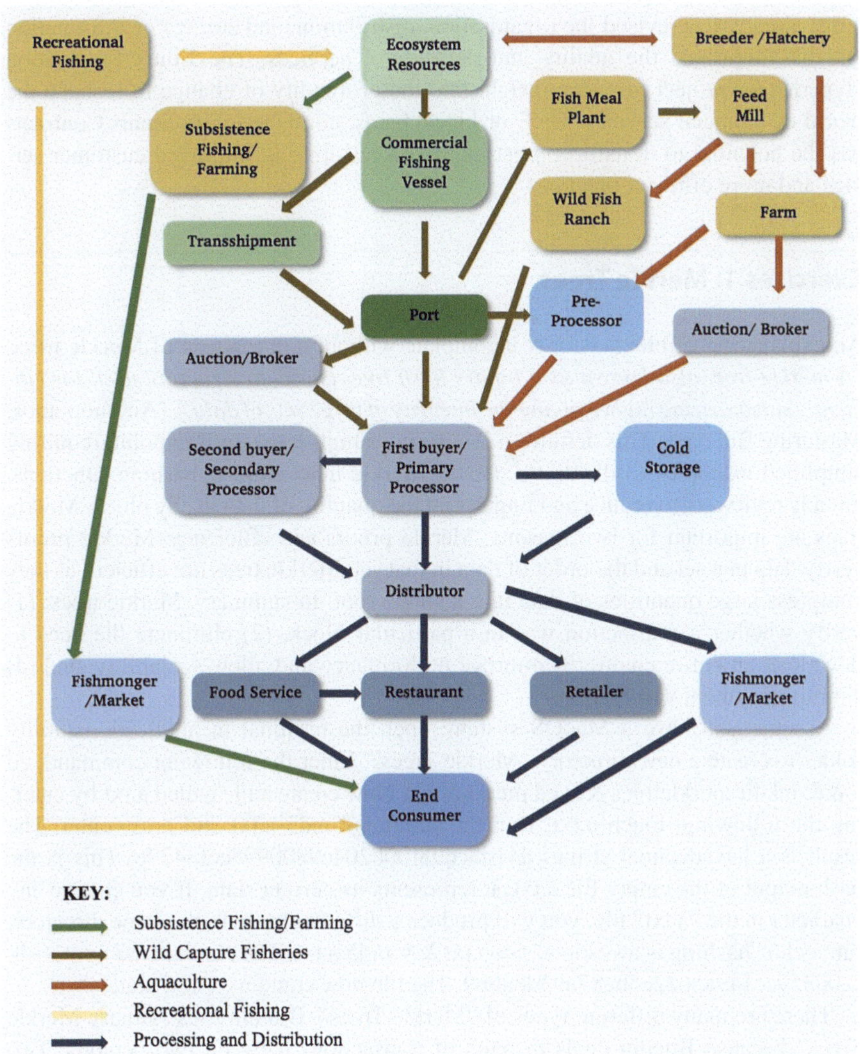

Fig. 11.10 The complexity of the seafood supply chain. (Source: Hyperledger White Paper v1.1 2018)

Conclusion

This chapter clarified the term "distributed ledger technology" using the work of the Cambridge Report. The definition then was applied to the Bitcoin Network to demonstrate that Bitcoin satisfied all sufficient and necessary conditions to constitute a DLT. The chapter then looked to subsequent "blockchain developments": Ethereum and Hyperledger, showing post-Bitcoin developments. Additional advancements inevitably will take place. Electronic ledger technology, applied to financial systems, already has revised the organisation, distribution, and storage of information and has improved the quality and delivery of services. The Linux Foundation Hyperledger project provides insight into the profundity of change to reshape the world of financial services. DLT, or blockchains, combined with Smart Contracts has the potential to transform most industries resulting in improved customer service and more efficient practices.

Exercises 1: Merkle Trees

An explanation of blockchain is incomplete without a discussion of Merkle trees. "*A merkle tree, also known as a binary hash tree, is a data structure used for efficiently summarizing and verifying the integrity of large sets of data*". (Antonopoulos, Mastering Bitcoin) "This definition is abstract, a high-level starting point, requiring simplified examples to illustrate." (Ibid.) Merkle trees employ hashing functions, already reviewed, to reduce and fingerprint the quantity of data in any block. Merkle trees are important for two reasons: Merkle proofs and efficiency. Merkle proofs verify data in a set and the order of data in that set. Merkle trees are efficient as they compress large quantities of data into a single root. In summary, Merkle trees: (1) verify whether a transaction was in a particular block, (2) eliminate the need to download an entire chain, (3) improve performance and allow scalability, and (4) simplify payment verification.

Assume you have a MacOS system: open the terminal in applications/utility folder to create a new directory "Merkle Trees". Enter the following command: cd ~ && mkdir merkletrees && cd merkletrees. Now create a file called a.txt by entering the following: touch a.txt. Run the command md5 a.txt and press enter. The result is a hexadecimal string: d41d8cd98f00b204e9800998ecf8427e. This is the hash output of the empty file a.txt; it represents its current state. If you change any character in the "a.txt" file, you will produce a different hash. In the same directory, run: echo "hashing is awesome" >> a.txt && md5 a.txt. The result is the new hash: ca00359cc149a5622c5ba87a93d8abb9. The file now contains a new state.

There are many different types of "Merkle Trees". Bitcoin uses "Binary Merkle Trees" because Bitcoin deals in pairs of transactions between two persons. Two inputs (transactions) are combined to produce one output. When multiple pairs are hashed and then combined with hash values of other pairs of transactions, we eventually obtain one hash value: the merkle tree root. Let's examine a Bitcoin tree structure:

We already have the hash value for a.txt abbreviated as ca00359. Open the terminal window and delete the previous text file a.txt and enter the following lines of code:

```
echo "Hello from a.txt" >> a.txt && md5 a.txt &&
echo "Hello from b.txt" >> b.txt && md5 b.txt &&
echo "Hello from c.txt" >> c.txt && md5 c.txt &&
echo "Hello from d.txt" >> d.txt && md5 d.txt
```

The result is the output:

```
MD5 (a.txt) = c95c68d91441ba192ada81c9cfb2abe7
MD5 (b.txt) = 80262782d5961c452eae5de9991af0fd
MD5 (c.txt) = 0bfe75f719adf6450bb8be8e10126383
MD5 (d.txt) = 10fa7f973f6ec6682e1a6f4570a89861
```

Next, we want to produce a single hash from the combined hashes of a.txt and b.txt, so we combine the two hashes into a single line of code: c95c68d91441ba192ada81c9cfb2abe780262782d5961c452eae5de9991af0fd. Then we run the md5 command to produce the following hash: c95c68d91441ba192ada81c9cfb2abe780262782d5961c452eae5de9991af0fd. We now need to run the md5 command again on this combined hash to produce the parent hash: md5 <<< "c95c68d91441ba192ada81c9cfb2abe780262782d5961c452eae5de9991af0fd". This function produces the parent hash: a3d71b58e08759e6245667fb6f4770b6, abbreviated "a3d71b5". If we repeat the process for c.txt and d.txt, we get the parent hash: 078791272b0b48b7bb7004ebc1b22123, abbreviated "078791". The last step is to combine the two parent hashes to obtain to produce the merkle root. When combined, run with the md5 command, the merkle root is: eaad1d42b754612a4249bcbd95f0b734, abbreviated "eaad1d4".

Exercise 2: Use Case for Hyperledger and/or Blockchain

Explain how Hyperledger/Blockchain may be deployed to improve post-trade processing of financial transactions. Alternatively explain how this technology may be used to simplify "repo transactions".

Notes

1. See, E-time Stamp, The On-line Notary at https://www.digistamp.com/technical/how-a-digital-time-stamp-works
2. The "white paper" as progressively developed is found here: https://github.com/ethereum/wiki/wiki/White-Paper#ethereum
3. A comprehensive explanation of the innovations in Serenity may be found at What is Serenity? Ethereum 2.0 explained! At https://nirolution.com/everything-about-ethereum-2-0/

4. The Linux Foundation Projects, Hyperledger Burrow at https://www.hyperledger.org/use/hyperledger-burrow
5. Kelly Olson, Mic Bowman, James Mitchell, Shawn Amundson, Dan Middleton, Cian Montgomery, Sawtooth: An Introduction, January 2018 at https://www.hyperledger.org/wp-content/uploads/2018/01/Hyperledger_Sawtooth_WhitePaper.pdf

Bibliography

Tobias Adrian and Tommaso Mancini-Griffoli, The Rise of Digital Money (2019 International Monetary Fund).

Andreas M. Antonopoulos, Mastering Bitcoin: Unlocking Digital Currencies (O'Reilly 2015).

Bank of International Settlements, Enhancing cross-border payments: building blocks of a global roadmap, Committee on Payments and Market Structures (July 2020).

Bybit Learn, Explained: What is Ethereum 2.0 (Serenity) & Its Importance, Nov. 26, 2020.

Imran Bashir, Mastering Blockchain (Packt> 3rd ed. 2020).

Vitalik Buterin, The Meaning of Decentralization (6 Feb. 2017) at https://medium.com/@VitalikButerin/the-meaning-of-decentralization-a0c92b76a274

Miguel Castro and Barbara Liskov, Practical Byzantine Fault Tolerance (1999).

Stuart Haber and W. Scott Stornetta, How to Time-Stamp a Digital Document, Journal of Cryptology, Vol. 3, No. 2 (1991).

Nick Szabo, Smart Contracts: Building Blocks for Digital Markets 1996.

Sid Coelho-Prabhu, A Beginner's Guide to Decentralized Finance (DeFi), Coinbase, Jan. 6, 2020.

Nirolution, What is an Ethereum Validator? ETH Validator Explained!, Sep. 13, 2018.

Leslie Lamport, Robert Shostak, and Marshall Pease, The Byzantine Generals Problem (1982).

The Linux Foundation, An Introduction to Hyperledger (2018).5. Neel Mehta, Adi Agashe, and Parth Detroja, *Bubble or Revolution* (Paravane Ventures 2020).

Satoshi Nakamoto, Bitcoin: A Peer-to-Peer Electronic Cash System (2008).

Michel Rauchs … Bryan Zhang, Distributed Ledger Technology Systems: A Conceptual Framework, University of Cambridge (2018).

Saarland University, Zero Knowledge Proofs, Great Ideas in Theoretical Computer Science (2014) at http://resources.mpi-inf.mpg.de/departments/d1/teaching/ss14/gitcs/notes6.pdf.

Dan Tapscott and Alex Tapscott, Blockchain Revolution: *How the Technology behind Bitcoin is Changing Money*, Business and the World (Penguin 2016).

Artificial Intelligence

12

Introduction

Artifical intelligence is a wide field composed of different domains of study. The base of AI reposes upon mathematics and programming. This chapter explains AI from a conceptual perspective and uses practical illustrations, thereby skirting mathematical and programming matters without diminishing its explanatory value. The chapter provides an overview of: [1] machine learning; [2] deep learning, [3] natural language processing, and [4] algorithmic trading, an application of AI to financial services.

AI is difficult to define, and a consensus has not been reached on using a single comprehensive definition. In 1956, John McCarthy coined the term "artificial intelligence" to capture the concept of "thinking machines". His proposal proceeded on the basis of the "conjecture that every aspect of learning or any other feature of intelligence can in principle be so precisely described that a machine can be made to simulate it" (John McCarthy, M.L. Minsky, N. Rochester, and C.E. Shannon 1955). Modern dictionary definitions focus upon AI as a subfield of computer science and speak of the ability of machines to imitate human intelligence, without becoming human. Industries provide specific definitions crafted around their business needs and applications: for example, Amazon, Google, IBM, and Facebook define the term "artifical intelligence" using inconsistent language.[1]

In general, "Artificial intelligence (AI) is the overarching discipline that covers anything related to making machines smart" (Sonix 2021).[2] If you make a physical object or software program smart, then that activity falls under the field of AI. More precisely, borrowing a definition from McKinsey Analytics, "AI is typically the ability of a machine to perform cognitive functions we associate with human monds, such as perceiving, reasoning, learning, and problem solving". Machine Learning (ML) is a subset of AI. ML refers to systems that can learn by themselves, subject to human oversight. ML is divided into discrete categories. "Most AI work now involves ML because intelligent behaviour requires considerable knowledge, and

J. JA Burke, *Financial Services in the Twenty-First Century*,
https://doi.org/10.1007/978-3-030-63967-9_12

learning is the easiest way to get that knowledge" (Sonix 2021) Deep learning (DL) is a sophisticated implemention of ML to develop a computer model of the human brain. Artificial neural networks use models of human neural networks to help computers learn. Natural language processing refers to machines that understand language and translate sentences from one language to another. Automated speech recognition uses computer hardware and software to identify and process a human voice. Algorithmic trading applies principles of AI to develop trading strategies for financial markets. We start with "machine learning", an immense field constituting one part of AI, and potentially the most significant source of innovation.

Machine Learning

A machine is "a mechanically, electrically, or electronically, operated device to perform a task" (Merriam Webster online dictionary); learning is "the activity or process of gaining knowledge or skill by studying, practicing, being taught, experiencing something" (Ibid). Machines learn by studying data to detect patterns for the purposes of classification, prediction, identification of unknown patterns and identification of anomalies or unexpected behaviour. The processes machines use to learn are called algorithms.[3] The question is what factors have permitted the advent of machine learning. Two factors mainly are responsible for the widespread adoption and development of machine learning: (1) archives holding immense collections of electronic data related to persons, financial transactions, biological information, and other data categories, and (2) the development of iterative computer programs called algorithms. An algorithm is a set of instructions designed to perform a specific task. "Different algorithms learn in different ways. As new data regarding observed responses or changes to the environment are provided to the machine, the algorithm's performance improves. Thereby resulting in increasing intelligence over time" (SAS Best Practices). These algorithms can observe large datasets, and identify patterns and relationships that cannot be identified by human beings. Critical to advances in machine learning were "big data" and computational power to process the data; both phenomena increased exponentially, and thus the ability of machines to learn increased exponentially.

Assuming a sufficient volume of data, machines detect patterns or apply known rules to a sufficient volume of data, and then: (1) categorize or catalogue as people or things, (2) predict likely outcomes or actions based on identified patterns, (3) identify formerly unknown patterns and relationships, or (4) detect anomalous or unexpected behaviours. "In this sense, algorithms learn from the past and use this learning to make valuable predictions about the future".[4] Three important data requirements are needed for a machine to learn. First, learning algorithms need large quantities of data, or examples, to provide reliable results. For example, supervised learning may require tens of thousands of examples. Second, since machine learning "aims to observe similarities or differences in data, the data can neither be too similar nor too random" (Keith McNulty 2018)Third, since machine learning "may operate in multi-dimensional space with each dimension associated with certain input variables" (Ibid), missing information creates empty space thereby preventing learning. Hence, the data must be complete.

There are four types of machine learning: (1) supervised, (2) semi-supervised, (3) unsupervised and (4) reinforcement learning. We start with supervised learning because it is frequently used in practice. Supervised learning starts with gathering data. "The data for supervised learning is a collection of pairs (input, output)" (Startup Engineer.IO 2021) That dataset comprises labelled examples. Each element of labelled examples is converted into a feature vector. "In machine learning feature vectors are used to represent numeric or symbolic characteristics, called features, of objects in a mathematical and easily analysable way" (Ibid). Machine learning "algorithms" require a numerical representation of objects to process information and to perform statistical analysis. An example of a "feature vector" is the "RGB" colour description that identifies a particular colour by specifying the amount of red, green, and blue in the colour. The feature vector would look like this: colour = (R, G, B). Inputs can be anything, for example, email messages, pictures, or sensor measurements. Outputs generally are real numbers, or labels (e.g. "spam", "not spam", "cat", or "dog"). In some cases, outputs are vectors, sequences of words, or other structures.

Supervised Learning

Supervised learning often is used to solve classification problems. Classification deals with teaching a machine to group together data by particular criteria. A common example is the detection of spam emails. A computer programmer may write a program to filter out spam emails. The training set comprises groups of spam-like emails labelled "spam" and groups of regular emails labelled "not-spam". The aim is to make an algorithm that can differentiate between spam email and regular email when the machine encounters an unlabelled new email. Tommi S. Jaakkala, professor of electrical engineering and computer science at MIT, uses prediction models to illustrate the process of supervised machine learning. Take the example of predicting movies a particular individual might like. The programmer enters data: movies liked and movies disliked. Assume the programmer provides synopses of these movies and labels them plus/minus one depending upon whether the movie is liked or disliked. The task of machine learning is to learn from these initial labelled datasets whether the individual would like one of tens of thousands of available movies. The learning process proceeds from the labelled data to accurate prediction. Practical examples of supervised learning are: (1) fraud detection, (2) risk assessment, (3) personalised marketing, (4) customer segmentation, and (5) image and speech recognition.

Supervised machine learning systems involve mapping from a set of inputs to a set of outputs. Examples follow (Fig. 12.1):

Input X	Output Y	Application
Voice Recording	Transcript	Speech Recognition
Historical Market Data	Future Market Data	Trading Bots
Photograph	Caption	Image Tagging
Drug Chemical Properties	Treatment Efficiency	Pharma R&D
Store Transaction Details	Is Transaction fraudulent?	Fraud Detection
Recipe Ingredients	Customer Reviews	Food Recommendations
Purchase Histories	Future Purchase Behaviour	Customer Retention
Car Locations and Speed	Traffic Flow	Traffic Lights
Faces	Names	Face Recognition

Fig. 12.1 Machine learning. (Source: Burkov)

Semi-supervised Learning

Semi-supervised learning falls between supervised learning where all data is hand-labelled, and unsupervised learning where all data is unlabelled. With one exception, semi-supervised machine learning is similar to supervised learning. The exception is that some data is labelled or tagged and other data is unlabelled or untagged. Semi-supervised learning is used when there is too much data to label or when the data contains subtle variations to deter the creation of a comprehensive set of examples. The algorithm thus is trained upon a combination of labelled and unlabelled data. The machine examines the "identified data" and then extrapolates or infers a function from the "unmarked data". One observer states, "The system doesn't figure out the right output, but it explores the data and can make inferences from datasets to describe the hidden structures from unlabelled data". (Expert.ai Team 2020)Semi-supervised is like having a teacher provide a student with a few concepts in class and then giving the student questions as homework based on similar concepts. Practical applications of semi-supervised machine learning are: (1) speech recognition, (2) web page classification, and (3) image recognition.

Unsupervised Learning

"Unsupervised learning deals with problems in which data doesn't have labels" (Andriy Burkov 2019). The absence of labels means that there is no "answer key" or "desired behaviour" for your model. Nevertheless, using specific algorithms, machines learn in an unsupervised context and build models that may be evaluated solely on the data as opposed to human judgment. Applying the algorithm to the unmarked data, the machine determines correlations by parsing data, drawing inferences, and clustering like things together. As the volume of data increases so does the intensity of machine learning.

Reinforcement Learning

The idea that we learn by interacting with our environment is probably the first to occur to us when we think about the nature of learning. When an infant plays, waves its arms, or looks about, it has no explicit teacher, but it does have a direct sensorimotor connection to its environment.

Reinforcement learning (RL) arguably is extremely close to the way a human being learns. RL creates an "agent" that interacts with its environment, receives positive or negative feedback for actions taken, and seeks to achieve goals. "Many of the core algorithms of reinforcement learning were originally inspired by biological learning systems" (Burkov). The "learning agent" is programmed to achieve explicit goals and objectives based upon a set of rules. The agent senses and experiences its environment and takes actions to maximise numerical rewards. The agent exploits its inherent rules to create a desired outcome. Not only must the agent exploit what it has already experienced to obtain a reward but also the agent must try new actions to determine whether they lead to a positive reward. It learns how to act within the context of its environment through a process of trial and error. The agent exercises judgment to achieve intended outcomes.

Take, for example, a master chess player. The master player is the learning agent, the game board is the environment, the rules are the rules of chess, and the objective is to win the game against an opponent. When the player makes a "move", "the choice is informed both by planning – anticipating possible replies and counter-replies – and by immediate, intuitive judgments of the desirability of particular positions and moves" (Burkov). This example illustrates reinforcement learning. The chess player, like a learning agent, is an "active decision-making agent interacting with its environment, within which the agent seeks to achieve a goal despite uncertainty about its environment". (Burkov)

Deep Learning

Deep learning is a subset of machine learning based on a network constructed to simulate the structure of the human brain. Deep learning relies upon progress in neuroscience. As neuroscientists learn more about the structure and functioning of "grey matter", data scientists may construct complicated networks and algorithms to reflect "human brain like" problem solving. The networks of algorithms are called artificial neural networks (ANNs). Deep learning requires a large quantity of high-quality data: unstructured and unlabelled. Differentiating between how a problem is solved by supervised learning, as opposed to deep learning, opens a gateway to understanding the latter. Assume the data consists of images of cats and dogs, and the problem is to train the machine to classify images correctly. In supervised learning, a data scientist structures or labels the pictures of dogs and cats defining specific features of both animals. This machine learning method is labour intensive. The algorithm "learns" upon the training set to distinguish between dogs and cats to correctly classify a new unlabelled image. "Deep learning networks ... take a different approach to solve this problem" (Hackernoon 2020) The machine is given images of cats and dogs, but the images are unstructured/unlabelled. The images pass through layers of the network. "The artificial neural networks using deep learning send the input (the data of images) through different layers of the network with each network hierarchically defining specific features of the image" (Ibid). "After the data is processed through layers within deep neural networks, the system finds the appropriate identifiers for classifying both animals from their images" (Ibid).

Natural Language Processing

The largest human-generated data source is unstructured text. According to an SAS report, 175 million pieces of text are generated each minute, providing an immense silo of data, and the amount is increasing exponentially. The unstructured text comprises tweets, posts, searches, text, and emails. Data scientists harvest this data by accessing the Internet and use unstructured text to teach machines to understand human language. "Natural language processing (NLP) is a branch of artificial intelligence that focuses on the understanding, interpretation and emulation of human language. NLP draws from many disciplines, including computer science and computational linguistics, in its pursuit to fill the gap between human communication and machine understanding" (SAS Visual Text Analytics 2018). NLP teaches a machine to analyse unstructured text, understand the text, and generate communication. NLP has produced popular applications such as chatbots, voice assistants like Siri, Alexa, and Cortana, voice-to-text applications like Dragon NaturallySpeaking and Google Docs, and computer-based translation applications like Google Translate. NLP has two constituent parts: natural language understanding (NLU) and natural language generation (NLG).

Applying AI to Markets: Algorithmic Trading

A logical application of AI to financial services is the development of programs to trade in financial instruments, based on machine and deep learning. Virtually all investors want to "beat the market": profit by purchasing undervalued securities and limit losses by selling overvalued securities. However, questions arise whether financial instruments are subject to mis-pricing and whether investors can "beat the market" in the short term. Arbitrageurs with millions to invest may profit from small pricing differences until the equilibrium price is reached. But arbitrage is beyond the financial means of average investors who are advised to park their money in a market index or investment fund and wait years to see the benefits of growth that, at best, likely will achieve historical returns of about 7% annually. A simple calculation shows the pessimistic environment confronted by the average investor: Assume an initial investment of $50,000, monthly additional savings of $200, and an annual return of 7%, it would take 36 years to reach $1 million. Ceteris paribus, this method is no way to become wealthy.

The Efficient Markets Hypothesis

A primary impediment to short-term trading gains is a theory called the efficient market hypothesis. In 1965, Eugene F. Fama published a paper entitled "The Behaviour of Stock-Market Prices" where he stated "on average, competition will cause the full effects of new information on intrinsic values to be reflected instantaneously in actual prices" (Fama 1965). The efficient market hypothesis (EMH) postulates that "the prices of securities in financial markets fully reflect all available information" (Mishkin 2018). However, before we examine the theory further, we need three definitions: market price, intrinsic value, and equilibrium price. The market price of a security is the current price of the stock. For example, on 10 September 2020, the price of a single share of Microsoft is $211.29. Intrinsic value is a more complex price as investors are assumed to know all information about the stock, including its expected future cash flows and risks. While prices of shares fluctuate around the "intrinsic value", the price changes with new projects and competition. The "equilibrium price" balances buy and sell orders at any given moment in time, that is, the quantity demanded and the quantity supplied are identical.

Let us look at the rates of return. The rate of return on a security equals the sum of the capital gain on the security (the change in price) plus any cash payments, divided by the purchase price. The formula is: $R = P_{t+1} - P_t + C/P_t$, where R = the rate of return on the security held for a particular period, say one year, P_{t+1} equals the price of the stock after the holding period, say one year, C = any cash payments received during the holding period, and P_t equals the original price paid for the security. P_t is known at the beginning of the period and we may assume the same of C; therefore, the only variable is the future price or P_{t+1}. If the expected price of the security at the end of the period is denoted P^e_{t+1}, the expected return is $R^e = P^e_{t+1} - P_t + C/P_t$. The efficient market hypothesis assumes that future prices are equal to optimal forecasts based on all available current information. In other words, the market expectations of future securities prices are rational, so that the expected return always equals the optimal return. The EMH states that it is impossible consistently to buy stocks that are undervalued or sell stocks that are overvalued. Profits and losses are caused by the direction of the market itself as a whole over a long period.

There are three forms of the EMH: strong-form efficiency, semi-strong efficiency and weak-form efficiency (Open Learn) The strong-form version implies that all information—both public and private—are reflected in the share price of the security, including inside information. Empirical research has produced results that contradict this form of EMH. The semi-strong version maintains that prices of shares incorporate all publicly available information but not private information. Prices reflect historical data, data published in firm financial statements, economic factors, and company announcements. The implication is that the investor is unable to profit from information available to everyone else. In addition, thousands of financial analysts following companies read obscure data or large amounts of data and thereby incorporate that information into the share price. Empirical research strongly supports the semi-strong version of EMH (Ibid) The weak-form version claims that prices reflect only historical data, not new or private information. Assuming that investors examine the identical information, one individual cannot profit from information to which everyone has access. The weak-form version supports decisions to buy or purchase based on "technical analysis". Empirical research has found substantial support for this version of EMH (Ibid).

Behavioural Finance: Flaw in the Efficient Market Hypothesis Theory

However, no theory is perfect. Empirical research has exposed a flaw in the EMH theory: it is based on the assumption of investor rationality. If investors do not behave rationally by failing to incorporate all information correctly into the share price, then markets are likely to be inefficient. Experts attribute this insight to the emergence of a new field of study behavioural finance. Concepts from other social sciences—for example, sociology and psychology— are borrowed to understand the behaviour of stock prices (Mishkin 2013). Mishkin states that the EMH assumes that "unexploited profit opportunities are eliminated by "smart money" market participants" (Mishkin). Smart money sells stocks when the price rises irrationally, with the result that the price falls to a level justified by the its fundamentals. The technique used is short sales. Smart money participants borrow shares from brokers and sell them in the market, on the premise that when the shares are re-purchased at a lower price and returned to the owner, the smart money participants earn a profit. However, is it possible for smart money participants to dominate the behaviour of all other investors. Short sales can result in large losses if the share price rises rather than falls as expected by the smart money.

Anecdotal evidence drawn from the current market does not bode well for short sellers. For example, Morningstar reported on 10 September 2020 the current price of the following shares: Tesla Inc. at $371.34; Amazon.com Inc. at $3175; Microsoft

Corp at $205; and Alphabet Inc. A at $1526. The prices of these shares as of 1 January 2020, a holding period of less than one year, were respectively: Tesla Inc. at $83.67; Amazon.com Inc. at $1804; Microsoft Corp at $157; and Alphabet Inc. A at $1432. Applying the formula described above, the rate of return for each share in percentage terms is: Tesla (346%); Alphabet (6.56%); Microsoft (30.57%); and Amazon (75.9%). These returns are astonishingly high especially given the short holding period. Had they been sold short at the beginning of 2020, the smart money participants would have incurred substantial losses in the absence of other hedging techniques. Since the evidence is anecdotal, it cannot be generalised into a rule. But it appears to support two propositions: investors act irrationally and short sellers cannot prevent collective irrational behaviour, especially in an environment where governments have imposed restrictions on short sales.

Automated Trading Strategies

A simple example of automated trading is high-frequency trading. High-frequency trading is a form of algorithmic trading made up of frequent turnover of many small positions of a security. The SEC identifies several characteristics of high-frequency trading: (1) high-speed sophisticated programs capable of generating routing and executing orders, (2) location of physical equipment in proximity of exchanges and, access to individual data feeds offered by the exchanges, (3) short time frames for establishing and liquidating positions, and (4) ending the day in a flat position, that is, not carrying risk overnight.

Prevalent high-frequency strategies include the following. A strategy called "leveraging structural differences" relies upon the firm obtaining data significantly sooner than other market participants and executing trades based on this information. A second strategy called "liquidity rebate trading" takes place when a market offers a reward to a firm for buying and selling large positions thereby making the market liquid. Firms seek to fill large orders partially and then sell those purchased positions in the market to receive the "rebate". A third strategy called "market making", a familiar practice, where firms take advantage of differences in prices between the asking price (the price at which the firm bought the security) and the bidding price (the price at which it is willing to sell the security). A fourth strategy called "statistical arbitrage" takes advantage of small difference in the price of the same security trading on different markets. An "under-priced" security trading in one market is immediately sold for a higher price in another market where the security trades.

The justification of high-frequency trading, available only to large institutional investors, is that it drastically increases liquidity, the degree to which assets can be quickly bought and sold, and reduces trading spreads. However, the strategy of "leveraging structural differences", often called front-running, is suspiciously similar to trading on inside information, that is, information likely to affect prices and not disclosed to the public. Traders often place trades on their own company's stock thereby arguably giving them an unfair advantage over investors not yet in possession of the information. Critics of high-frequency trading maintain that the practice increases market volatility as positions are held only for seconds. The opposite of high-frequency trading is low-frequency trading. Investors take a long position, for example by borrowing in a currency with a low interest rate and using the funds to purchase assets in a high interest rate market. Assume you can borrow Yen at 1% and buy assets denominated in British Pounds paying an interest rate of 6%. This strategy exposes the trader to currency risk.

Origin of Rules Trading

Rule trading derives from mathematics. Most trading rules comė from complex mathematical principles applied to create models for financial markets. We can start by looking at three simple strategies: Moving Average, Mean Reversion, and Pairs Trading. The simple Moving Average strategy averages the closing price of a single security over the last "x" periods of time. Periods of time may vary from the short term of five days to the long term of 200 days. Let's use Microsoft as an example by looking at its closing price over a five day period (4 September 2020, 8 September 2020, 9 September 2020, 10 September 2020 and 11 September 2020): 213.35, 206.25, 206.88, 213.30, and 205.35. To calculate the moving average, we add the five closing prices and divide by the number of periods: 209.026. A trader using this model constructs a time series of prices using on-going 5 day averages. Price movements are used to identify "downtrends" or "uptrends" in prices of securities. Technical analysts use "peaks" and "troughs" as signals to buy or sell a security, assuming that movements represent something more than random factors.

Mean Reversion, also known as pullback trading, incorporates the idea that a stock that has made a strong downward move in the last few days is likely to bounce back up to its average price, based on a calculation of moving averages. Mean reversion assumes that extreme changes in the price of a security are like to be followed by a return to its previous state. Pairs trading looks at shares of stock that are highly correlated, meaning most of the time these stocks move in the same direction, and generally these stocks are companies within the same industry, like Pepsi and Coca-Cola, or Ford and General Motors. When the prices of these correlated stocks diverge, a trading opportunity is presented. The strategy is to buy the underperforming stock and short-sell the outperforming stock. When the purchased underperforming stock returns to its average trading price, traders sell the security. When the outperforming stock that is short-sold is purchased at a cheaper price, traders return the shares to the original owner.

Introduction to Modelling: Algorithmic Trading

The information contained in this section is not designed to teach you how to build an algorithmic trading model, but is designed to help you understand models used in the industry. Every model starts with mathematics. Financial models apply mathematics to describe patterns and then to predict future price movements. The simplest example of mathematical modelling is taken from Euclidean geometry: Pythagoras' theorem. Pythagoras explained the relationship between three sides of a right angle triangle, by the equation $c^2 = a^2 + b^2$ or $c = \sqrt{a2 + b2}$. If you know the values of a and b you can compute c. Hence, c is the dependent variable and a and b are the independent variables. This theorem can be generalised to Y = f(x) where Y is the dependent variable, x is the independent variable, and *f* is the function describing the relationship between H and x; *f* can be a mathematical equation or a surface (Wolberg 2000). "Data modelling is the process in which data is used to determine a mathematical model" (Ibid).

All models fall into two categories: parametric and non-parametric. The term "parametric equation" defines a group of quantities as functions of one or independent variables. It assumes the value of a parameter for analysis. In effect, the term *f*(x) is known. "Parametric models are those starting from a known functional form for *f*(X). Probably the most well-known parametric method is the *method of least squares*" (Wolberg). If *f*(X) has a known functional form, it can serve as a powerful modelling technique. An example is the count rate of a radioactive isotope measured as a function of time. Wolberg gives the following equation: $Y = A\ e^{-(kx)} + B$. The dependent variable Y is the count rate; A is the amplitude of the count rate originating from the isotope; x is the independent variable, here it is time, and B is the background count rate. Nonlinear least squares are used to determine the values A, *k*, and B (Wolberg).

In some problems, however, *f*(X) is unknown. Wolberg gives two examples: a mathematical model to predict the probability of rain tomorrow. Weather forecasting cannot be based upon "simple analytical functional forms for *f*(X). Hence, the alternative for weather forecasting is to develop computer models based on data that yield predictions. A second area where it is impractical to apply function forms for *f*(X) is financial markets. Wolberg states, "It would be lovely to discover a simple equation to predict the price of gold tomorrow or next week, but so far no one has successfully accomplished this task". In spite of this inability, billions are invested daily based on computer models for predicting movement in the financial markets. These non-parametric models are referred to as "data-driven" methods. In addition, in a data-driven method, the model is never error-free; hence, a programmer building a financial model seeks "a signal with enough predictive power to make the model useful" (Wolberg).

Nir Vulkan, associate professor of business economics at Said Business School University of Oxford, has developed principles used to build an algorithmic trading and principles used to assess the model (Oxford 2018). He presents the principles in two sets of four. There are four rules for building an algorithmic model: (1) understanding how the model makes money, (2) identifying and quantifying the opportunity in the model, (3) testing and verifying the model, and (4) building the model and connecting it to markets. First, money can be made in three ways: (1) better forecasting or prediction of what will happen in markets, (2) better execution strategy, or (3) better risk management. Second, in building a model, the creator must be able to explain the value of the model to investors; for example, is the model taking advantage of an abnormality in the market. Third, the model must be tested and verified, especially against "out-of-sample" data. If the model fails to work on out-of-sample data, then the model must be rebuilt or modified. Fourth, the model must be introduced to the real world and watched for performance, for example, unforeseen costs. From the perspective of an investor, the four principles used to evaluate an algorithmic trading model are: (1) avoiding excessively optimistic claims, for example, "if it's too good to be true, then it probably is", (2) the promoter must be able to explain in basic economic terms how the model works, as algorithmic trading models capture behavioural finance patterns, (3) did the programmers overfit the data, and did they test the data on sufficient out-of-sample data?, and (4) was the model tested in different markets and how did the model perform in bad times?

Algorithmic trading models seek to predict future movements of a time series, the changes in a security's value over time. Assume market M and it is known that conditions X, Y, Z affect M. However, what is not known, are the relationships among X, Y, and Z. The latter factors also constitute time prices. Wolberg suggests using "candidate predictors" to "form the basis of your modelling process." Suppose you are trying to predict the price movement of Security ABC one day into the future called "Y"; then a table may be constructed to track the price movement of this security over say 15 days. Y is the one-day forward price. Price changes for different periods may be calculated as: n = 1, n = 2, and n = 3, and designated respectively X1, X2, and X3 (Fig. 12.2).

That "candidate predictors" in this table illustrate how one would begin to develop an algorithmic trading model.

A Valid Model

Assume, contrary to reality, we have built a model. The question arises: how to tell whether it is valid. The best test is that it works in reality. But there are other methods as well: out-of-sample and back-testing. Preliminarily, an understanding of "overfitting" is required. The term "overfitting" refers to a situation where, when the model fails, the builder adds more parameters to "fit in" the data that the model works. Factors other than the rules in the model are accounting for its predictions. These variables are called "noise". Adding more parameters gives equal weight to the noise. Nir Vulkan gives the following illustration. You want to predict the winner of a horserace taking place the next day. There is a room of six people: one expert on horseracing, and five who know nothing of value or even hold false information. You decide on a strategy of selecting the horse recommended by the majority. The analogy demonstrates the effect of noise. The only opinion that should have been incorporated into your decision was the opinion of the expert; the other five opinions should have been ignored (Elite Data Science 2016–2019). Out-of-sample testing (OOS validation) is a good way to test the model's assumptions and compare its performance against competing models. OOS validation examines the model's performance on data that was not used in the model's construction. Here is an OOS selection (Fig. 12.3):

Day	Price	Y	X1	X2	X3
1	100	5			
2	105	-1	5		
3	104	-5	-1	4	
4	99	-19	-5	-6	-1
5	80	26	-19	-24	-25
6	106	14	26	7	2
7	120	30	14	40	21
8	150	-27	30	44	70
9	123	-13	-27	3	17
10	110	1	-13	-40	-10
11	111	-11	1	-12	-39
12	100	-10	-11	-10	-23
13	90	11	-10	-21	-20
14	101	11	11	1	-10
15	112		11	22	12

Fig. 12.2 Candidate predictors. (Source: University of Oxford)

First, the model is tested against the data in Portion A, called the estimation period, to examine the parameters of the model. Then, the model is tested against Portion B, the validation data, the OOS validation period. Because this data is at the end of the range, it would be necessary to select randomly a few years within the time period (Fildes and Makridakis 1995: 292). OOS validation is not an exact science, the subject of immense study, and essential to testing models.

Back-testing simulates a "model based on historical market data using computers." The model is tested against existing empirical data. Markets are not deterministic, meaning there are no clearly defined causes and effects for all market movements. Hence, if a model works on historical data, the model has discovered a

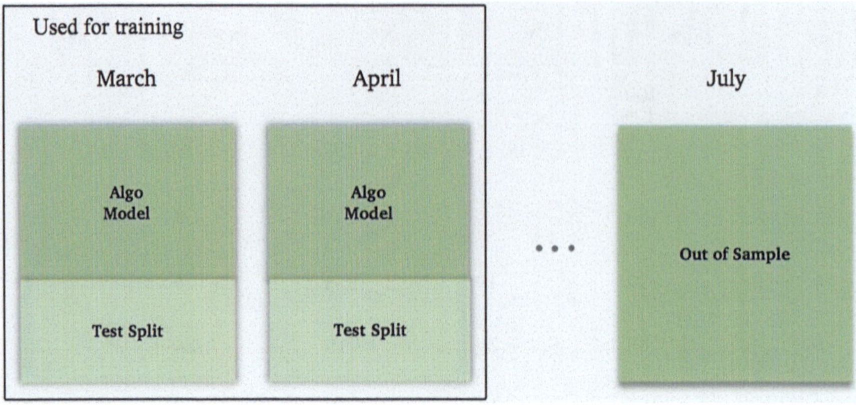

Fig. 12.3 Out-of-sample testing. (Source: stats.stackexchange.com)

particular market characteristic that produces a positive return over time. Although the model cannot predict that a trade will be the right move, back-testing indicates that the model should return a profit a majority of time.

Chatbots

An existing application of AI to financial services is the use of chatbots to improve customer experience. A "chatbot" is artificial intelligence software able to simulate conversation with human users, particularly over the Internet. Financial services providers already deploy "chatbots" to take telephone calls, route the user to the correct department, and provide basic account information. Artificial intelligence combined with robotics is likely to replace administrative functions in the financial services and other industries. Professional and personal assistant robots already are on the market.

Conclusion

This chapter introduced the field of artificial intelligence and indicated how AI may be applied to financial services. The applications run from the simple to the complicated. In addition, most text written in the chapter will be obsolete by the time of publication. While "chatbots" often fail to understand requests or demands for information, the programs will evolve and improve over time.

Appendix

Fundamental Analysis

There are two primary forms of market analysis: fundamental analysis and technical analysis. Fundamental analysis uses financial and economic analysis to calculate the "intrinsic price" of a stock. Study takes place at three levels: the macroeconomic level—global growth estimates, economic trends, innovations, and political stability; the company level—financial data, managerial competence, and strategies to develop the company; and the industry level—competition, and supply and demand. The three steps to be followed are: macroeconomic analysis focusing upon the context in which the company is operating, emerging market competition, factors likely to expand or impede growth external to the company. Industry analysis compares a company to its competitors. Questions answered are what are the core competences of the company vis-à-vis its rivals; does the company have strategic advantages such as brand power, government subsidies, the market presence, and size. Situational analysis looks at the company's current state, its capabilities, its current and potential clients, and business environment. Financial analysis is the core of fundamental analysis as it concentrates on the company's financial statements—balance sheet, income statement, cash flow statement, and equity statement—and compares the results to those of competitors. Qualitative analysis covers the managerial system, personnel development, and corporate governance. Fundamental analysis is a strong long-term tool.

Technical Analysis

Technical analysis "is the science of predicting stock-price movements based on historical data" (Oxford). Technical analysis assumes that the results of fundamental analysis already are factored into the price of the security. Hence, technical analysis focuses on the historical data of stock price movements, seeking to find repetitive patterns of momentum and decline, based on investor behaviour. They trade with support and resistance points, since stocks tend to never exceed a point where they have risen, or trade below a point where they have fallen. Support models tend to indicate the lowest price of a stock at which it usually trades, while resistance models reflect the highest price at which a stock generally trades. For example, assume a trader named Mia notices that Stock XYZ peaked at \$80 per share in the last year. Therefore, the price of \$72 is XYZ's resistance level. Mia also notices that the price of XYZ has not fallen below \$50; therefore \$50 is the support model. Based on this information, Mia places an order to buy say 1000 shares of XYZ at \$51. The premise is that the price of XYZ is unlikely to descend below \$50, and Mia stands to gain when the share price approaches its resistance model. This is a strategy for short-term traders. Technical analysis implicitly relies upon investor sentiment or how personality bias manifests in stock data. An analyst following Tesla uses technical analysis to forecast a future price of \$75.[5]

Questions

1. Artificial intelligence is a broad field of science. What business applications in the domain of finance may benefit from the use of AI?
2. Explain how "deep learning" works. The answer to this question requires independent research.
3. Amazon has a service called Amazon Web Services. Explain how AWS deploys AI to deliver services.

Notes

[1]McKinsey Analytics, An Executive's Guide to AI, 2018 McKinsey & Company, found at https://www.mckinsey.com/business-functions/mckinsey-analytics/our-insights/an-executives-guide-to-ai. Examples provided are: robotics and autonomous vehicles, computer vision, language, virtual agents, and machine learning.

[2]Sonix, What's the difference between artificial intelligence (AI), machine learning (ML) and natural language processing (NLP)?, found at https://sonix.ai/articles/difference-between-artificial-intelligence-machine-learning-and-natural-language-processing

[3]Algorithms are extremely complex and will be discussed later in this chapter. However, algorithms can perform simple processes, such as multiplying two numbers, or complex processes such as playing a compressed video file. Search engines, like Google, use algorithms to retrieve information.

[4]Keith McNulty, What is Machine Learning? https://towardsdatascience.com/what-is-machine-learning-891f23e848da, 8 Aug. 2018.

[5]AG Thorson, Tesla Stock Crash Targets $75.00, FX Empire, 11 September 2020 at https://www.fxempire.com/forecasts/article/tesla-stock-crash-targets-75-00-671907. The article provides an excellent illustration of using technical analysis to forecast the price of a security.

Bibliography

Andriy Burkov, The Hundred Page Machine Learning Book (2019).

Erik Brynjolfsson and Andrew McAfee, The Business of Artificial Intelligence: How AI fits into Your Science Stream, Harvard Business Review 21 July 2017, found https://hbr.org/cover-story/2017/07/the-business-of-artificial-intelligence.

McKinsey & Company, Dorian Pyle and Cristina San Jose, "An executive's guide to machine learning", McKinsey Quarterly June 2015, (need link).

Data Science, Shweta Bhatt, "Reinforcement Learning 101", Mar. 19, 2018, found at https://towardsdatascience.com/reinforcement-learning-101-e24b50e1d292.

A.M. Turing, Computing Machinery and Intelligence, Mind 49: 433-460 (1950).

Kimberly Nevala, The Machine Learning Primer, SAS Best Practices ebook (2017).

Richard S. Sutton and Andrew G. Barto, Reinforcement Learning: An Introduction (2nd ed. 2018).

Patrick Hall, Wen Phan, Katie Whitson, "The Evolution of Analytics: Opportunities and Challenges for Machine Learning in Business (SAS Best Practices 2017).

John R. Wolberg, Expert Trading Systems: Modelling Financial Markets with Kernel Regression (John Wiley & Sons, Inc. 2000).

Elite Data Science, Overfitting in Machine Learning: What It Is and How to Prevent It at https://elitedatascience.com/overfitting-in-machine-learning

John McCarthy, Marvin L. Minsky, Nathaniel Rochester, and Claude E. Shannon, A Proposal for the Dartmouth Summer Research Project on Artifical Intelligence, August 31, 1955 at https://doi.org/10.1609/aimag.v2714.1904.

Robert Fildes and Spyros Makridakis, The Impact of Empirical Accuracy Studies on Time Series Analysis and Forecasting, International Statistical Review 1995, 63, 3, 289–308.

Frederic S. Mishkin, Kent Matthews, and Massimo Giuliordi, The Economics of Money, Banking, and Financial Markets (Pearson 2013).

Sonix, What's the difference between artifical intelligence (AI), machine learning (ML) and natural language processing (NLP)? 2021.

Startup Engineer.IO. Institute of Entrepreneurship, TU Hamburg, Machine Learning Fundamentals 2021.

Keith McNulty, What is Machine Learning?, Towardsdatascience 2018.

Expert.ai Team, What is Machine Learning? A Definition, 6 May 2020.

Hackernoon, Deep Learning vs. Machine Learning: A Simple Explanation, Oct. 27, 2020.

SAS Visual Text Analytics, Snapshot Demo, Youtube, 1 Feb. 2018.

Open Learn, The Efficient Markets Hypothesis, Part 3.

Useful Links

Timeline https://www.computerhistory.org/timeline/ai-robotics/.

Wired https://www.wired.com/story/guide-artificial-intelligence/.

Andreessen Horowitz https://www.youtube.com/watch?v=ht6fLrar91U.

Popular Mechanics

https://www.popularmechanics.com/technology/robots/a28380/everything-to-know-about-ai/?utm_source=digg&utm_medium=email.

Machine Learning (Towards Data Science)

https://towardsdatascience.com/a-lay-persons-guide-to-the-algorithm-jungle-2bc77dc30faf.

https://towardsdatascience.com/trash-or-treasure-how-to-tell-if-a-classification-algorithm-is-any-good-cb491180b7a6.

https://towardsdatascience.com/bluff-the-bots-a-glossary-of-key-terms-in-machine-learning-3d528c8d86f4.

Part IV

The Future of Financial Services

13 BRICS

Introduction

The history of the BRICS begins prior to the 2006 formation of the informal grouping of the countries comprising the acronym. The beginnings are rooted in the 2001 observations of the Head of Global Economic Research at Goldman Sachs: economist Jim O'Neill. The question arises what did O'Neill see in 2000–2001 that prompted him to publish his paper "Building Better Global Economic BRICs". O'Neill took a high-level macroeconomic view of world economic growth and observed that select emerging economies accounted for a significant share of global GDP, vis-à-vis the G7, at the end of year 2000, and that forecasts for the next decade indicated that the economies of Brazil, Russia, India, and China would grow faster than the economies of the G7 thereby increasing their share of global GDP and raising questions about the G7's hegemony over global economic policy.

"At end-2000, GDP in US$ on a PPP basis in Brazil, Russia, India, and China (BRIC) was about 23.3% of world GDP".[1] Considering four different scenarios to predict likely developments between the G7 and the BRICs, O'Neill projected that by 2010 "the relative weight of the BRICs would rise from 8% at present (in current US$) to 14.2%, or from 23.3% to 27%, converting at PPP rates".[2] O'Neill also projected increased membership in the European Union, and subsequently, the European Monetary Union increased from 12 to 25 member countries. O'Neill reasoned that this increased membership "should be accompanied by a decreased representation" by the EU at the G7 from three countries to one, and that the G7 should be realigned to reflect the new economic reality by expanding the G7 to include China, Brazil, Russia, and possibly India.

Parenthetically, in 2003, Goldman Sachs published a second paper on BRICs entitled "Dreaming with BRICs: The Path to 2050". In 2010, Goldman Sachs declared the first decade of the twentieth century to be "the decade of the BRICS". However, the enthusiasm was short lived. Both the original and 2003 publication were written for investors and therefore focused on BRICs from the point of view of

J. JA Burke, *Financial Services in the Twenty-First Century*,
https://doi.org/10.1007/978-3-030-63967-9_13

return on investments for the firm and its clients. Neither paper discussed a future informal or actual grouping of the four countries. The 2003 paper is not discussed here since its projections were overly optimistic and inaccurate thereby invalidating the modelling used. For example, Goldman Sachs projected real GDP growth rates for Brazil for the years 2013 through 2018 were: 2013 (4.0%), 2014 (4.0%), 2015 (3.9%), 2016 (3.9%), 2017 (3.8%), and 2018 (3.8%). Brazil's actual GDP growth rates were: 2013 (3.01%), 2014 (0.51%), 2015 (−3.55%), 2016 (−3.47), 2017 (0.98%), and 2018 (1.40).

At the time of O'Neill's publication, data for year 2000 shows GDP current prices (US$2000 billion) for the G7 and BRICs. This baseline data provides a basis to evaluate the strength of O'Neill's projections (Figs. 13.1 and 13.2).

The 2000 data, based on nominal GDP, demonstrates that the People's Republic of China is larger than Italy and Canada thereby supporting O'Neill's proposal to reform the country composition of the G7. The next table reproduces Table 5 [O'Neill's paper] setting forth O'Neill's "projected average 10-year nominal GDP" based on the four scenarios (metrics) used to make the projections. The table is entitled "Share of World GDP (all in %) (Fig. 13.3).

In all four scenarios, China's relative standing in terms of economic size vis-à-vis the G7 strengthens considerably, rising to the second largest economy under GDP PPP analysis under Scenario D "converting projected GDP trends using PPP conversions rather than estimated end-2011 current US Dollars". In all four scenarios, Brazil moves closer to Italy, though Russia remains in eleventh position.

G7 Country	GDP current prices 2000 US$ bn
United States	9,963
Japan	4,760
Germany	1,878
United Kingdom	1,417
France	1,289
Italy	1,077
Canada	699

Fig. 13.1 G7 GDP. (Source: O'Neill 2001)

G7 Country	GDP current prices 2000 US$ bn
Brasil	588
Russia	247
India	474
China	1,080

Fig. 13.2 BRICS GDP. (Source: O'Neill 2001)

Country	Current GDP		PPP		Scenarios							
					A		B		C		D	
United States	1	33.1	1	24.0	1	34.2	1	32.5	1	31.5	1	26.5
Japan	2	15.8	3	8.0	2	11.0	2	10.5	2	9.7	3	7.3
Germany	3	6.3	5	5.0	3	6.1	3	7.7	3	6.6	4	5.6
United Kingdom	4	4.7	7	3.4	5	4.6	5	4.8	5	5.2	8	3.6
France	5	4.3	6	3.5	6	4.2	4	5.3	6	4.5	6	3.9
China	6	3.6	2	12.6	4	5.6	5	4.8	3	6.6	2	16.1
Italy	7	3.6	8	3.4	7	3.5	7	4.4	7	3.8	7	3.8
Canada	8	2.3	11	2.2	10	2.4	9	2.3	10	2.1	10	2.5
Brazil	9	2.0	9	2.9	9	2.5	8	2.5	8	3.0	9	3.2
India	10	1.6	4	5.1	8	2.6	10	1.2	8	3.0	5	5.4
Russia	11	0.8	10	2.7	11	1.3	11	0.6	11	1.6	11	2.3

Fig. 13.3 Share of world GDP (all in %). (Source: O'Neill 2001)

Looking back from year 2020, we can compare reported data for 2010 in real GDP and O'Neill's projected data and rankings. The following table shows GDP (constant 2010 US$) for the G7 and BRICs (Fig. 13.4).

United States	14.992 T
Japan	5.7 T
Germany	3.396 T
France	2.643 T
United Kingdom	2.475 T
Italy	2.134 T
Canada	1.613 T
Brazil	2.209 T
Russia	1.525 T
India	1.676 T
China	6.087 T

Fig. 13.4 2010 GDP (constant 2010 US$) for G7 and BRICS. (Source: IMF database)

The 2010 real GDP data exceeds that of O'Neill's projected forecasts. China is the second largest economy in the world, surpassed only by the United States. The economies of Brazil and India are larger than those of Canada and Italy. The size of the Russian economy approximates that of Canada. The rise of the BRICs is captured by calculating its share of real global GDP in 2010. In that year, world GDP was $66.113 trillion. The combined real GDP of BRICs in 2010 amounted to $20.334 trillion or 30.7% of world GDP. By comparison, the combined real GDP of the G7 in 2010 amounted to $30.726 trillion or 46% of world GDP. Together, the G7 and BRICs accounted for 76% of world GDP.

Adjusted for PPP in 2010, the 2000 rankings are shaken at their foundations as illustrated by the following table (Fig. 13.5).

The 2010 data on a PPP basis illustrates more dramatically the rise of the BRICs. China is the second largest economy, moving close in economic size to the United States. India is the third largest economy, and Brazil and Russia are the fourth and fifth largest economies.

United States	14.992 T
Japan	4.481 T
Germany	3.188 T
France	2.336 T
United Kingdom	2.283 T
Italy	2.085 T
Canada	1.361 T
Brazil	2.799 T
Russia	2.927 T
India	5.229 T
China	12.379 T

Fig. 13.5 2010 GDP PPP (weights 2010 US$) for G7 and BRICS. (Source: IMF database)

The following table shows the most recent data for real GDP in year 2019 (Fig. 13.6).

While the United States remains the largest economy in the world, China is the second largest economy being approximately three times larger than Japan, the third largest economy. Germany is the fourth largest economy, while India is the fifth largest, followed by the United Kingdom, France, Italy, Brazil, (Russia and Canada are equal in size), and South Africa. A re-constituted G7, based on economic size, would comprise: United States, China, Japan, India, United Kingdom, France, and Italy.

The 2018 data for GDP (PPP) for the 15 largest economies is set forth in the following table (Fig. 13.7).

This table provides empirical support for O'Neill's prediction that within one or two decades the size of the BRICs economies would exceed those of the G7. If the G7 were expanded to G8, every BRIC country would be a member while the United States, Japan, and Germany would be the only surviving G7 States. The surprise new member is Indonesia, overlooked by the Goldman Sachs team in the first decade of the twenty-first century. While no person can predict the future, there is

United States	21.428 T
Japan	5.082 T
Germany	3.846 T
United Kingdom	2.827 T
France	2.716 T
Italy	2 T
Canada	1.736 T
Brazil	1.84 T
Russia	1.7 T
India	2.875 T
China	14.343 T
South Africa	351.432 B

Fig. 13.6 2019 GDP for G7 and BRICs. (Source: IMF database)

substantial evidence that global economic policymaking requires representation by large emerging countries. This also evidences a shift toward a more multi-polar world, a shift resisted by Nation States with vested interests rooted in history.

G7

In 1975, in response to the oil crisis and collapse of Bretton Woods, the President of France, Valéry Giscard d'Estaing, and the Chancellor of the Federal Republic of Germany (West Germany), Helmut Schmidt, invited the heads of state and governments of France, West Germany, the United States, Japan, the United Kingdom, and Italy, deemed the leading industrial nations of the world, to meet at Chateau de Rambouillet to discuss the ways out of the global recession. At the first summit, the G6 adopted "a 15-point communiqué, the Declaration of Rambouillet, and agreed

Rank	Country	GDP [2018, PPP]	Share of World	Change [vs. nominal rank
1	China	25.4 T	18.6%	+1
2	United States	20.5 T	15.06%	-1
3	India	10.5 T	7.7%	+4
4	Japan	5.5 T	4.0%	-1
5	Germany	4.5 T	3.3%	-1
6	Russia	4.0 T	2.9%	+5
7	Indonesia	3.5 T	2.6%	+9
8	Brazil	3.4 T	2.5%	+1
9	United Kingdom	3.1 T	2.3%	-4
10	France	3.1 T	2.3%	-4
11	Italy	2.5 T	1.9%	-3
12	Mexico	2.5 T	1.9%	+3
13	Turkey	2.4 T	1.7%	+6
14	Korea	2.1 T	1.5%	-2
15	Spain	1.9 T	1.4%	-1

T – trillion US$

Fig. 13.7 The 2018 data for GDP (PPP) for the 15 largest economies. (Source: IMF database)

to meet once a year in the future, under a rotating presidency".[3] In 1976, Canada joined the group, making it the G7. In 1991, the G7 invited the then General Secretary of the Communist Party of the Soviet Union to "talks in London, parallel to the G7 summit. In 1998, Russia was formally admitted to the group, making it the Group of Eight leading industrial nations. In 2014, after reunification of the Republic of Crimea with the Russian Federation, the G7 kicked Russia out of the group. Hence, the G7 is a self-selected international group, assuming the mantel of solving global economic problems, without any attention to open election procedures. The current Presidency is held by the United States and the summit, originally scheduled for June 2020, has been postponed to autumn, due the Covid-19 pandemic.

In addition to its role as caretaker of global economic problems, the G7 also deems itself the judge of democratic government. John Kirton, Director of the G7 Research Group stated:

> The G8 [lecture given prior to ejection of the Russian Federation] has addressed its basic political purpose and associated problem-solving functions by engaging in the six dimensions of global governance that most international institutions perform. The first is domestic political management, where G8 governors give their own and global citizens the confidence that open democratic societies can solve the many profound problems they face. The second is deliberation, where G8 governors meet face to face to foster transparency, understanding, trust and attention over the particular problems that require solutions from global governance in an increasingly globalizing world. The third is direction setting, by defining on a democratic foundation new principles of fact, causation and rectitude, and norms for proscribing and prescribing what states and other actors should do as a result. The fourth is decision making, by collectively committing to specific, future-oriented actions that put these principles and norms into effect. The fifth is delivering these commitments by having the members individually comply afterward with what they have collectively promised to do. The sixth is developing global governance, by generating a new system of international institutions to meet the new needs of the global community in a rapidly globalizing age.[4]

Notwithstanding this glowing review, the G7 no longer represent the leading industrial world powers. The self-selected group is an anachronism. The G7 refuses to expand its membership, though it permits observers. Countries like China and India that have larger economies than many members of the G7 never received an invitation to join the elite institution.

This anomaly did not go unnoticed. In 1993, Paul Martin, Canada's Finance Minister, started to attend the G7's finance minister meetings. It "struck him that while the group was meant to represent the most powerful economies in the world, crucial voices were missing from the discussion: countries such as China and India were not there, nor were representatives from the emerging economies of South America, Asia or Africa."[5] He raised the issue with his G7 counterparts, but the latter were not keen altering the composition of the group. In 1997, the Thai baht crisis caused a major financial crisis in Southeast Asia, Russia, and Brazil. The G7's response to the Asian countries was "essentially clean up your own act".[6] Martin resolved to take action. In 1999, Martin and United States' Treasury Secretary Lawrence Summers, established a second, self-selected, multilateral body, the Group of Twenty. Its members are: Argentina, Australia, Brazil, Canada, China,

France, Germany, India, Indonesia, Italy, Japan, Mexico, Russia, Saudi Arabia, South Africa, South Korea, Turkey, the United Kingdom, the United States, and the European Union.[7] Collectively, the G20 "represent about two-thirds of the world's population and account for 80 percent of global GDP".[8]

G20

In 1999, the finance ministers and central bank governors of the G20 met in April and proposed "to (1) establish a new mechanism for informal dialogue in the framework of the Bretton Woods institutional system, to (2) broaden the dialogue on key economic and financial issues among systemically significant economies and to (3) promote cooperation to achieve stable and sustainable world economic growth that benefits all".[9] For several years subsequent, efforts to hold G20 attend summits at the heads of state level failed, but then the 2008 financial crisis threatened the global economy. Convened by the then President of the United States George W. Bush, the leaders of the G20 met in Washington in November 2008 and then in London in April 2009. Finally, on 22 October 2009, Bush called the first G20 Leader's Summit for November 14–15 in Washington, D.C., "with the goal of trying to mitigate some of the severity of the economic fallout by acting in a coordinate fashion".[10] The decisions to develop coordinated monetary and fiscal stimulus packages cemented the new stature of the G20, and later, leaders would refer to the G20 as the "premier forum for international economic co-operation."[11] Whether the G20 can sustain this role going into the decade of 2020 is open to question.

BRICS Inter Se

Now, it is time to turn toward the BRICS inter se. A starting point is the question of how a term coined by an economist became a multilateral international group. Whether O'Neill's acronym and publications strongly influenced Brazil, Russia, India, and China is an open and unanswered question. Prior to the BRICs, there was RICs: Russia, India and China drawn together since 2001 by regional security interests following the United States' invasion of Afghanistan. Putin suggested adding Brazil to this group: RICs + Brazil. Observers note that the Goldman Sachs ambitious predictions about the economic growth of the group likely precipitated its formation and institutionalisation, but the group had independent common ground to form their union: a new global monetary and financial order reflecting the actual importance of economic size of countries.

Whatever the underlying impetus, the BRICs held their first ministerial meeting on 20 September 2006. A decision was taken to expand multilateral cooperation and subsequently to hold annual meetings. At the 2007 meeting, Brazil proposed that the group "study the possibility of organizing a stand-alone summit and dedicating more time and energy towards exploring opportunities to cooperate."[12] In response, Russia agreed to hold a stand-alone meeting of foreign ministers. On 16 May 2008, the foreign ministers of Brazil, Russia, India, and China met in Yekaterinburg. The timing was propitious as the sub-prime mortgage crisis, that would lead to a global recession, had already begun to unfold. The 2008 meeting in Yekaterinburg resulted in the issuance of a joint communiqué that called for reform of international structures and strengthened multilateralism within the United Nations. The 2008 financial crisis opened the door for the BRICs by allowing them to "use this opportunity to adapt global structures in their favour."[13] *The Economist* wrote at the time, the largest emerging markets were "recovering fast and starting to think the recession may mark another milestone in a worldwide shift of economic power away from the West."[14] During the period 2006–2008, the BRIC nations had an average annual economic growth rate of 10.7%. Numerous meetings at the ministerial level continued to be held throughout 2008 in response to the financial crisis until in late November, Russian President Dimitry Medvedev and Brazil's Luiz Inácio Lula da Silva announced that the heads of state of the BRIC countries would hold their first summit in Russia in 2009.

Prior to holding the summit, the BRICs foreign ministers and central bankers took advantage of the financial crisis by preparing a common agenda to be submitted at the G20 summit to be held 2 April 2009. The BRICs stated:

> We called for the reform of multilateral institutions in order that they reflect the structural changes in the world economy and the increasingly central role that emerging markets now play. We agreed that international bodies should review their structures, rules and instruments in respect of aspects like representation, legitimacy and effectiveness and also to strengthen their capacity in addressing global issues. Reform of the International Monetary Fund and of the World Bank Group should move forward and be guided towards more equitable voice and participation balance between advanced and developing countries. The Financial Stability Forum must immediately broaden its membership to include a significant representation of emerging economies.[15]

The coordinated platform demanded reform of the global financial structure, including increased IMF funding and modification of IMF quotas to give BRIC Nation States influence and representation on the board equivalent to their economic stature. The BRIC platform found its way into the G20 declarations. On 16 June 2009, the BRIC countries' leaders met and published a joint statement articulating their common view that the international order must be changed. Paragraph 3 states: we seek reform of "international financial institutions, so as to reflect changes in the global economy. The emerging and developing economies must have greater voice and representation in international financial institutions, whose heads and executives should be appointed through an open, transparent, and merit-based selection process".[16] Presaging their position of de-dollarisation, the joint statement in paragraph 12 states: "We underline our support for a more democratic and just multi-polar world order based on the rule of international law, equality, mutual respect, cooperation, coordinated action and collective decision-making of all states".[17]

The G20's and BRIC's calls for reform of the IMF were not in vain. In 2010, the IMF adopted changes consistent with the demands of the BRIC Nation States: all

BRIC countries would be top ten IMF shareholders, quota share would be shifted by more than 6% to emerging markets and developing countries, and all Executive Directors would be elected. Under the reform, China became the third largest shareholder. However, in spite of these adjustments, IMF Board votes remained out of sync. For example, Brazil the 10th largest economy had 1.38% of IMF Board votes while Belgium, one third in economic size, had 2.09%. Like proposals were made to the World Bank. The largest shareholder of the World Bank remains the United States, enabling the latter to appoint the President. The next four largest shareholders are the UK, France, Germany, and Japan. China nominates its Executive Director as a single country. Russia and the Syrian Arab Republic nominate their director jointly. Other BRICS members nominate their director collectively in groups comprising other countries. The World Bank retains its Bretton Woods agreement profile, observing and recording changes in global order, without overhauling its internal structure.

In late 2010, South Africa joined the BRICS. Observers, especially O'Neill, questioned the suitability of this choice, remarking that South Africa was not in the same league as the original BRIC members. Countries like Nigeria and Indonesia appeared better choices but were overlooked. South Africa wanted to join the BRIC nations to advance its national ambitions. South Africa argued that "South Africa's destiny is Africa's destiny". Evidence supporting the claim is founded on South Africa's influence on African affairs and its role in BASIC (Brazil, South Africa, India, and China) and IBSA (India, Brazil, and South Africa). Existing working relationships justified the selection of South Africa as well as its geographical position: the African continent. Inclusion of South Africa gave the BRICS representation on several continents and five civilisations. Given O'Neill's refusal to modify his acronym, the inclusion allowed BRICS to co-opt ownership of the original idea.

In 2014, the BRICS established the New Development Bank (NBD) and entered into a Treaty to establish a BRICS Contingency Reserve Arrangement (CRA). The bank's initial subscribed capital was $50 billion and an initial authorised capital of $100 billion. Its main purpose was to finance infrastructural and sustainable development projects in BRICS and other emerging market economies. The CRA, initially funded at $100 billion, was created to rectify balance-of-payments pressures or, when necessary, provide liquidity in the markets of any member. The NBD has funded projects within the following areas: clean energy, urban development, environmental efficiency, transport infrastructure, water resource management and sanitation, and social infrastructure.[18] The BRICS Action Plan for Innovation Cooperation (2017–2020) demonstrates that the BRICS efforts on the global scene surpass reconstruction of the financial order. While BRICS cooperate in multi-domains, the group recognises the importance of science, technology, and innovation, and has established the BRICS Science Technology Innovation and Entrepreneurship Partnership to achieve the Action Plan's objectives.

Notwithstanding the deepening ties among the countries, a common denominator accounts for its gravitational centre: the commitment to de-dollarise global trade and shift the financial centre from the United States. The European Union has joined this objective, as every time a transaction is required to be cleared through the United States, a country becomes subject to US jurisdiction and is vulnerable to economic sanctions. A recent example is Washington's unilateral withdrawal from the Iran nuclear deal in 2018, followed by restoration of sanctions on Tehran. "That situation left European multinational companies vulnerable to punishment from Washington if they continued to do business with Iran".[19] Europe wants to do business with Iran giving Europe a strong motivation to shift away from the dollar. Russia has sold most of its dollar reserves and China has internationalised the Chinese Yuan, introducing yuan-denominated crude oil futures referred to as "petro-yuan". It comes down to a basic notion: no country wants to be told it cannot do business with another country because the US doesn't like it.

Conclusion

"The underlying narrative that made the rise of the BRICS concept possible – the transition from unipolarity to multi-polarity – is irreversible."[20] The Bretton Woods financial institutions and the hegemony of the US dollar as the global reserve and trade currency are unsustainable as currently constituted. Countries with economic value equivalent to, and surpassing, the economic output of the G7 will seek to impose their own "distinctive set of rules, institutions, and currencies of power".[21] If IMF forecasts through 2024, based on PPP, are roughly accurate, the largest seven economies will be: the United States, China, India, Japan, Germany, Russia, and Brazil. The G7 status as the "leading industrial nations" is imperilled. Equally imperilled is its hold over the global financial system.

Questions

1. Why is the organisation called BRIC?
2. When was South Africa added to the organisation and what were the justifications for its inclusion?
3. Critics state that the BRICS countries are too different in terms of culture, political interests, economic resources and development, and trade relations to constitute a meaningful regional bloc. What are your views as to the potential of the BRICS?
4. In your view, do the BRICS countries have the political and financial weight to create a multi-polar financial world?

Appendix

Table 13.1 General indicators on the BRICS countries

	GDP, current prices (billions US dollar)	GDP per capita, current prices (US dollar)	Inflation, average consumer prices (percent change)	Population (millions)	Current account balance (percent of GDP)
Brazil	2055	9895	3.4	207.7	−0.5
Russia	1527	10,608	3.7	144.0	2.6
India	2611	1983	3.6	1316.9	−2.0
China	12,015	8643	1.6	1390.1	1.4
South Africa	349	6180	5.3	56.5	−2.3
Germany	3685	44,550	1.7	82.7	8.0
USA	19,391	59,501	2.1	325.9	−2.4
					BertelsmannStiftung

Source: IMF world economic outlook database (April 2018)

Notes

1. At year-end 2000, on a current GDP basis, BRIC share of world GDP was 8%.
2. Insert Scenario D
3. See https://www.g7germany.de/Webs/G7/EN/G7-Gipfel_en/Geschichtlicher-Ueberblick_en/historical-overview_node.html
4. John Kirton, The Case for G8 Reform, June 26, 2008, http://www.g8.utoronto.ca/scholar/kirton_reform_080629.pdf
5. Centre for International Governance Innovation, Catherine Tsalikis, *Can the G20 Save Globalization's Waning Reputation?*, 27 November 2018, https://www.cigionline.org/articles/can-g20-save-globalizations-waning-reputation?utm_source=google_ads&utm_medium=grant&gclid=EAIaIQobChMIkLby-Lnv6gIVDLLICh1qIgYDEAAYASAAEgLJ1vD_BwE
6. Id.
7. Nigeria was an original member but never joined due to structural problems. Therefore, the EU became the 20th member.
8. See https://www.cigionline.org/articles/can-g20-save-globalizations-waning-reputation?utm_source=google_ads&utm_medium=grant&gclid=EAIaIQobChMIkLby-Lnv6gIVDLLICh1qIgYDEAAYASAAEgLJ1vD_BwE
9. Id.at 3.
10. Id.
11. Id.
12. Stuenkel, Oliver. The BRICS and the Future of Global Order (Emplacement du Kindle 433). Lexington Books.
13. At 483.
14. Stuenkel, Oliver. The BRICS and the Future of Global Order (Emplacements du Kindle 480–481).
15. Id.
16. BRICS Information Centre http://www.brics.utoronto.ca/docs/090616-leaders.html
17. Id.

18. New Development Bank, https://www.ndb.int/about-us/essence/history/ "The Bank shall have an initial authorized capital of US$100 billion. The initial subscribed capital shall be US$50 billion, equally shared among founding members. The first chair of the Board of Governors shall be from Russia. The first chair of the Board of Directors shall be from Brazil. The first President of the Bank shall be from India. The headquarters of the Bank shall be located in Shanghai. The New Development Bank Africa Regional Center shall be established in South Africa concurrently with the headquarters."
19. Eustance Huang, A 'growing club' of 'very powerful countries' is steering away from using the dollar, Oct. 302,019, https://www.cnbc.com/2019/10/31/de-dollarization-russia-china-eu-are-motivated-to-shift-from-using-usd.html
20. BRICS book at 4174.
21. Naazneen Barma, Ely Ratner, and Steve Weber, A World Without the West, National Interest, July 1, 2007 http://www.highbeam.com/doc/1G1-166934087.html

Bibliography

Joint Statement of the BRIC Countries Leaders (Yekaterinburg, Russia, June 16, 2009) at https://infobrics.org/document/3/

Jim O'Neill, *Building Better Global Economic BRICs*, Global Economics Paper No:66 Goldman Sachs 30 Nov. 2001.

Gillian Tett, *The Story of the Brics*, FT Magazine 15 Jan. 2010.

Oliver Stuenkel, The BRICS and the Future of Global Order (Lexington Books 2015).

Dominic Wilson and Roopa Purushothaman, *Dreaming with BRICs: The Path to 2050*, Global Economic Papers No:99 Goldman Sachs 1 Oct. 2003.

Modern Monetary Policy 14

Introduction

MMT applies to any country that is a monetary sovereign. A monetary sovereign is a Nation State that: (1) is the monopoly issuer of a fiat currency, (2) does not peg its currency to anything, whether a second currency, a basket of currencies, or metal, and (3) does not borrow funds in a foreign currency. Any Nation State meeting these three criteria is a monetary sovereign. The United States is the example *par excellence* of a monetary sovereign. Congress has explicit powers to spend and tax, under Article 1, Section 8 of the United States Constitution. The US dollar is a floating currency, its value is not pegged to anything, and the United States, when it borrows, it borrows in US dollars. No person or entity other than the United States government can create dollars.[1] In addition, since the 1950s as a result of Bretton Woods, the dollar, though no longer linked to gold, remains the world's pre-eminent reserve and trade currency. Other monetary sovereigns include the United Kingdom, Japan, Australia, and Canada. The European Union is not a Nation State but a *sui generis* legal entity brought into existence by treaties. Although the European Central Bank has the sole authority to issue the euro, Member States of the European Union that have adopted the euro are not monetary sovereigns. A monetary sovereign has the ability to deploy MMT by the act of spending.

The "Six" Pernicious Myths

The foundational principle of MMT is that a monetary sovereign need not budget itself like a household. Monetary sovereigns are not required to balance their budgets, seeking external funding to finance debts. Monetary sovereigns run deficits, since debts are repaid by creating more fiat currency. In addition, spending by monetary sovereigns is restrained only when additional spending produces harm in the real economy. The first myth that governments must behave like households and

J. JA Burke, *Financial Services in the Twenty-First Century*,
https://doi.org/10.1007/978-3-030-63967-9_14

balance budgets is intuitive, deeply ingrained in political thought, and fundamentally wrong. The conventional view of fiscal policy is that the taxpayer sits at the centre of the sovereign's financial universe. Tax receipts fund government spending. When government spends more than its receives in tax payments, which is usually the case, the government runs a deficit. The deficit is financed by borrowing thereby giving rise to the model of tax and borrow to spend or TABS. The underlying assumption is that the government does not have any money. The exact opposite is true. Taxpayers and lenders do not have any fiat currency unless the currency is first brought into existence by the monetary sovereign. The conventional view stands common sense on its head and gets fiscal policy backwards. As the Federal Reserve Bank of St. Louis put it, the US government is "the sole manufacturer of dollars" (Kelton).

Notwithstanding this fact, the conventional view is widely held by government leaders and experts in economics. In a now-famous speech from 1983, British prime minister Margaret Thatcher declared that "the state has no source of money, other than the money people earn themselves. If the state wishes to spend more it can only do so by borrowing your savings or by taxing you more" (Kelton). Thatcher stated restraints on government finance were identical to restraints on personal finances. Subsequently, Theresa May expressed the same view. However, the simple and incontrovertible fact is that monetary sovereigns produce their currencies and these currencies have no other provenance. Whether Thatcher or May actually believed what they said is unknowable; the statements may have been politically expedient.

Nevertheless, the conventional view has proponents in the United States Congress. Nancy Pelosi reinstated a budget rule known as "pay as you go" or PAYGO in 2018. PAYGO prohibits borrowing to finance new expenditures, leaving taxation as the only source to cover proposed new spending.

Recourse to taxes to pay for what may be called the "public good" pervades political thought. The general concept is let's tax the rich people. For example, Senator Bernie Sanders insisted that a financial transactions tax would cover the "cost of making public colleges and universities tuition-free" (Kelton). Equally convinced that taxing the rich was the best solution, Senator Elizabeth Warren claimed "that a 2 percent tax on fortunes above $50 million would raise enough revenue to wipe out student debt for 95 percent of students and also pay for universal childcare and free college" (Kelton). The truth is that taxing the rich is unnecessary. The government, as a monetary sovereign, can spend to make education free and wipe out student debt.

Economic thought appears to be equally under the spell of the first myth. Frederic S. Mishkin in his textbook *The Economics of Money, Banking, and Financial Markets* states: "Because the government has to pay its bills just as we do, it has a budget constraint. We can pay for our spending in two ways: We can raise revenue (by working), or we can borrow. The government also enjoys these two options: It can raise revenue by levying taxes, or it can go into debt by issuing government bonds" (Mishkin). This restates the conventional view of equating government and household budgets. While Mishkin qualifies his general statement by noting government has a third option, that is, create money and use it to pay for goods, he states that the financing of a persistent deficit by means of money creation will lead to sustained inflation, even hyperinflation (Mishkin). The QE programmes advanced by Japan, the European Union, and the United States, that, in the aggregate, created and introduced trillions of yen, dollars, and euro into their respective economies did not produce inflation. Indeed, QE has failed to stimulate growth and achieve sustained progress in job creation. Although more empirical data is needed, Mishkin's statement taken globally is inaccurate. MMT's fundamental principle—that when monetary sovereigns are involved, distinctions must be made between currency issuers and currency users—is difficult to refute.

The second myth is that deficits are evidence of overspending. Borrowing from Mosler, Kelton asks readers to imagine two buckets respectively marked "Government" and "Non-government". Assume the government spends $100 into the economy and collects $90 in taxes. The government has a deficit of $10. But this view of the deficit requires closing one eye. Accounting principles reveal that, if the government is in deficit, something or someone else must be in surplus. In the example, the non-government "bucket" has a surplus of $10, that is, the economy is in surplus, which is a good thing. By contrast, when the government is in surplus, it logically follows that the real economy is in deficit. This raises the question: why would governments deliberately restrain their economies? Hence, overspending, though subject to limits, is not inherently harmful and, without evidence of harm, is beneficial to the economy, where people live, work, produce, and create value. Overspending poses a problem only when it leads to inflation. Politicians that are mired in the second myth may push to cut expenses in programmes such as Social Security and Medicare, programmes essential for millions of people to survive.

The third myth is that deficits burden the next generation. The argument runs as follows: future generations of citizens of the monetary sovereign will inherit deficits, or more broadly the national debt, and must pay off debt to the detriment of alternative productive uses of income and capital. Kelton cites history to dispel this myth, at least as to the United States. "As a share of gross domestic product (GDP), the national debt was at its highest—120 percent—in the period immediately following the Second World War" (Kelton). Yet, the post-World War Two period in the United States was a period of unprecedented growth and prosperity. "In the 60 years after World War II, the United States built the world's greatest middle class economy, then unbuilt it" (Weissmann, Jordan 2012).[2] In the 1950s and 1960s, the poorest fifth of all households fared the best (Weissmann). If deficits harm future generations, then it naturally begs the question why the largest deficit in recent US history resulted in prosperity for the poorest households in America. Consequently, the claim that deficits will efface the fortunes of future generations is not written in stone.

The fourth myth is that deficits crowd out private investment and undermine long-term growth. The myth relies upon the faulty assumption that monetary sovereigns must compete against other borrowers for access to a limited supply of funds. The premise is that government borrowing takes away funds "that would otherwise have been invested in private sector endeavors that promote long-term prosperity"

(Kelton). However, as noted, fiscal deficits increase private savings and do not obstruct private sector borrowing.

"The fifth myth is that deficits make the United States dependent on foreigners" (Kelton). Countries, like China and Japan, holding large positions of US debt presumably have leverage over the United States, as creditors of private enterprise have leverage over their debtors. This myth fails to understand the principle of monetary sovereignty, where, under the three conditions already specified, monetary sovereigns are always able to pay off debt. In fact, monetary sovereigns are debtors but suppliers of their own currency to foreign Nation States. The supply of currency to third countries allow those countries to purchase goods and services in international trade from the monetary sovereign and to offer a safe investment asset. The United States could wipe out all external debt with a computer keystroke.

The sixth myth, at least in the United States, is that entitlement programmes, like Social Security, Medicare and Medicaid, "are propelling us toward a long-term fiscal crisis" (Kelton). However, this proposition does not hold water as the United States as the quintessential monetary sovereign can never run out of money. Rather, the question posed should not engage a debate about insolvency but about how the money is being spent. Kelton asks: "What will that money buy? Changing demographics and the impacts of climate change … could put stress on available resources". The obligation of government is to maximise the use of its existing resources, develop more sustainable methods of production, and to promote innovative solutions to problems in the real economy, rather than focusing upon balance sheets.

The Real Crises and How They Are Managed

The real crises in the United States are unrelated to federal deficits or entitlement programmes. To name a few, they are: (1) 17.8% of the population of the United States lives in poverty as defined by the OECD (the country has the second highest poverty rate among OECD countries),[3] (2) infrastructure is graded at D+, (3) inequality of income and capital as already demonstrated by Piketty is at a level not seen pre-World War One, (4) workers have not experienced a real growth in wages since the 1970s, or approximately 50 years, and (5) total household debt, including mortgages, automobile loans, credit card, and student debt amounted to $14.3 trillion in the first quarter of 2020. According to Brookings, household assets in 2018 amounted to $113 trillion, making it appear that households could easily pay off all existing debt. However, it is clear that the average American household has no possibility to pay off its debt. "The average American now has about $38,000 in personal debt, excluding home mortgages."[4] Credit card debt accounts for 25% of all debt, and approximately 20% of Americans spend 50–100% of monthly income on debt repayment. These problems represent critical crises in the United States.

Conventional Monetary Policy

The United States government entrusts its central bank, the Federal Reserve System, to manage the economy. The Federal Reserve mandate is to keep inflation at 2%, and to maintain a substantial level of employment. From the perspective of the central bank, a certain percentage of unemployment is deemed essential to control inflation. Economists call this the "natural rate of unemployment": the non-accelerating inflation rate of unemployment (NAIRU). The Federal Reserve Bank of New York president William C. Dudley explains: "we do not know with much precision how low the unemployment rate can go without prompting a significant rise in inflation. We do not directly observe the non-accelerating inflation rate of unemployment, or NAIRU. Rather, we only infer it from the response of wage compensation and price inflation as the labour market tightens" (Kelton). The problem is that the natural rate of unemployment, if it indeed exists, is impossible to calculate.

Conventional monetary policy uses "a key interest rate to manage inflationary pressures". The explanation of the "key" interest rate is drawn from publications of the Bank of England, due to clarity and lucidity of their language. The UK Central Bank defines monetary policy as "actions the central bank or government can take to influence how much money is in the economy and how much it costs to borrow" (UK Report 2020). The UK Central Bank uses two main tools: (1) setting the "bank rate" and (2) creating money digitally to purchase government or corporate bonds, asset purchases known as "quantitative easing" (QE). The UK Central Bank has an inflation target of 2%; it also supports the aim of economic growth and employment. The UK model is similar though not identical to how central banks operate in the United States, Japan, and the European Union through the European Central Bank and therefore is a useful pedagogical instrument.

The "bank rate" is the single most important rate in the UK economy. The "bank rate" determines the interest rate the central bank pays to commercial banks holding money with the central bank. By consequence, the "bank rate" influences the interest rate commercial banks charge other people or businesses to borrow or to pay on savings accounts. Monetary policy is grounded on a chain of correlations. A change in the "bank rate" (1) affects how much economic actors spend, and (2) how much economic actors spend (3) influences how much things cost; thus (4) changes in the "bank rate" *can* influence prices and inflation. For example, a fall in the "bank rate" *tends* to increase borrowing and reduce savings, while a rise in the "bank rate" *tends* to reduce spending and incentivise savings. The terms *italicise*d stress that monetary policy is not an exact science. Rather it is based on central bank knowledge of how people are behaving under current market interest rates and how they might behave if the central bank either lowers or raises the "bank rate" to meet its targets. In addition, the "bank rate" is not the only factor to determine interest rates in the market, particularly long-term interest rates. Whether based on mathematical models, historical trends, or technical patterns, when the central bank announces changes in the "bank rate", the decision is informed but not scientifically based.

In the United States the fight against inflation conflicts with the goal of full employment. The Federal Reserve Board takes the position that full employment and low inflation rates involve a paradox. There must always exist a "natural rate of unemployment" to control inflation. Hypothetically, the policy means that millions of people who want work are cut off from the labour market for the sake of low inflation. In other words, people wanting work are nailed to the "cross of inflationary pressure". As discussed, modern monetary policy takes a different view. However, prior to embarking on the programme of modern monetary policy, an understanding of inflation is valuable.

Causes of Inflation: Two Models

The most widely known types of inflation are: (1) cost-push inflation and (2) demand-pull inflation (Mishkin, Frederic S. 2019). Cost-push inflation results from a negative supply shock or a push for an increase in wages unjustified by productivity gains. A negative supply shock decreases output and causes prices to rise. Negative supply shocks may occur due to unexpected events constraining output in the supply chain, for example, a natural disaster affecting the production of oil. The decreased supply of oil, for example, in conjunction with a pre-crisis stable demand for oil, pushes up the price of oil. Alternatively, workers may decide to press employers to raise wages either to increase their wages in real terms (i.e., workers can buy more goods and services) but the wage increase is not consistent with increased productivity, or anticipating inflation, workers demand wage increases to maintain purchasing power. Both scenarios lead to higher prices. Cost-push inflation may result in a destructive cycle whereby every wage increase is accompanied by higher prices, and higher prices induce workers to demand wage increases, until the cycle becomes unsustainable and firms begin to reduce the workforce. Policy activities intervening to reach high levels of employment may exacerbate the spiral of wage increase followed by price increase.

Demand-pull inflation occurs in an economy running at full speed within its limits. This economy is at or virtually close to full employment, causing firms to increase wages to employ more workers to meet overall aggregate demand. When aggregate demand rises faster than aggregate supply (productive capacity), firms push up the prices of products, resulting in inflation. As with cost-push, workers lack enough real purchasing power to maintain their standard of living. The economy also may have too much money in supply leading to the phenomenon of "too much money chasing too few goods". The causes of demand-pull inflation may result from easy credit (low interest rates) whereby workers/consumers borrow to make large purchases such as real property, driving asset prices higher. The "positive wealth effect" boosts consumer spending in general, an irrational euphoria, and workers again demand higher wages. Eventually, the "dervish" dance comes to a stop and the economy enters a recession.

In spite of these types of inflation. A former Federal Reserve governor, Daniel Tarullo, has stated: "the FED (Federal Reserve) has no reliable theory of inflation guiding its day-to-day decision-making. It has various conjectures, assumptions, and models, but many of these are unproven or indeed improbable" (Kelton). In addition, the Federal Reserve acts pre-emptively to prevent inflationary pressures from arising; thereby the Federal Reserve tries to predict the future. In the process, the Federal Reserve may fail to hit its inflation target or vice versa to fail to stimulate economic growth. The Federal Reserve prefers to keep the Federal Funds Rate within a 2.0–5.0% "sweet spot" to maintain a healthy economy, however the latter term is defined. Historically, the Federal Funds Rate reached a high of 20% during the 1980s and has reached historic lows subsequent to the 2008 financial crisis where rates dropped essentially to zero. Due to the impact of Covid-19, the Federal Fund Rate is virtually zero percent and the Fed has announced that zero rates may hold until 2022.

Modern Monetary Policy: Explained

MMT starts from the premise that monetary sovereigns are not subject to household budgeting constraints, since monetary sovereigns have the power to create money by spending. In theory, there is no upper deficit or debt limit. In reality, there are limits, but these limits are grounded in actual adverse economic effects, such as inflation, but these limits do not include "running out of money". Thus, "MMT opens the door to a new way of thinking about how we could run our economy" (Kelton). MMT is not a panacea for all economic ills but it is a "description of how a modern fiat currency works" (Kelton). After establishing "an accurate picture of how a monetary system works", MMT moves to its "prescriptive, policy-making side" (Kelton). The primary focus of MMT is to search the economy to find untapped potential in what is called "fiscal space". If, as Kelton proposes, there are millions of unemployed workers and the economy has the capacity to produce more goods and services without raising prices, "then we have the fiscal space to bring those resources into production" (Kelton). MMT demotes "monetary policy in its current form and elevates fiscal policy as the primary tool for macroeconomic stabilization" (Kelton). MMT decouples spending from the need to raise money by taxing or borrowing.

Kelton explains the implementation of MMT in the context of the US government and economy. First, she notes that there are two parts to the federal budget: discretionary and mandatory. Congress has discretion to regulate the amount of money it puts into programmes annually: for example, defence, education, transport, and environmental protection. However, the largest percentage of the federal budget is mandatory that, for example, requires spending on Social Security, Medicare, and unemployment insurance. "In total, mandatory spending accounts for 60 percent of federal expenditures, and interest accounts for another 10 percent" (Kelton). Seventy percent of the federal budget is on automatic pilot while 30% "is under discretionary control of lawmakers" (Kelton). Needless to say, Congress has the authority to amend federal law thereby changing the composition of the federal budget, but it has elected not to do so. In addition, Congress has the authority to remove all self-imposed constraints on spending such as PAYGO, the debt ceiling, and the Byrd rule, but it has elected not to do so.

Kelton's experience working for Congress provides examples of futile Congressional activity seeking to fathom a source of funding to pay for proposed legislation. Members would tinker with the tax code to demonstrate that this or that amendment would generate enough revenue to pay for the cost of whatever expense was contained in the draft legislative document, though even members of Congress did not consider these measures plausible. Kelton observes: "It's all a game, really, rooted in the flawed mental model (TABS) that holds back so much of our potential" (Kelton). However, there were noted exceptions. For example, in 1917 when the Senate was voting on a 1215-page bill, called the National Defense Authorization Act, the Senate simply authorised the spending of $737 billion more than requested by the White House. There was no hint about where the money was going to come from. In the words of Congresswoman Ocasio-Cortez, "we write unlimited blank checks for war" or tax cuts.

The core idea of MMT is to create a new "automatic stabilizer" in the form of a federal job guarantee. "Automatic stabilizers", called a "driverless fiscal response", comprise government spending programmes that automatically kick in when an unforeseen and adverse event occurs. For example, when the economy encountered the 2008 financial crisis, taxes fell, workers lost jobs, and firms struggled against insolvency. Yet, spending rose because of programmes like "unemployment insurance, food stamps, Medicaid and other safety net programs" (Kelton). Because the federal job guarantee would function like a "driverless fiscal response", "the steering wheel will always turn in the right direction at the right moment in time". MMT thinks of taxes as a means to provision government with services it wants like armies, hospitals, and infrastructure. "Unemployment is defined as people seeking paid work in the government's unit of account. The US dollar is basically a tax credit. MMT is the only macroeconomic approach" that adopts this approach toward taxation.

MMT would eliminate domestic unemployment by "offering to hire the unemployed" (Kelton). Recall that conventional monetary policy eschews full employment and targets NAIRU, the natural rate of unemployment. Unemployment is dealt with by unemployment insurance. MMT would follow a different approach unless the government chose to keep a certain percentage of domestic working population unemployed. The job guarantee programme would constitute an open-ended commitment to "provide job seekers access to the currency in exchange for performing public service work". MMT economists recommend that these jobs pay a living wage and that the work serves the public good. The federal job guarantee would become a mandatory federal spending programme, flexibly employing people when needed and letting the people exit the programme when the job no longer is needed. "From a purely economic standpoint, the major advantage is its ability to stabilize employment over the business cycle" (Kelton). Instead of the Federal Reserve adjusting the Federal Funds Rate up or down during the business cycle, the government would create jobs during a recession and eliminate them in a period of prosperity. "In short, the job guarantee is the MMT solution to our chronic jobs deficit" (Kelton).

Equally important is how government uses its discretionary spending power. Without a "mental reset", MMT cannot work. MMT also recognises that while spending capacity is infinite, the economy's productive capacity is not. The constraint is to live within a nation's biological and material means. "The good news is that because we chronically run our economy below its maximum speed limit, there's almost always room to rev up spending without risking an acceleration in inflation" (Kelton). While the federal job guarantee has historical predecessors, such as FDR's New Deal and programmes in Africa and South America, each of these precedents was exercised during a crisis and were temporarily imposed. The MMT federal job guarantee would be permanent. In the end, MMT is about human imagination and the creation of a people's economy.

Conclusion

This chapter provided a cursory review of modern monetary policy as opposed to conventional monetary policy. MMT is available to any Nation State that is a monetary sovereign. MMT demystifies the strongly held idea that monetary sovereigns must behave like ordinary households when developing a budget. MMT also corrects several subsidiary misconceptions based on the first mistaken viewpoint. It diminishes the role of central banks and shifts management of the economy to government and fiscal authority. Consistent with the pervasive theme of this textbook, MMT is designed to mitigate human suffering through full employment, maximisation of natural resources, and reliance upon transformative thinking.

Questions

1. Compare the Federal Reserve System, the UK Bank of England, and the European Central Bank. Identify similarities and differences. How does each central bank conduct its monetary policy?
2. Critically examine the proposition that a monetary sovereign is not required to balance its budget.
3. What are the two principal types of inflation? Explain Milton Friedman's quantity theory of money.
4. MMT states that full employment will not lead to inflation. Assess this claim.

Notes

1. The Federal Reserve System created by Congress has the authority to issue Federal Reserve Notes and is charged with maintaining the stability of the currency, that is, controlling inflation, keeping unemployment low, and influencing long-term interest rates. But, the Federal Reserve cannot tax nor can it spend.
2. Jordan Weissmann, *60 Years of American Economic History, Told in 1 Graph*, The Atlantic August 23, 2012 at https://www.theatlantic.com/business/archive/2012/08/60-years-of-american-economic-history-told-in-1-graph/261503/

3. Source: Statista, Poverty Rates in OECD countries as of 2017 at https://www.statista.com/statistics/233910/poverty-rates-in-oecd-countries/
4. Megan Leonhardt, "Here's how much debt Americans have at every age", Aug. 20, 2018 (CNBC) at https://www.cnbc.com/2018/08/20/how-much-debt-americans-have-at-every-age.html

Bibliography

Kelton, Stephanie, *The Deficit Myth: Modern Monetary Theory and How to Build a Better Economy*, (John Murray Press 2020).

Mishkin, Frederic S., *The Economics of Money, Banking, and Financial Markets* (12th ed. Pearson Education Ltd 2019).

Rule, Garreth, *Understanding the Central Bank Balance Sheet*, Centre for Central Bank Studies, Bank of England 2015.

Weissmann, Jordan, *60 Years of American Economic History, Told in 1 Graph*, The Atlantic August 23, 2012.

Impact of FinTech: A Prediction

15

Introduction

This chapter reflects upon developments in the financial services industry that have taken place since the post-2008 financial crisis. The proliferation of technology-based banks, insurance companies, lending platforms, and new fund-raising concepts demonstrates the potential of financial innovation and the use of new technologies to reinvent an industry produced by a confluence of un-coordinated historical events. Excepting Asia, the prediction that "BigTech" would enter and dominate the field has not yet occurred, but it is too early to make any conclusion as the pace of change in financial services is ferocious. For example, Apple, Amazon, and Google [Bigtech] offer payment solutions. The United States remains the financial centre of the world and the goal of making the world a multi-polar financial market faces daunting challenges. For more than 70 years, the United States has served as the financial crucible of the world and will never surrender this authority, without a political, economic, and conceivably, military struggle. US financial authority fits seamlessly with its agenda of leading the world into the future, in terms of its political, economic, and social policies. Without diminishing the importance of FinTech, DLT, and cryptography, artificial intelligence may be the instrument of greatest change in financial services.

However, these positive conceptual and institutional developments compete against powerful governments and multi-national companies. For example, Facebook announced a plan to launch a digital currency named "Libra" with the support of major financial and non-financial institutions: eBay, Mastercard, Visa, and Stripe. When the US government signalled its disapproval of the project, the financial institutions withdrew, fearing the prospect of heightened oversight by regulators. Although the "Libra" project is not dead, it is a ghost of its original incarnation. Governments react with caution to new developments often imposing misguided regulations that have the capacity to deflate rising expectations that accompany change. Multi-national companies, including banks and technology companies, have the financial strength to "buy out" innovation. Nation States and

J. JA Burke, *Financial Services in the Twenty-First Century*,
https://doi.org/10.1007/978-3-030-63967-9_15

multi-national companies pose the greatest threat to the potential and promise of financial innovation. In addition, governmental and non-governmental institutions have multi-faceted agenda, including control of data, meaning control of human conduct. Existing intrusions into privacy of citizens and customers bode ill for the creation of a free electronic space imagined by Nick Szabo, firewalled from Nation State interference.

The Dream Vision

The cypherpunks, Satoshi, and Buterin sounded a call for a revolution not only in financial services, but in the creation of digital spaces, free from the constraint and surveillance of large enterprises and especially government, a world built upon a *tabula rasa* based on a cryptographic tech system. Szabos' reference to Galt's Gulch captured the spirit of this revolutionary thought, and more extremely, Timothy May's "The Crypto Anarchist Manifesto", in which he suggested open markets for everything, including illegal activity and the proceeds of crime. While lacking the intellectual stature of Marx, Lenin, and Mao, especially in terms of practical application of theory, nevertheless, the founders of electronic cashless payment systems and blockchain recognised the contradictions and conflicts between the "haves and have-nots". These are class conflicts as Piketty's work demonstrates. The democratic pulse underlying the "dream" runs completely contrary to how financial services are delivered (dictated) by extant institutions.

However, the dream has taken a detour, if not a transformation into a nightmare. "When Satoshi Nakamoto set out his vision for Bitcoin, he envisioned a world where currency was no longer in the control of banks and governments and people could build a financial system without having to trust any powerful institution. Most cryptocurrencies since have had a similar ethos" (Mehta). Distributed ledger technology opened the door to expand freedom from governmental and bank control, including non-financial aspects of individual life, such as transferring back to individuals control of their private information, for example, identity and personal history. With sufficient imagination, the novel technologies offered the promise of a new world of human action based on democratic principles, absent third-party interventions. The questions arise: What went wrong? Is there a solution to achieve the founders' aspirations?

Several factors impede the development of a digital "nirvana". First, Nation States, as elaborated in Chap. 1, are the most significant impediments to substantial change especially when change is likely to deprive them of control, over their currency, and their populations. Even modest proposals, such as the prohibition of the misuse of financial services systems serving dubiously legal and definitively harmful purposes, cannot inch forward in the context of the United Nations. Second, the heavy hand of history hangs like an albatross around the neck of any new idea. "If you created a colony on Mars and declared from the outset that all money would be cryptocurrency and all asset ownership, contracts, products, and services would use the blockchain, that might just work. The problem is that Earth is nothing like that:

our economic, social, and political systems have formed over millennia. Changing them is extremely difficult and slow, and most people want a system that just works over a chaotic, untested new system" (Mehta). The creators of cryptocurrencies and distributed ledger technology were too optimistic given the social institutions produced by history. The conventional wisdom, that always may be challenged, states: "you can't just "disrupt" governments that oversee millions of people, banks that handle billions of dollars, and economies that move trillions of dollars a year" (Mehta). Third, the vanguard of the "financial and personal" revolution lacked a global and compelling plan. Rather, the "revolutionary thinkers" acted independently creating thousands of cryptocurrencies, hundreds of FinTech institutions, and numerous novel market places. But these "creations" are not woven together into a single tapestry. The piecemeal approach cannot produce a global unified financial space when the agents of resistance are governments with almost unfettered power and firms managing trillions of assets.

In the most pessimistic scenario, "the ultimate irony of crypto … is that crypto is succeeding by doing exactly the opposite of what it was originally intended for. Non-government-run cryptocurrencies like Bitcoin and public blockchains like Ethereum stay close to the founding ethos of decentralization" (Mehta). Coinbase arguably has become the "trust" intermediary for Bitcoin thereby hollowing out the central concept: no financial intermediation. However, government-run cryptocurrencies (tokenised currencies) and private blockchains are likely to prevail. "Crypto will make governments and big corporations more, and not less, powerful—consider how the blockchain helped titans like Walmart and Microsoft grow their profits, or how China can dominate more of the world's countries and economies thanks to tokenized currency" (Mehta). The verdict of Mehta, Agashe, and Detroja is *Feuerbachian* pessimism. But these experts, compelling as are their arguments, represent one view, and it is perhaps not too late to make meaningful change.

The Reality

Facts speak with authority and the facts are not so gloomy as forecasted by Mehta et al. The following table shows the world's ten largest banks as of 2020 (Fig. 15.1):

Hence, the world's top ten banks have assets totalling $19.371 trillion. Turning to FinTech companies, comparisons based on assets are not possible because of lack of data but comparisons based on market capitalisation may be made on sound ground. Subject to this qualification, the top ten FinTech companies in the world in 2020 were (Fig. 15.2):

In terms of market capitalisation, a few FinTech firms are larger than some of the ten largest banks in the world. This is a significant development showing that, contrary to the pessimistic outlook of Mehta et al., challenger institutions can compete for the customer base of incumbent institutions, and potentially put them out of business. "Even JPMorgan, whose CEO famously called Bitcoin a "fraud," announced it would start trading Bitcoin futures, which are contracts saying a buyer will buy a certain number of items for a certain price at a certain time." Not quite what Satoshi imagined, but a positive acknowledgement.

Rank	Name	Market Cap	Country
1	JPMorgan Chase	$459.27 B	USA
2	Bank of America	$306.06 B	USA
3	ICBC	$282.80 B	China
4	China Construction Bank	$207.98 B	China
5	Agricultural Bank of China	$172.15 B	China
6	Wells Fargo	$153.90 B	USA
7	Citigroup	$141.54 B	USA
8	Bank of China	$129.89 B	China
9	Royal Bank of Canada	$126.83 B	Canada
10	National Australia Bank	$126.25 B	Australia

Fig. 15.1 The ten largest banks by Market Cap 2021. (Source: companiesmarketcap.com, 2021)

FinTech's Landscape

An analysis of FinTech must start with a review of WeChat Pay (WCP) (owned by Tencent), Alipay (AP), and M-Pesa (MP). WCP and AP "fundamentally transformed Chinese commerce and are game-changing global actors in the Fintech mosaic" (Bradley 2019). WCP's payment volume alone is seventy times bigger than PayPal's worldwide mobile payment volume (Ibid). In China, smartphones are used ubiquitously to make payments virtually anywhere, usually by means of a QR code, stored on the smartphone or merchant's scanner. Importantly, payments are not processed or settled through card networks such as Visa or Mastercard. Rather, nonbank transactions are settled and cleared through a Chinese government clearing centre (NUCC). Not only does this allow WCP and AP to avoid US controlled network systems but also reduces the cost of the transaction. The Merchant Discount Rate is generally 6 basis points or 0.06%, compared to US debit card transactions at a cost of 100–125 basis points or 1.00–1.25%.

Foreigners may find it difficult to understand the Chinese attachment to WeChat. Ben Thompson of *Stratechery* states: "For all intents and purposes WeChat *is* your phone, and to a far greater extent in China than anywhere else, your phone is everything" (Jack Vale 2019). "There is *nothing* in any other country that is comparable, particularly the Facebook properties (Facebook, Messenger, and WhatsApp) to which WeChat is commonly compared." WeChat is "integrated into the daily lives of nearly 900 million Chinese." (Vale quoting Ben Thompson) MP is the FinTech

Rank	Name	Country
1	Ant Financial	China
2	Adyen	Netherlands
3	Qudian	China
4	Xero	New Zealand
5	SoFi	USA
6	Lufax	China
7	Avant	USA
8	ZhongAn	China
9	Klarna	Sweden
10	Oscar	USA

Fig. 15.2 The world's top ten FinTech companies 2019. (Source: investopedia.com, 2019)

(FT) phenomenon in Africa. MP is a phone-based P2P money transfer service. Like Mars, parts of Asia, Africa, and South America lacked the "economic, social, and political systems [that] have formed over millennia." The lack of infrastructure was a blessing not a curse.

Select FinTech Banks: Lack of Universality

A review of FinTech companies, including "neo-banks", considered in the top ten reveals their strengths and weaknesses. The overarching "Achilles heel" is that these digital businesses are not necessarily licensed banks and generally offer limited services and operate in niches. The common framework is that these FinTech companies use platforms or digital business models to offer their services, including often third-party developer offerings. Like platform businesses, the FinTech companies generate network effects: the more apps, the more customers; the more customers, the more apps. The following short descriptions confirm these claims. However, the reader is cautioned: the evolving ecosystem of FinTech companies quickly renders information inaccurate or obsolete.

NEAT	www.neatcommerce.com

Summary: A Hong Kong-based FT (not a bank) specialising in entrepreneurs, start-ups, small and medium-sized businesses. In Hong Kong, Neat Limited holds a Money Service Operator License, Trust or Company Service Provider License, and Money Lenders license. Neat Ltd enables individuals to incorporate in Hong Kong. It offers multi-currency accounts, corporate cards, payment gateway, spending cheques, and worldwide bank transfers. Fees are stacked on its prepaid Mastercard. In the UK, Neat Global Ltd is an agent of PayrNet Ltd, an e-money institution authorised by the Financial Conduct Authority. Its scope of operations is limited as it does not operate in 143 countries. Funds are not insured, but protected, that is segregated.

Doconomy	www.doconomy.com

Summary: Doconomy AB, founded in 2018, is a company registered in Sweden. The FT start-up is geared for environmentalists. Using United Nations estimates of how to reduce carbon emissions by year 2030, Doconomy limits your spending not by financial ability to pay but by exceeding recommended emission targets. The bank card thus allows users to track their carbon footprint.

Doconomy offers a banking service for managing your personal finances and your everyday climate actions. Banking services are provided by Alandsbanken Abp, authorised by the Finnish Financial Supervising Authority. With Doconomy, you get a savings account, a payment and credit card, funds and climate compensation. Future DO members' savings will be covered by the deposit insurance scheme."

Nubank	www.nubank.com.br

Summary: Founded in 2013, it is the "leading" FT bank in Brazil, though it is not a bank but an electronic money institution. According to its web page: "We are a fintech that develops simple, secure and 100% digital solutions for your financial life. Today, we are the largest independent digital bank in the world and we have more than 20 million customers in all 5,570 municipalities in Brazil [Brazil has a population of 209.5 million, meaning that Nubank has more than 10% of the population]. We are NUs, that is: fair and transparent in conduct, direct and objective in communication, and we treat each client as a person. We are against expensive and inefficient bureaucracy, paperwork, agencies and call centers. We are in favor of listening and valuing your opinion, and of earning your trust as a customer." The bank has more than 20 million customers across Brazil.

The digital account provides a Mastercard credit card. The PJ account is for legal entities: no annual or maintenance fee, free and unlimited transfers between Nubank accounts, free and unlimited transfers to and from any bank, online bill payment, payment of taxes, billing data to customers. It operates 24/7. Brazil's Central bank created a new means of payment called Pix, making it possible to send and receive money in ten seconds. PIX is implemented.

N26	www.n26.com

Summary: Founded in 2013 in Berlin, Germany, the N26 is a GmbH and a bank licensed under BaFin, Germany's financial regulator. N26 has over 26 million users in the Eurozone, the United Kingdom, the United Arab Emirates, and the United States. The "standard" account is free, comprising a checking account, funded by making a bank transfer using what is called MoneyBeam, and a debit Mastercard, that may be used without fees in the Eurozone. A smart feature automatically categorises your spending and "real-time push notifications" keep track of your finances. N26 also has a relationship with "Transferwise" to assist in international funds transfers.

There are two alternative personal accounts: N26 You and N26 Metal, both charging fees. N26 You debit card costs €9.90 monthly and N26 Metal costs €16.90 monthly. Both cards remain debit cards. The standard account allows three free ATM withdrawals in the Eurozone; N26 You allows five and N26 Metal allows eight. Additional withdrawals in the Eurozone cost €2 per withdrawal. As to withdrawals abroad, there are no fees when using the N26 You and N26 Metal, but the standard account charges 1.7% of the amount withdrawn. Travel insurance and lifestyle insurance are features available only with the paid accounts.

Then, N26 offers a feature called "Spaces" where the user may create subaccounts for purposes such as savings, or organising business expenses. While cross-border, fees are expensive and services are limited, for example, absence of lending.

Up	www.up.com.au

Summary: Founded in 2017 in Melbourne, Australia, UP partnered with existing Australian banks to avoid the bank licensing process. UP claims to excel in clarifying users' spending habits. The "everyday" account is free for standard uses, including international ATM withdrawals. The user may create a "saver", an account, at this date, paying 1.60% (divided between a base interest rate of 0.10% and a bonus rate of 1.50%). The bonus is paid provided the user performs five or more card purchases per month, excluding ATM transactions. The company website is not clear on whether interest is compounded. "Up" services are available only to Australian residents.

Tangerine

Summary: Tangerine is a direct bank located in Canada. Tangerine is wholly owned subsidiary of Scotiabank of Canada. Tangerine offers checking and savings accounts, investment and mutual funds (through a subsidiary) and mortgages, a service that most competitors do not provide.

Starling Bank	www.starlingbank.com

Summary: Founded in 2014 by Anne Boden, and based in the UK, "Starling Bank is an award-winning and fully licensed bank". The bank offers "four different account types: personal, business, joint and euro – and a pioneering payment services proposition for businesses". Since inception, the bank has raised £363 million. It has more than 1.5 million customers with over £3 billion in deposits. An informative history of the bank is found here: https://www.starlingbank.com/about/road-to-starling/. Unlike most FT banks, Starling bank offers personal loans up to £5000, and business loans up to £50,000. Starling Bank is available only to UK residents. However, post-Brexit, Starling intends to obtain a banking license in Ireland to take advantage of the EU banking passport. Starling also has a developer offering at developer.starling.com.

Revolut	www.revolut.com

Summary: Founded in the UK in 2015 by Russian entrepreneurs Nik Storonsky and Vlad Yatsenko, Revolut is licensed as bank in Lithuania thereby enabling the company to passport its services into other Member States of the European Union. In the UK, Revolut has obtained a limited banking license allowing it to offer a select suite of services. Historically, in 2016, Revolut had 100,000 personal customers and raised $15 million in a Series A offering (venture capital and/or private equity). In 2017, Revolut launched its business product, a platform for crypto-trading, and raised additional funds. In 2018, Revolut offered Revolut Metal, and raised $250 million in a Series C offering. Revolut offers services in other markets, e.g. Australia, Singapore, having partnered with a local bank, the United States. Revolut has a developer offering at developer.revolut.com.

Chime	www.chime.com

Summary: A US West Coast-based FT accepting salary deposits and other payments immediately. Chime is available to residents of the US states and District of Columbia. This FT mobile banking app works in cooperation with Bancorp Bank, N.A. Chime offers mobile app services and a debit card. Chime works with Google Pay, Apple Pay, and Samsung Pay.

Monzo	www.monzo.com

Summary: UK's leading challenger bank, with planned operations in the United States in conjunction with Sutton Bank. Its customer base is almost 5 million. Monzo offers a variety of accounts: Current, Plus, Business, Joint, and 16–17 accounts. The Monzo current account is a full UK current account with no monthly fees. The current account offers loans up to £3000 with an APR of 26.6%, and provides an interest-bearing savings account paying up to 0.74% AER. Monzo Plus (£5 monthly) provides all features of the free account, with these select features: 1.00% AER on accounts up to £2000; holographic debit and virtual card (a card that hides details to protect against fraud when paying online), and credit tracker. ATM withdrawals abroad are free up to £400 every 30 days.

In sum, these FinTech companies, some of which are neo-banks, use the term "bank" very loosely. While these FinTechs have improved the delivery of financial services to customers by using digital and mobile technologies, they do not serve a global customer base nor offer a full range of banking services, especially lending. For example, neo-banks do not finance real estate transactions, a financial services used by most people to purchase property. Though potential customers need not visit a physical branch, neo-banks require, in addition to a passport or national identity card, a physical address in a jurisdiction where it is licensed to operate and a telephone number in that jurisdiction. The mobile citizen is excluded.

Hence, the distinction between FinTech institutions and legacy banks are that the former are first-movers to use mobile devices and applications to make banking transactions easier. While the use of a mobile phone, laptop, or watch to conduct banking business is substantially innovative, when one looks under the hood of the FinTech bank, they do not differ significantly from legacy banks and no FinTech yet offers the full range of services of legacy banking. This statement is not a criticism of FinTech development, but a clarification of its current limitations. The layered structure of PayPal illustrates. PayPal claims it is a P2P payment system, but its infrastructure is firmly rooted in legacy banking and shows the fallacy of the claim. A PayPal user must have a bank account, a debit or credit card, and a PayPal account. The strategy and implementation cater to customer experience, but PayPal reposes upon the banking system and card payment networks.

The Future Bank: Planet Mars

Following Brett King, I construct an ideal bank, using "first principles thinking", as if no bank had ever previously existed. A prerequisite to building a bank *tabula rasa* is to create a customer profile. The profile of our customer is predicated on the mobile citizen or "Citizen M". Let us assume, an expatriate, born in Ireland, naturalised in the United States, and educated in three countries. Our Citizen M has lived and worked in seven different countries, and owns real property in France, where he resides. At time of retirement, Citizen M will receive pension benefits and medical insurance from the USA government and a German firm. Citizen M expects to retire in Spain. Citizen M now lives and works in Russia. We will not complicate matters with family dependents. However, we note that purportedly we live in a Global Village. Hence our profile of Citizen M is not far-fetched and is likely to become more common in future generations.

A bank provides four fundamental functions: (5) payments, (6) savings, (7) lending, and (4) risk management. Let us start with payments, as most FinTech banks or financial services firms have done. A payment is a transfer of something of value from one individual or entity to another generally in exchange for a good or service or to discharge a debt. Setting aside discussions of cryptocurrency and blockchains, excepting direct payments between individuals in physical currency, payments require a payments system, involving not only financial institutions but also central banks. The extant payment system is composed of numerous parochial fragments held together by various mechanisms and relationships, with pieces governed by diverse regulations or rules. It is beyond repair. Primarily for political reasons, a global seamless payment system cannot be constructed. However, freed from these constraints, in theory, such a global payment system could be constructed, just not on planet earth.

Let us take *FinTech Magazine*'s top ten FinTech banks. The first problem each entity addressed was the failure of legacy banks to respond to customer demand for fast, easy, and reasonably-priced payments. Without diminishing their collective efforts, we are stunningly far from a global payment network. Take Nubank, an incredibly successful FinTech in Brazil, about to roll out a new payment system called "Pix", in conjunction with the central bank, where payments will be made real time in ten seconds or less. The problem is that, to open an account, the customer must be a resident of Brazil. Other top ten FinTech banks despite claiming worldwide payments, impose similar residency or geographical restrictions upon customers allowed to open accounts, contradicting the claim to be able to make payments anywhere. Citizen M certainly is left out of the equation.

Savings is the second function of a bank. However, savings assumes that an individual has income or capital, as defined by Piketty. FinTech banks that offer a "savings account" pay modest annual interest rates, the best being about 2%. According to Statista, the global rate of inflation in 2020 is expected to be 2.99%. While inflation varies, interest rate payments on savings account cannot lead to a substantial increase in funds. The wealthy, as Piketty reminds, do not use typical bank accounts to invest their money. This deficit raises the more fundamental problem to correct: an alternate distribution of national income and capital among residents of the world. Our Citizen M would need to seek alternative measures to save and invest, most likely through a brokerage house. However, Citizen M would run into physical residency requirements to open accounts. We assumed income from the United States, while Citizen M lives abroad. Without a US address and US mobile telephone number, Citizen M cannot open an account with any financial institution in the United States. The same restrictions are imposed by FinTech firms like LendingClub that currently pay attractive rates on high-quality loans.

Lending is the third major function of a bank. At the retail level, individual customers often seek debt to purchase real property. Without referring to the myriad middle persons, both private and public officials, involved in the loan agreement and separate agreement governing the pledge, banks lend in the physical territory where they are located. Assume Citizen M in anticipation of retirement seeks to purchase real property in Spain, Citizen M would have to use a Spanish, or at best, a UK financial institution. In spite of the EU banking licence that applies anywhere in the EU, there is little, if any, cross-border mortgage lending at the retail level. Assuming licensing is not an impediment, the question arises why banks do not offer cross-border loans to purchase property, unless they do so through a subsidiary as found in countries like Estonia and Latvia where the major banks are Scandinavian.

In addition, the process of purchasing real property is painful, to say the least. Let us take the French experience, for example. When Citizen M finds a suitable property and Citizen M and the seller agree on price, then the parties proceed to a Notaire who prepares a "Compromis de Vente", a pre-agreement to purchase the property that usually contains a "condition suspensive de l'obtention d'un état hypothécaire", a mortgage contingency clause. Unless otherwise specified, the buyer takes the property "as is", excepting "vices cachés", hidden defects the seller is obligated to reveal. Assuming Citizen M finds financing, a firm prepares an "Expertise", a report that covers three items: termites, asbestos, and radon. If Citizen M wants a complete evaluation of the condition of the property and its adherence to all regulations both local and national, then Citizen M, at his/her expense, must retain the services of an engineer. When financing is settled, then the parties proceed to sign the "Acte de Vente", the final sale agreement whereby transfer of title takes place between seller and buyer. The Notaire is responsible for the preparation of the document. The Notaire makes a presentation of key points before the parties prior to signature. The buyer is responsible for payment of Notaire fees, about 7% of the sales price. The process takes months. For historical reasons, governments treat sales of property in an almost sacrosanct manner, while other transactions of equal or greater value may be executed in seconds, for example a sale of €250,000 in equity on a recognised market is executed instantaneously, though settlement takes a few days. Our hypothetical process of sale and purchase is similar in other countries.

Risk management is the fourth function of banks. From the individual customer point of view, risk management tends to focus on governmentally insured accounts. The amounts insured vary from jurisdiction to jurisdiction. Risk management internal to the bank depends upon compliance, prudential management, and the ability to withstand unforeseeable uncertainty. FinTech companies that are banks claim compliance with their regulator, and some offer governmental insurance against funds held with the bank in certain accounts.

Now, we construct the hypothetical bank. The "Bank of Mars" exists in a world where the historical detritus developed over millennia is swept aside. The first question is how to form it. We propose a decentralised/distributed autonomous organisation (DAO) existing on a "Genesis" distributed electronic ledger. The DAO contains the protocols matching the foundation document. The protocols allow for amendments to be made to the foundation document when approved by a "consensus" procedure adopted by its owners and embedded in the protocol layer. The foundation document sets out the principles of organisation, management, operation. The DAO is owned by customers of the bank and is not a for-profit seeking entity.. The bank's overall purpose is to serve the financial needs of its customers across the spectrum of financial services: savings, lending, investing, insuring, and developing customised financial road maps based on customer profiles. The bank would be "crowdfunded" at an amount set by the initial founders sufficient to pay for human and technical resources needed to implement the idea.

The jurisdiction of the Bank of Mars is the "Ether" because if earth bound, Nation States will kill the concept from inception. The bank has no physical presence as it exists nowhere and everywhere. The bank is established on distributed ledger technology. We call this the "Genesis" network. All data about the bank is transparent to anyone, including its financial statements. The protocols governing the bank comprise the trust required of a bank that now falls to government regulation, regulatory oversight, and compliance with hundreds if not thousands of discrete rules emanating from the myriad jurisdictions in which the bank operates. Like Ethereum and other decentralised/distributed ledger technologies, the Bank of Mars develops a set of protocols to mitigate, if not eliminate, the risk of fraud and theft. Personnel may be divided into three categories: (5) management, (6) technical, and (7) operational.

Sub-networks are built upon and run parallel to the "Genesis network". The first sub-network contains customer accounts. Opening an account requires a customer to provide a current passport issued by an earth based authority. Identity is verified by using digital technology like iris scans. Verifying sources of funds would depend upon the amount funded to open the account. For example, sums less than $25,000 would not be subject to verification requirements, as that amount of money is miniscule in the world in which we live. Vetting the sources of funds relies upon applications to identify the source of "unexplained wealth" and the provenance of the funds. For example, assume a politically exposed person applied for an account, the account would be opened only if amounts to be deposited had a relationship to the salary payable to that person in his/her official position. In addition, since customers are owners, there is less incentive to steal or use the bank as a means to legitimate "dirty" funds. The second sub-network consists of all financial services offered by the bank. The two sub-networks are linked to the "Genesis network" to build a virtual single rail of delivery of financial services.

The Bank of Mars may take advantage of Cloud Computing. "The cloud itself is a set of hardware, networks, storage, services, and interfaces that enable the delivery of computing as a service. Cloud services include the delivery of software, infrastructure, and storage over the Internet (either as separate components or a complete platform) based on user demand" (Hurwitz et al. 2010). The cloud has the potential to reduce costs, construct firewalls where necessary, link devices to software, and link software to large servers, say two racks.[1]

In the imaginary world of the "Bank of Mars" payments would take place instantaneously, borrowing from scalability technology being developed by Ripple, Ethereum Serenity, and be Mars worldwide. The type of currency depends on client demand, and its practical use as a means of payment among users of the system. The end objective of the bank is to provide returns to customers now available only to the wealthy in a modest attempt to reduce inequality of distribution of income, and inequality of capital (essentially a stock of income). Earnings are used to invest in the bank to improve infrastructure, services, and retain talent to keep the bank always at the cutting edge.

Conclusion

The 2008 financial crisis opened the door to disruption in the financial services industry. The facts show that new technologies and philosophies have already impacted the incumbent financial institutions. Most progress has taken place where financial institutions did not exist or did not serve well, since as experts agree, FinTechs and alternative financial services were easier to establish in the absence of what financial services institutions history produced for advanced economies. The fate of cryptocurrency as "money" depends upon time to clear and settle transactions measured in seconds. A customer purchasing a cup of coffee and the merchant cannot wait five minutes before a block is validated. Should crypto fail to reach transaction speeds equal to Visa and Mastercard networks, then the use of this currency may be limited to very large value transactions, since distributed ledger technology can move money cross-border faster and safer than existing institutions. In addition, if cryptocurrency is not accepted as a means of payment, then it likely will function as an investment vehicle subject to regulation that now applies to financial instruments. Distributed ledger technology and artificial intelligence have already proven their ability to deliver existing and novel services efficiently at both the retail and wholesale level. But private and permissioned networks used by industrial giants are likely to crowd out public and permission-less networks, contrary to the original ideal. While the anarchists' dream may not be realised, without the contribution of their revolutionary thought and work, it would not have been possible to destabilise the financial services industry.

Questions

1. Describe how FinTech, DLT, and AI may be used in combination to improve financial services?
2. Do you agree that Nation States, and their individual regulations, prevent the creation of a global financial system?
3. Following the hypothetical of the "Bank of Mars", construct a planet-wide financial service financial services system.

Note

[1]https://www.cloudbanking-services.com/

Bibliography

Henri Arslanian and Fabrice Fischer, The Future of Finance: The Impact of FinTech, AI, and Crypto on Financial Services (Palgrave Macmillan 2019)

Michel Bradley, WeChatPay and Alipay: The Future of Fintech or Uniquely Chinese?, Medium Jun. 5, 2019 at https://medium.com/@jbradle021988/wechatpay-and-alipay-the-future-of-fintech-or-uniquely-chinese-a15269051b06.

Judith Hurwitz, Robin Bloor, Marcia Kaufman, Fern Halper, *Cloud Computing for Dummies* (Wiley Publishing, Inc. 2010)

Jack Vale, The rise of WeChat and its role in the workplace, Guild Mar. 18, 2019 at https://guild.co/blog/the-rise-of-wechat-and-its-role-in-the-workplace/.

Neel Mehta, Adi Agashe and Parth Detroja, *Bubble or Revolution?: The Present and Future of Blockchain and Cryptocurrencies* (Paravane Ventures 2020)

Conclusion

16

Introduction

First, this textbook was designed to encourage students to think critically about the accepted fundamentals found in textbooks generically dealing with economics, money, and banking. Central banks and financial services institutions are human creations and are not the function of tentatively valid scientific generalizations. Therefore, they may be changed and replaced to serve the public good, without becoming public institutions. Second, the expanded reliance upon existing and developing technologies should continue to push change in the industry, and the post-Covid-19 environment may result in the survival of the fittest: businesses best able to survive in an environment of incessant change. The cloud and the introduction of 5G technology may push existing boundaries further. However, there are many sources of resistance: Nation States, and capital-heavy existing financial institutions.

Third, the conventional idea of the "financial circular flow model" that existing savings are passed via a bank to productive borrowers is false. Banks create money and sources of funds used by financial institutions broadly defined are more complex. In addition, the link between finance and economic growth requires more empirical evidence. In addition, economic growth results from non-financial factors, for example, demographic components, innovation, and labour productivity. Fourth, US dollar hegemony is unlikely to be challenged or changed in the foreseeable future, thereby allowing the US to use its financial system for political and economic ends.

Fifth, Piketty provides a compelling narrative of the inequality of distribution of capital and national income. The tyranny of merit has met its most effective enemy. Piketty also shows how the financial sector plays a role in his narrative through tax havens harbouring 10% of global GDP, excess capital to burden consumers with debt, and creating conditions for financial crises. Sixth, it remains unknown whether a digital currency can or will replace fiat currencies as a reserve or trade currency.

J. JA Burke, *Financial Services in the Twenty-First Century*,
https://doi.org/10.1007/978-3-030-63967-9_16

Assuming Nation States adopt Central Bank Digital Currencies, the implications for individual privacy are substantial. In conclusion, this textbook provides extensive material to consider the function of financial services in a complex fast-changing business and technological environment and to understand the evolution of financial services in the twenty-first century.

Bibliography

Anders la Cour, *Bank to the Future*, Banking Circle (2020).

Index[1]

[1] Note: Page numbers followed by 'n' refer to notes.

J. JA Burke, *Financial Services in the Twenty-First Century*, https://doi.org/10.1007/978-3-030-63967-9

The manufacturer's authorised representative in the EU is Springer Nature Customer Service Centre GmbH, Europaplatz 3, 69115 Heidelberg, Germany. If you have any concerns regarding our products, please contact ProductSafety@springernature.com

Printed and bound by CPI Group (UK) Ltd, Croydon, CR0 4YY
13/08/2026
02196027-0001